Ourselves in Our Work

Ourselves in Our Work

Black Women Scholars of Black Girlhood

Edited by Toni Denese Sturdivant with Altheria Caldera

PETER LANG
New York · Berlin · Bruxelles · Chennai · Lausanne · Oxford

Library of Congress Cataloging-in-Publication Data

Names: Sturdivant, Denese, Toni, editor. | Caldera, Altheria, editor.
Title: Ourselves in our work: Black women scholars of Black girlhood /
[edited by] Toni Denese Sturdivant, Altheria Caldera.
Other titles: Black women scholars of Black girlhood
Description: New York: Peter Lang, [2024] | Includes bibliographical
references and index.
Identifiers: LCCN 2023041307 (print) | LCCN 2023041308 (ebook) | ISBN
9781433194528 (paperback) | ISBN 9781433194535 (hardback) | ISBN
9781433194511 (epub) | ISBN 9781433194504 (pdf)
Subjects: LCSH: African American girls—Social conditions. | African
American girls—Race identity. | African American girls—Research. |
Women's studies—Biographical methods. | African American women—Race
identity. | African American women—Social conditions.
Classification: LCC E185.86. O89 2024 (print) | LCC E185.86 (ebook) | DDC
305.48/896073—dc23/eng/20230907
LC record available at https://lccn.loc.gov/2023041307
LC ebook record available at https://lccn.loc.gov/2023041308
DOI 10.3726/b21228

Bibliographic information published by the Deutsche Nationalbibliothek.
The German National Library lists this publication in the German
National Bibliography; detailed bibliographic data is available
on the Internet at http://dnb.d-nb.de.

Cover design by Peter Lang Group AG

ISBN 9781433194535 (hardback)
ISBN 9781433194528 (paperback)
ISBN 9781433194504 (ebook)
ISBN 9781433194511 (epub)
DOI 10.3726/b21228

© 2024 Peter Lang Group AG, Lausanne
Published by Peter Lang Publishing Inc., New York, USA
info@peterlang.com - www.peterlang.com

All rights reserved.
All parts of this publication are protected by copyright.
Any utilization outside the strict limits of the copyright law, without the permission of
the publisher, is forbidden and liable to prosecution.
This applies in particular to reproductions, translations, microfilming, and storage and
processing in electronic retrieval systems.

This publication has been peer reviewed.

Contents

Acknowledgments	vii
Introduction Ourselves in Our Work: Black Women Scholars of Black Girlhood	1
TONI DENESE STURDIVANT AND ALTHERIA CALDERA	

Part I Positionality: My Identity, My Work   11

1 *To See and Be Seen:* Living and Loving the Complexities of Black Girlhood	13
DARLENE ANITA SCOTT	
2 *The Project of Black Girlhood:* Reimagining Interconnectivity and Indivisibility between Black Women and Girls	25
LOREN S. CAHILL AND NOOR JONES-BEY	
3 *Positioned to Listen*	37
IMANI S. R. MINOR	
4 *Seeing through Silence:* The Memory of We	51
STEPHANIE POWER-CARTER	

Part II Revelations: What I've Learned or Unlearned from Studying Black Girls   65

5 *Setting the Trend:* What Black Girls Taught Me about Showing Up and Dancing with Complexity	67
CHARLENE M. BROWN	
6 *Revelations:* What I've Learned from Black Girls	81
JANINE JONES	

7 The Road So Far: My Unlearning and Relearning about Black Girls in Educational Spaces   95
    LATEASHA MEYERS

Part III Being a Scholar of Black Girls and Black Girlhood   107

8 But Some of Us Are Brave: Exploring How Black Girlhood Origin Stories Shape Sister Scholarship   109
    DANIELLE K. WRIGHT AND RASHIDA GOVAN

9 (Re)membering Black Girlhood: My Journey to Working with and for Black Girls   123
    MISHA N. INNISS-THOMPSON

10 Why I Do This Work: "I Was Built for This"   133
    TAMIKA GAFFORD-CARTER

11 Defining Ourselves, for Ourselves: The Embodiment of Critical Mentoring Pedagogy as Praxis in Black Girlhood Studies   147
    TARYRN T. C. BROWN

Part IV Continuing the Work: The Future of Black Girlhood Studies   161

12 Continuing the Work of Black Girlhood Studies: Culturally Centered Program Development and Evaluation   163
    NISAA KIRTMAN AND KIMBERLY BRYANT

13 Into the Future: Researcher's Role in Black Girlhood Methodology   183
    JANELLE GRANT

Notes on Contributors   197

Index   201

Acknowledgments

There are more scholars of Black girlhood than have contributed to this volume. We would like to acknowledge all of the Black women scholars who have worked to make Black girlhood safer and freer through partnering with Black girls.

Introduction Ourselves in Our Work: Black Women Scholars of Black Girlhood

TONI DENESE STURDIVANT AND ALTHERIA CALDERA

The idea for this book originated during a focus group I (Altheria) was conducting with Black girls about the ways they show-up, or are forced to show-up, in schools. As the girls shared with me the ways they are often misperceived by teachers and administrators, I saw my own experiences as an academic in institutions of higher education reflected in their stories, a topic I wrote about in my reflexive notes. I wrote, "When Shameka described how she monitors the loudness of her voice so that she's not perceived as angry or ghetto, I felt as if her words were my own." When the pandemic caused me to halt this project, I relistened to the recorded interviews and focus group discussions and continued to write about how my work with Black girls had shed light on my own lived experiences as a Black woman and about why their stories motivate me to focus part of my scholarship and activism around Black girls. I remember hurting for the Black girls in my study because I knew that their transition to Black womanhood would only offer them more of the same institutional failures. I wondered if other Black women had felt what I felt or had had similar experiences in their research with Black girls. I began to search for articles or books that illuminate the ways Black women find themselves in their work with Black girls and did not find any publications that solely focused on the experiences of Black women who study Black girls. I knew then that I wanted to create a space that would encourage Black women to reflect on their experiences—how they and their work have been shaped by their work with Black girls.

In the hurry to meet institutional publication demands, oftentimes scholar-activists do the work and do not pause to critically reflect upon the work we're doing and why they're doing it. Academia, and sometimes community, demand that we move along to the next project, as there is always more work to be done. This book represents a breathing space, both an inhale and exhale, that encourages Black women to look back and to look forward. I think of this project as a purposeful pause, an intentional interlude. In Part I, we've created a shared space for Black women to examine themselves in relation to their work with Black girls. For example, Darlene Scott discusses society's inability to understand her, and Black girls in general, as nuanced individuals belonging to a distinct cultural group. She discusses the bliss of early childhood in distinct opposition to the realization that she would be expected to manifest and downplay parts of herself as she learned more about her world beginning in 4th grade. Further, Dr. Stephanie Power-Carter details, among other things, the necessity of remembering. She describes the wisdom of remembering who she is and who her ancestors were when engaging in her research and how this act of remembering, of making research personal, is not always accepted as valid and yet it is key.

For Black women, writing ourselves into our scholarship is often devalued, but we insist on its significance by creating womanist prose (Walker, 1983), Black Feminist Autoethnography (see Brown-Vincent, 2019; Boylorn, 2016; Griffin, 2012), and Black Women's Autobiography (Ards, 2015). Similarly, many Latinx women scholars employ similar methodologies like testimonio (The Latina Feminist Group, 2001) and autohistoria (Anzaldua, 2000). We as editors join this push back—resisting this artificial separation between our personal lives, our scholarship, and our communities. When theorizing about identity, Anzaldua reminds women of color that our lives are not little stuffed cubbyholes. She describes identities as flowing between and over aspects of a person (Keating, 2009). Simply stated, we believe in "me-search as research" because knowledge rooted in and derived from lived experiences is important (Gardner et al., 2017). This bridging between seemingly disparate aspects of our lives is necessary in order for us to bring our authentic selves to any settings in which we find ourselves. Writing about the overlap between our work and our lives is a step towards this authenticity. The following sections describe the kind of work in which the contributors engaged and why it matters.

Critical Reflexivity in Qualitative Inquiry

Much of the scholarship centering Black girls is qualitative in nature. This fact alone speaks to the importance Black women scholars give to understanding lived experiences and the value they place on individual stories. Qualitative inquiry requires researchers to reflect on their positionality, the sociopolitical and historical ways our identities shape our experiences in society, as well as our biases to acknowledge how these aspects of ourselves may play a role in our interpretations during data collection and analysis (Creswell, 2014; Repko & Szostak, 2017). Reflexivity makes manifest the underlying worldviews and beliefs that a researcher might hold in order for the reader to better frame the research within the context of the researcher (Merriam & Tisdell, 2016). In the case of this volume, Black women doing research with Black girls, examined the ways in which their past as a Black girl and their current state as a Black woman might play a role in the lenses used in their work. Yet, this process that is regarded as an essential aspect of ensuring the validity of qualitative research, can offer more than simply providing readers with information to determine if they should trust the study. Critical reflexivity allows readers to gain new and deeper insights into the lived experiences of the researcher, to understand them as a person with real world experiences rather than simply a data collection and analysis being. Reflexivity allows Black women scholars to arrive at more nuanced understandings about themselves, their work, the world in which we find ourselves and can lead to further avenues of exploration for future study.

In critical qualitative research, in particular, reflexivity is essential in that it acknowledges the power relations inherent in the researcher-participant relationship and causes researchers to not only reflect on how we might impact the research but also how the research may shape us. By having this time to reflect on our lived experiences, Black women have the opportunity to confront past actions and actors within our own lives, to question what they believe about Black girlhood. In Part II, which focuses specifically on learning and unlearning through research with Black girls, Janine Jones reveals what she learned about the ways Blackgirls challenge hegemonic rules and consequences which fail to consider their full personhood.

Probst and Berenson (2014) stated that "reflexivity is generally understood as an awareness of the influence the research has on what is being studied and, simultaneously, of how the research process affects the researcher. It is both a state of mind and a set of actions" (p. 814). Our work, however, expands the work of reflexivity to include not just the ways Black women's positionalities shape their work but also how their work with Black girls impacts their lives. It might be thought of as reverse reflexivity.

This shared aspect of positionality, gender, and race serves as an asset in critical research around Black girlhood in that Black women researchers may be viewed as safer or more trustworthy in also having social identities that are marginalized and a shared identity of being Black and femme.[1] As Black girl participants may feel comfort in a researcher that shares identity markers with them, Black women researchers may also feel a kinship with participants. This connectedness may force us to ponder ways in which the experiences of our participants reflect our experiences as Black girls and even as Black women.

Research as a Mirror to the Self (Healing through Reflection)

According to Spencer (2006), the Phenomenological Variant of Ecology Systems Theory (PVEST) conceptualizes identity development as a cyclical process that occurs throughout a person's lifespan, being influenced by both internal dispositions and external factors. As Black women conduct research involving Black girls, we do not simply collect data and mechanically analyze it. Instead, Black women researchers must observe phenomena, take notes or recordings, read and reread transcripts, analyze our data, and draft manuscripts detailing what we found. The research process forces researchers to spend a considerable amount of time with a topic, and these moments have the potential to serve as external factors that can shape internal dispositions about self.

The very act of conducting research, especially critical research, has the power to shape any researcher's views of themselves and society at large. In conducting research in which many social identities are shared, the research, that is, the phenomena, the data, and the findings, though external factors, can serve as a mirror, reflecting the shared experiences of the researcher and the participants. In enacting the steps of our specific research methodologies, Black women researchers are given the opportunity to reflect on not only our data as we seek to answer research questions but also to reflect on our own lived experiences and how they are similar to or different from what we are currently observing, writing about, or analyzing.

Self-reflection is a tool for healing (Thorpe & Barsky, 2001). Therefore, as we researchers are forced to grapple with our lived experiences through the research process, we may also find that we allow ourselves to heal from past trauma and harmful actions and situations. Further, according to Thorpe and

---

[1] We use femme to encompass cisgender and transgender women and girls.

Barsky (2001), "through extensive self-reflection, women are able to make sense of their lives, and often make decisions that mark the beginning of new structures fostering meaning and commitment to those choices" (p. 761). Therefore while going through the research and subsequent reflection process, Black women researchers that conduct research with Black girls may progress through stages of our lives, moving into a more informed, intentional, and healthy state than before we embarked on the journey.

Shared Positionality

This book is significantly about positionality, defined as a researcher in relation to the social and political context of the study—the community, the organization, or the participant group (Coghlan & Brydon-Miller, 2014). In this case, contributors examine their identities in relationship to the Black girls they study, a task that is characterized by complexity and nuance. In their exploration of positionality, Caldera, Rizvi, Calderon-Berumen, and Lugo (2020) named research conducted by women of color with participants who share many aspects of their cultural identity as *women of color intimate research*. Research that intersects with the self, such as the scholarship done by Black women who study Black girls, deserves careful examination.

While Black girlhood and Black womanhood are two distinct stages, there are commonalities and shared struggles within both. The chapters in this book illustrate this continuum. For example, in Part I, Imani Minor states that as a woman in her early twenties, she does not yet feel like a full adult and therefore contemplates the boundaries around Black girlhood and womanhood as she reflects on how to position herself as she navigates higher education spaces and research. In reflecting on her research, she states, "as I continue to reflect on my work, I realize the unique lens that this betweenness offers me as I listen to Black girls while also honoring the profound ways that these young Black girls have affected my own growth process." But the connection between the two stages is not limited to young adults. In fact, Dr. Loren S. Cahill & Noor Jones-Bey write about how the two stages are, in fact distinct but are also intertwined and interdependent with shared joy and resilience due to shared struggles and oppression. Black Feminist Theory (Hill Collins, 2000) and Critical Race Feminism (CRF) posit that the intersectionality of being both Black and a woman or girl comes with both racialized and gendered experiences (Wing, 2003). Essentially, Black femmes are oppressed under a system of racism and patriarchy concurrently. For example, Carter Andrews, Brown, Castro, and Id-Deen (2019) found that Black girls are often "adultified" and sexualized in schools, unfortunately pushing the distinct stages closer together and creating an unnecessary shared experience. Dagbovie-Mullins (2013) writes about the interconnectedness of sexual objectification in Black girlhood and womanhood.

> At the same time that black girls are oversexualized and considered sexually aberrant in the media, black women are infantilized, viewed as play things who are endlessly sexually available and childlike, particularly in popular culture media where images of black women are most prominent: reality television and music videos. The prevalence and acceptance of these damaging images (black girls as women and black women as girls) in popular culture suggests that black girls aren't really girls. The dangerous entangling of woman and girl prompts us to think about black girls in two interrelated and degrading ways: they are forgettable and invisible and yet highly visible, hypersexual, and repelling. (p. 746)

Black girls are robbed of childhood due to being sexualized, while Black women are robbed of the agency typically afforded to adults by being reduced to sexual objects.

Further Black women and girls both experience discrimination based on appearance due to society's negative views of phenotypical features common in Black women and girls (Caldwell, 2003). This combination of racial and gender discrimination impacts both Black women and girls. Black women have reported losing their jobs due to their natural hair being seen as unprofessional and Black girls have faced discrimination in schools due to their natural hair and cultural styles being seen as dress-code violations (Donahoo, 2021). Further, Black girls as young as preschool-aged have shown an awareness of the undesirability of their natural hair (Earick, 2010; Sturdivant, 2020) and skin color, using play as a vehicle to make themselves more desirable by white supremacist ideology standards (Sturdivant, 2020). From early childhood through adulthood, Black femmes must confront the idea that society's Eurocentric-based beauty standards tend to render their traits undesirable and less feminine.

Apart from being discriminated against for natural appearance and being objectified and sexualized, Black women and girls are also often seen as hyper-aggressive and face the consequences of this stereotype rooted in Eurocentric notions of proper behavior. In schools, Black adolescent girls are likely to face punishments for acting what is deemed inappropriate. For example, Wun (2016) describes Black girls that were issued office referrals for showing agency at school by expressing their displeasure or disagreement with instructions that they found unfair. This idea that Black femmes should fall in line and not assert themselves is not limited to children. Black women are also characterized as being angry and aggressive, and this stereotype is enacted in private spaces as well as professional settings. Jones and

Norwood (2017) detail experiences in which coworkers take steps to silence Black women as they speak up about real issues in their workplace. Both Black women and girls are put in positions in which they must determine if they want to challenge unfair systems and possibly face reprimand and negative labeling or continue to suffer in silence.

Black women and girls share an experience of being oppressed under a system of white supremacy as well as under patriarchy. The shared experience of being both Black and femme in our society leads to shared struggles. Some of these are identical such as discrimination based on hair texture, while others are similar yet more nuanced, such as the ways in which both groups are sexualized or how each is punished for her agency.

Scholarship as Activism (Social Justice Aims)

One of the ways that Black women have responded to this dually oppressed status, and sometimes more than dually oppressed when considering Queer, differently-abled, and other oppressed social identities that can be held by Black women, is through scholarship. By engaging in research that allows Black women and girls to tell their counterstories and center their everyday struggles, joys, and realities, Black women scholars push back against the status quo. Centering the voices of marginalized communities is an exercise in freedom as it creates a space in which Black girls' lived experiences, thoughts, and actions can be presented without the threat of punishment due to not aligning with Eurocentric ontology and epistemology. Further, the shared struggles and social identities of Black women researchers and our Black girl participants equips Black women to ask questions and to design studies that serve to highlight social ills with the intent of eventually eradicating them. The work of Black girlhood studies is largely performed by Black women. Therefore, we thought it important to delve into why these women do this work. In Part III, several contributors described their work in ways that work toward the liberation of Black girls–and women. For example, Dr. Misha N. Inniss-Thompson explains her use of a cultural-asset perspective in her research as she strives to make manifest the voices of Black girls in a way that is often not done.

Quaye, Shaw, and Hill (2017) argue that "not engaging in activism is irresponsible and does not lead to social change" (p. 383). In fact, it is the shared struggles between Black women and Black girls that make scholar activism such a paramount exercise. Because Black women researchers tend to have experienced similar injustices and discrimination, we are uniquely equipped to produce the scholarship that best illuminates and critiques the systems and policies that created the inequities. According to Repko and Szostak (2017), critical research aims to take a political stance as it advocates for groups that are marginalized, such as Black girls. Black women scholars can use our experiences to help make changes in the lives of future Black women.

Looking to the Future

As we look into the future of this expanding field, we invite the reader to imagine the potential paths that Black girlhood studies could take. Janelle Grant invites the reader to reflect on methodology as we move forward with our work and to challenge long-held beliefs about research and how that serves or fails the work of Blackgirlhood studies. The work of Blackgirlhood studies is ongoing. The valuable insights that have been published and discussed as we have listened to Black girls have led to implications for ourselves as well as the world in which we find ourselves. These implications can lead to imagining a better future to consciously celebrating our past and present. Janelle Grant posits that the future of Blackgirlhood studies research must include subjectivity, creativity, hope (and joy), and inspiration.

This volume itself works toward some of these aims for the future. Creating space that honors subjectivity, and lived experiences and explains why this pushback against dominant conceptualizations of "good research" is vital and inextricable from the findings arrived at through traditional data collection and analysis methods. We argue that our voices, counterstories, imaginings, rememberings, and conclusions are valid. As our work pushes back against ideology and practices that silence Black girls, our work within this volume also pushes back against another form of silencing, the silencing of our stories and learning as Black women researchers. Our voices and reflections are not simply useful for ourselves to be left out of our manuscripts only to be felt within our bodies, whether consciously or not, but also for those that find themselves existing in places in which our bodies and energy takes up space. Thus this writing is simultaneously for our past, present and future selves and also for those who bear witness to the transformation of Black femmes through our research, reflection, and collaboration.

References

Anzaldúa, G. E. (2000). Writing: A way of life: An interview with Maria Henriquez Betancor. In A. Keating (Ed.), *Interviews/Entrevistas* (pp. 235–250). New York, NY: Routledge.

Ards, A. (2015). *Words of witness: Black women's autobiography in the post-Brown era*. University of Wisconsin Press.

Boylorn, R. (2016). On being at home with myself: Blackgirl autoethnography as research praxis. *International Review of Qualitative Research, 9*(1), 44–58. Retrieved June 1, 2021, from https://www.jstor.org/stable/26372178

Brown-Vincent, L. D. (2019). Seeing it for wearing it: Autoethnography as Black feminist methodology. *Taboo: The Journal of Culture and Education, 18*(1). https://doi.org/10.31390/taboo.18.1.08

Caldera, A., Rizvi, S., Calderon-Berumen, F., & Lugo, M. (2020). When researching "the Other" intersects with the self: Women of color intimate research. *Departures in Critical Qualitative Research, 9*(1), 63–88.

Caldwell, P. M. (2003). A hair piece: Perspectives on the intersection of race and gender. In Adrien Katherine Wing (Ed.), *Critical Race Feminism: A reader* (2nd ed., pp. 309–317). New York University Press.

Carter Andrews, D. J., Brown, T., Castro, E., & Id-Deen, E. (2019). The impossibility of being "perfect and white": Black girls' racialized and gendered schooling experiences. *American Educational Research Journal, 56*(6), 2531–2572.

Coghlan, D., & Brydon-Miller, M. (2014). *The SAGE encyclopedia of action research* (Vols. 1–2). London: Sage Publications. https://doi.org/10.4135/9781446294406.

Collins, P. H. (2000). *Black feminist thought: Knowledge, consciousness and the politics of empowerment* (2nd ed.). New York, NY: Routledge.

Creswell, J. W. (2014). *Research design: Qualitative, quantitative, and mixed methods approaches* (4th ed.). Sage Publications.

Dagbovie-Mullins, S. (2013). Pigtails, ponytails, and getting tail: The infantilization and hyper-sexualization of African American females in popular culture. *Journal of Popular Culture, 46*(4), 745–771. https://doi.org/10.1111/jpcu.12047.

Donahoo, S. (2021). Why we need a national CROWN Act. *Laws, 10*(2), 26. https://doi.org/10.3390/laws10020026.

Earick, M. E. (2010). The power of play and language on early childhood racial identity in three U.S. schools. *Diaspora, Indigenous, and Minority Education, 4*(2), 131–145. https://doi.org/10.1080/15595691003635955.

Gardner, S. K., Hart, J., Ng, J., Ropers-Huilman, R., Ward, K., & Wolf-Wendel, L. (2017). "Me-search": Challenges and opportunities regarding subjectivity in knowledge construction. *Studies in Graduate and Postdoctoral Education, 8*(2), 88–108. https://doi.org/10.1108/SGPE-D-17-00014.

Griffin, R. A. (2012). I am an angry Black woman: Black feminist autoethnography, voice, and resistance. *Women's Studies in Communication, 35*(2), 138–157, https://doi.org/10.1080/07491409.2012.724524.

Jones, T., & Norwood, K. (2017). Aggressive encounters & white fragility: Deconstructing the trope of the angry Black woman. *Iowa Law Review, 102*(5), 2017–2069.

Merriam, S. B., & Tisdell, E. J. (2016). *Qualitative research: A guide to design and implementation* (4th ed.). Jossey-Bass Publishers.

Probst, B., & Berenson, L. (2014). The double arrow: How qualitative social work researchers use reflexivity. *Qualitative Social Work, 13*(6), 813–827.

Quaye, S. J., Shaw, M. D., & Hill, D. C. (2017). Blending scholar and activist identities: Establishing the need for scholar activism. *Journal of Diversity in Higher Education, 10*(4), 381–399. https://doi-org.proxy.tamuc.edu/10.1037/dhe0000060.

Repko, A. F., & Szostak, R. (2020). *Interdisciplinary research: Process and theory.* Sage Publications.

Spencer, M. B. (2006). Phenomenology and ecological systems theory: Development of diverse groups. In D. Kuhn & R. S. Siegler (Eds.), *Handbook of child psychology* (6th ed.). John Wiley & Sons.

Sturdivant, T. (2020). *Developing while Black: An exploration of racial discourse found in the play of Black preschool girls* (Publication No. 27832257). [Doctoral dissertation, University of Texas at San Antonio]. ProQuest Dissertations Publishing.

The Latina Feminist Group. (2001). *Telling to live: Latina feminist testimonios.* Duke University Press.

Thorpe, K., & Barsky, J. (2001). Healing through self-reflection. *Journal of Advanced Nursing, 35*(5), 760–768. https://doi.org/10.1046/j.1365-2648.2001.01908.x.

Walker, A. (1983). *In search of our mothers' gardens: Womanist prose.* Harcourt.

Wing, A. K. (Ed.). (2003). *Critical race feminism: A reader* (2nd ed.). New York University Press.

Wun, C. (2016). Unaccounted foundations: Black girls, anti-Black racism, and punishment in schools. *Critical Sociology, 42*(4–5), 737–750. https://doi.org/10.1177/0896920514560444.

Part I Positionality: My Identity, My Work

The contributors in this section reveal how their work with Black girls has shaped their identities as Black women. They explore how their positionality impacts their work with Black girls. Said differently, they "locate" themselves in their scholarship and/or practical experiences with Black girls.

1 *To See and Be Seen:* Living and Loving the Complexities of Black Girlhood

DARLENE ANITA SCOTT

I did not know how to smile in 4th grade. In my 4th-grade school picture I look like I'm grimacing. I am wearing my favorite turquoise sweater, a gift from the best aunt to ever "aunt," and the collar of a white blouse peaks from under the crew neck. For some reason my mother also chose to tie a red bow around my neck. My bangs barely touch my forehead; my glasses take up a great deal of my face.

I am in 4th grade when my oldest sister begins her first semester at Delaware State University, the nearby HBCU. She rims her eyes with eyeliner and wears the best brands. That year I gratefully collect and wear the clothes whose style or size, usually style, she outgrows. Another sister, five years my senior, aspires to challenge Roxanne Shanté on the urban radio station Power 99. The rap contest invites amateur artists to answer the rapper's infamous response to the UTFO single "Roxanne." Imitating her, I dutifully record lyrics in spiral notebooks—none of my lyrics are my own though. I memorize Whodini and New Edition songs. As a 4th grader I am not especially interested in romance but I am in love with every member of New Edition, especially the lead singer, Ralph. And I am in love with Shawn. In 4th grade I aspire to be a graffiti artist like my rapping sister's classmate Shawn. I go to the movies for the first time in 4th grade—to see *Beat Street*, a film about hip hop culture that covers all the elements—the music, the art, the deejay, and the dancing. My mom lets us choose our favorite boxed candy from McCrory's department store next door to the theater and we smuggle our contraband under our coats. She buys a tub of popcorn that we share and this affair is quite a big deal. We are seven altogether and poor, though I am not aware of it. So important is this affair that I record it in the journal I write in class—lined paper stapled between two dark blue pieces of construction paper. In my sloppy cursive I also note that year, that my dad has stopped smoking and has joined the church choir.

In 4th grade I commit my life to Christ a few times. At least once, I repent my sins at the vacation Bible school held at the church behind our house. The white pastor and his wife, who disappear from the neighborhood as quickly as they appear, deliver short Bible stories and provide snacks and miniature Bibles to us and our neighborhood kickball/hide & go seek/jump rope partners. I am similarly compelled at the perennial summer sessions held on the corner of my grandmother and grandfather's street where we learn gospel songs under Mrs. Cannon's raspy direction.

In 4th grade, I discover Langston Hughes in my classroom library. We share a birthday and with this much I am smitten. Plus, nothing that has been called poetry that I have heard outside the church—to this point "Ego Trippin'" by Nikki Giovanni and "The Creation" by James Weldon Johnson—is so explicitly *Black*. I love things that are Black.

In 4th grade my huge glasses are usually broken from rolling down the hill with my white best friend Jayne after the bell rings at 3:18. Jayne is the daughter of one of the town's two local florists. She is wealthy but does not show it. She matches her name. I'm not sure how or when she comes to be my best friend; we don't see or talk to each other outside of school. Except in those few minutes between the bell and when my mother calls home to confirm we have arrived home safely. Sometimes, my twin sister and I even sneak with Jayne into the school superintendent's yard that backs up to the elementary school playground before Jayne walks west to her neighborhood and we walk east to ours. Our school is named after a Black man, Benjamin Banneker. It was the town's middle grade school for Black students before integration, so it is bordered by Black neighborhoods. But the superintendent is a white man whose daughter called my twin sister and I niggers two years before during an afterschool dance class. And according to Jayne, whose family attends church with his family, he does not want Black kids in his yard. He spots us and unleashes his dog to attack us on the supersized trampoline.

I am a 4th grader and a Black girl. My world is split between the default whiteness of my school and the default Blackness of the blocks I call my neighborhood. It is like having presbyopia—through the corrective contact lenses I wear to correct it, each eye on my face does not see the same thing at the same time, yet they converge to give me a full image of myself and my world.

In 4th grade, I am certain of many things: my feet on wheels, my agility on the monkey bars, my sisters' divinity, and all the lyrics to "Cool It Now." I love to eat, read the *Ebony* pictorial histories on my grandmother's bookshelf, jump rope well and skate well too despite having only one pair of skates to share with my twin and our other sister who most people mistake for our triplet. When I am in 4th grade, she is in sixth and able to wear her hair "out" more often than on Easter and picture day. Her bangs meet her eyebrows. My certainty comes from being self-aware. I am not yet as aware of the other eyes that will impose on me, try to make me self-conscious and force me to shrink into their gaze.

In 4th grade, I am not yet made an academic outlier in my school district that has decided there can only be one—maybe two—Black students tracked as academically gifted in any given grade level in any given year. Or better, I am not yet aware. In 4th grade, I wear fewer barrettes and balls but will have to endure the breakage from a couple of over-strength relaxers before my first professional hair style which I will choose from a shiny hair magazine influenced by the other women in my life who will include my sisters, their college friends, and the video models after whom they style themselves. Beginning in 4th grade I will begin to collect more and more evocative costume jewelry—eventually graduating to chandelier, chunky bamboo, and Nefertiti earrings—the bigger the better—multiple rings, and a series of gold chains. My public presentation will speak much louder than I, and what I choose to say will not always align with whatever trope into which I am placed based almost solely on this public presentation. I will learn not so many years from 4th grade, sometime in the murk of puberty for sure, that my identity is relegated to codified identifiers not of my choosing. Fourth grade is the last year of my life in which I am unable to be oblivious to my Black girl-ness as social currency, not that I was not being perceived that way all along. It is not the only time I will see myself fully but after 4th grade I will become conscious of how often I am challenged by society's inability to see me the same way.

My experience is not unique. Black girls and the fullness of their identities have historically been erased, minimized, or absorbed into abstraction, theory, or the background. Black girls, too often, are unseen. This doesn't mean that they are invisible but rather that the reduction of their identities disappears them into stereotypes and caricatures that are used to justify their exploitation and dispossess them of the agency to fight it. In the early 1970s, political scientist Mae C. King (1973) writes on the function of this stereotyping: "Every political system has its myths. Some are more dominant than others. These myths serve as a means of explaining and justifying the way of life of a society." Sociologist Patricia Hill Collins (1986) names these myths "controlling images" just over a decade later and posits that they are worse than stereotypes in their capacity to normalize and codify the exploitation of Black women. While their scholarship speaks to Black womanhood, Black girlhood has been collapsed into adulthood since Black people were brought to this country as chattel. Black children's labor and sex were as exploited as adult women disrupting and effectively eliminating Black girlhood. So, to this day, as Dr. Monique Morris (2016) notes in *Pushout: The Criminalization of Black Girls in Schools*, "Black girls are likened to adults," and the adultification "renders Black girlhood interchangeable with Black womanhood." The danger in failing to see Black girls as girls, in the fullness of all their iterations, or only as these inaccurate images, is that unless they are seen, which is to say, perceived, they do not receive appropriate attention and investment and the exploitation they face is considered inevitable.

In 2016 I launch a multimedia project of visual art and poetry, *Breathing Lessons,* to locate 4th grade me and who she is to become in the immediate years after; to help her navigate an iteration of Black girlhood, the good girl, that given all the dominant imagery of Black girlhood seems to deny her a place. Language is the first to be implicated—*black* necessarily invalidates *good* in the widely accepted connotation. History is implicated in tandem—the disembodiment of Black womanhood inaugurates tropes like the Jezebel and mammy figures that originate from what would contemporarily be described as "fast" girls and "prudes," the former supposedly performing sexual desire and prowess beyond her age and the latter performing asexuality or non-cis-gender specific sexuality. Each trope diminishes Black girls to their sexual; ergo, reproductive capacity. Since the enslavement of African-descended women, their bodies; their sex have been commodified. They are both capital and capital-producing through their reproduction of children who will also be raised as chattel and investments in them are only made to that end. So, 4th grade me is tracked as academically gifted; groomed to be currency: a credit.

The project's origin story begins before 2016 though. Between leaving 4th grade to enter the crucible of puberty and landing on the other side in early adulthood, I begin relating to the good girl though I generally realize, but reject, that I might be one. If I am to locate the origin of *Breathing Lessons,* though, it would probably be with my rejection of a romantic partner's all too familiar name calling. He calls me a good girl although in my mid-20s, I am a full-grown woman. My rejection likely also has to do with the fact that within the interlude between 4th grade and our conversation, I had never heard or imagined the identification in the representations of Black girlhood I knew. I reject the moniker based on the imagery of what I believe I know to be a good girl—white, not especially attractive or popular enough to make adolescence less of a chore—and she is not appealing or familiar to my notions of Black girlhood.

If I decide to stuff my adolescent life into Freytag's Pyramid of plot structure, my rejection is probably somewhere in the falling action even though I cannot identify the climax where the decision *had* to be made—either I was going to be a good girl or I was not. The denouement is fairly plain now that I am more than a few years removed from adolescence and my ex-partner calling me out. I am returned to 4th grade; I do not reject or embrace who I am. I just am. This is what it can mean to see and be seen. Despite active messaging, policy, and behaviors that would deny Black girls this kind of agency, a fully realized Black girl is not impossible. Moreover, it is critical that she be recognized in her fullness so that she can be invested in appropriately and can grow into a fully realized person. I now notice how often I was compartmentalized to suit social, academic and other constructions not of my choosing and worse, how often they delimited me.

There are ways of contextualizing Black girls that can either affirm or destabilize them. In a family anecdote, my mother describes the kindergarten screening process for my twin sister and me. One of the tasks is for potential students to draw themselves. My twin sister and I are six years old and begin searching the table for brown crayons to complete the task. As we color ourselves, the screener looks to my mother with what my mother has described as surprise. She explains to my mother that she is impressed that we choose to color ourselves brown, apparently ignoring the fact that we are in fact brown. The screener's attention reveals that she notices our self-realization, but her recognition comes tethered to an expectation of erasure by absorbing ourselves into a default whiteness. Imagine coloring the cream-colored construction paper appropriately being perceived by the screener as divergent. Our ability to see ourselves is remarkable? This low-stakes erasure has high stakes implications. It informs the high stakes decisions made about and for Black girls.

Fourth grade marks the last year the stakes are as low—or so my teachers threaten when they tell us what will no longer be acceptable in "middle" school from our personal presentation to how we present our assignments. For Black girls, of course, the stakes have always been high even if we have been unaware of how high.

Fifth grade is the year that we begin to change classes. No longer in the care of a single teacher, we will travel from subject to subject independently. The middle school halls I am expected to navigate are a mixing bowl of three elementary schools poured into a single building. This year, my classmates are even more likely to be white and belong to a family of local prominence. Navigating the new people, new classes, new halls, and the larger lunchroom are their own challenges. There is no acclimation like the year of half-day kindergarten provided for my introduction to elementary school, but my 5th grade year begins the day after Labor Day, so blessedly the first week is not a full week.

In 5th grade, I am allowed to join the band. I am also allowed to choose the instrument I want to play. I choose the xylophones. So does my elementary school friend, Jayne. This is the most expensive instrument on the list of choices; my parents cannot afford to buy or rent the practice set but they do not deny me my selection. Instead, they contract with the band instructor to allow me to use a dated set she owns. The set does not contain all the keys, and the keys it does contain often move off track so that the notes are dampened by the strike of my mallets.

In 5th grade, we are still allowed recess. The playground does not have a set of monkey bars so I settle on the swings. In 5th grade recess can be denied for infractions that were previously inconsequential. In 5th grade, dress codes are implemented, academic tracking is fixed, and social vetting begins. As a Black girl, this means I can lose my recess because of my public presentation. For us Black girls this means our public presentation will be stifled or criminalized for the first of many times in our lives; we will be expected to diminish ourselves in some or many ways; we will be unicorn'ed by teachers and counselors for being anything other than the prescribed defaults of Black girlness, and we will likely be sexually propositioned by our peers and for this too, we will likely face criminalization, no protections, or else we will determine to stifle anything in us that points to our perceived fast-ness.

The "fast" girl trope is a contemporary repurposing of the Jezebel and the Sapphire as their daughter. The caricatures are rooted in the institution of slavery where Black girls and women are dehumanized as unfeminine and wont to behaviors typically assigned to animals like sexual wantonness and aggression, the main features of the Jezebel and Sapphire. The imagery is codified to justify the exploitation of their bodies for physical and reproductive labor and sex.

An anti-abolition tract contends: "Their very virtues, with their affectations and industry, are those of well-trained domestic animals" (Hunt, 1866, p. 20) describing the prevailing opinion of Black women at the time. The opinion is codified into practice when Congress prohibits the import of Africans in 1808. Enslaved Black women are forced to "breed" like animals to maintain the enslaved population. Their fecundity is justified by sexual proclivities assigned to them by the white men who exploit them. One white planter recounts:

> I knew all about the sexual act, but not until I was twelve years old did I know that it was performed with white women for pleasure; I had thought that only

Negro women engaged in the act of love with white men just for fun because they were the only ones with the animal desire to submit that way. (hooks, 1981, p. 63)

Even science supports and corroborates the imagery. As sites of curiosity, Black women's bodies are used for research and any element of their physical presentation that is dissimilar from the white woman's body is used as further scientific evidence of Black women's sexual appetite. Famously, Saartje Bartmann, a Khoekoe woman, is paraded throughout Europe, her buttocks and genitals displayed as "evidence" of Black women's erotic lives.

Like the Jezebel, the Sapphire violates prescribed physical and psychosocial notions of femininity and is punished for it (Pilgrim, 2012, para. 1). She is not passive; is even aggressive and antagonistic—especially to Black men—when she perceives injustice or moral defect. Her dominant personality excludes her from protection from exploitation and is even blamed for it. Enter Black girls policed for infractions like insubordination or talking back and denied protection when the perception of their corporeal presentation—in this case, their vocal expressions including volume, inflection, and speech patterns are treated as aggressive, not feminine and as evidence of maturity so not in need of protection.

A 2018 study of Washington D.C. public schools, *Dress Coded: Black Girls, Bodies, and Bias* demonstrates these stereotypes at work in the policing of Black girls' bodies. Dress codes often target female anatomy, how clothing fits rather than the attire itself. Seventeen-year-old Samantha O'Sullivan complains, "two people be wearing the same thing and then like if you, if you're like curvier then they'll tell you to change because it looks inappropriate." Inappropriate becomes code for mature; aging too "fast," and mature is proxy for sexual as Kristine Turner, a 16-year-old student, points out about her middle school's no make-up rule and its implications: "They said lipstick was distracting. [Long] nails were just considered too grown."

I am a middle schooler, in 5th grade. Enter school dances where slow songs queue performances of awkward adolescent courtship conventions. The Black girls, and only the Black girls, will be criminalized for them based on any aspect of their public presentation to their style of dance that betrays them as "fast." Because of the persistence of the stereotypes, their bodies and their uses of them, like dance, are treated as sexually provocative and therefore out of the bounds of girlhood—femininity and youth. Reinforced by applications like the "mistake of age" defense in cases of statutory rape (Thompson, 2022, p. 979), out of these bounds, they are also unprotected from exploitation. Older offenders often escape criminal liability by claiming their victims appear older than their age.

The constriction of adolescent expression for Black girls is what Lakisha Michelle Simmons (2015) describes as a "double bind." Simultaneously sexualized and expected to be respectable—fundamentally chaste—Black girls are adultified by both tenets. Implying that they have some kind of "knowing" and moreover should "know better" betrays maturity and denies them the formative experience of adolescence.

As a 5th grader, I get my first training bra although there is little to "train." I call attention to the half shirt by pulling on the straps, an invitation to the boys at my table who graciously oblige with hypersexual quips they have heard somewhere before but clearly do not understand. My homeroom teacher ignores the lot of us as if the overly sexual language is typical age-appropriate chatter. I uncomfortably offer the boys a toothless "shut up." When I am in 5th grade, my twin sister has boyfriends; I do not. As puberty reshapes our bodies, dress styles, some Black girls perform to the trope; for some puberty will take longer—or never—to visit, confusing their place in the corpus of Black girlhood.

According to my school picture, I learn to smile in 5th grade. In 5th grade, I am allowed to style my own hair, and I always make sure my earrings match my outfit. They are not very large yet. In 5th grade, peg-legged jeans are the style and I wear a pair my oldest sister has gifted me more times than many. As a 5th grader, I am as interested in my presentation as ever but I simultaneously emerge from the year as an introvert though I am without the language to call it that.

I am in the 5th grade when I receive a series of coming-of-age books and a period starter kit that consists of a calendar, maxi pad, and a booklet that tells me how and when to change the pad. In the school library I have access to so-called teen magazines that offer free samples of pads and tampons which I collect religiously; they also talk about how to kiss boys, what to wear for the season, and profile pop stars that never appear in my favorite: *Right On*. The models look like my classmates who have parties at the skating rink, are selected for the cheerleading squad, and clump together at the dances giggling but never dancing like the kids from my neighborhood who form a circle and cheer for whoever is confident enough to enter it and showcase their skills. (I am not one of them). As a 5th grader, I am learning to be more critical of my image in the mirror.

The changes in my self-awareness are subtle so they are probably absorbed into the expectations of adolescence. As a 5th grader I am awarded for my grades; I love to read and write and create the "reports" that are our 5th-grade versions of theses. My instructors act impressed by my ability to perform so well in their academic system and say as much to my mother at the biannual parent conference nights that I attend with her mostly so I can eat the complimentary cookies. I am affirmed by their compliments; my mother is gracious but underwhelmed by the attention they shower on me. My teachers use the opportunity to ply me with books and enter my writing into contests. In Social Studies, I write about Crispus Attucks for one of the contests and argue that he was probably placed in the front of the firing British on purpose. Mrs. Kelly gushes.

Where I am not in the circle of attention at dances, I am treated as a unicorn in the not-so-subtle academic tracking system. Through their lens, I am Mammy's daughter: the Special Black Girl. Opposite the Jezebel, Mammy is also a similar distortion of Black femaleness and investment in her is only as capital and capital-producing. I am clearly being tracked to attend college so that I can eventually participate in society as a producer of services or goods or "be something." The Mammy is considered respectable due to her proximity to the ideals perceived as whiteness which include her ability to be a "productive" member of The Community (versus her community) and her public presentation that allows her to absorb into The Community. In the academic environment investments are made in Black girls that are perceived as the Mammy figure to place them in stark relief against the "fast" ones. Make no mistake, these girls will not be protected any more than the "fast" girls. Any safety they experience is due to their proximity to whiteness which is always protected. In fact, because of this proximity, protection is not expected to be required. While the violence enacted on the Special Black Girl is not necessarily over-sexualizing or over-policing as it is with the Fast Girl, the violence is in the disembodiment she is expected to perform; the Special Black Girl is expected to amputate or compartmentalize her Black girlness in these spaces. Or, she can resist. There is danger in her resistance of course. To refuse to disassemble is a threat to the opportunities reserved for Special Black Girls and as she risks being excluded from The Community, she also risks exclusion from her community for whom these privileges are denied.

In most of my classes I am usually one of two Black students, and my classmates have convinced themselves that my introversion is an opportunity for exclusion. I am okay with it. I am most comfortable on Mr. Stevenson's bus that picks us up at the porch of my grandmother's and grandfather's house and drops us off on our street corner. These kids are my peers. Our parents attended the local Black middle, now elementary, school together so we are practically related. Most of us buy our fruit roll ups with food stamps and begrudgingly accept the disruption of our summer escapades that is our annual tour of Vacation Bible School at the various churches on the surrounding block determining which one is taking the best end-of-session field trip or offering the best snacks. In my 5th-grade year, I have yet to meet a book that centers Black people that I do not like; I also know most of the lyrics to "We Are the World" but don't especially believe them.

Only one of my teachers is Black, a woman named Mrs. Harris who also attends the Black middle, now elementary, school with my parents and teaches or more accurately facilitates gym. Gym is my least favorite class; I do not like playing the team sports or the required clothing change we are expected to make in the outdated locker rooms. I walk the length of the fitness test's required mile, refuse to change positions in volleyball, and if I am lucky Mrs. Harris pretends to believe my headache excuse and lets me sit on the stage of the gymnasium during class reading my books and watching the others in the auditorium sweat well before the end of the school day only to smell rank for the rest of it.

As a 5th grader, I love Attilio's pizza and admiring blisters that I develop while skating at the roller-skating rink during quarterly parties my mother's company holds for employees and their families. I aspire to host a birthday party there but must settle for attending the parties of a couple of classmates whose parents have the money to fund them. In 5th grade I do not go to my best friend's birthday party and mine is not a public affair. Like most birthdays, it is an intimate family meal of my choosing and homemade cake. In another year, when we prepare to turn 13, another friend, also white, who will be attending Jayne's party tells me as we sit on the swings in our last year of having recess that Jayne's father does not want her to have a Black best friend. We never discuss it again. Jayne will receive her first make up kit and a perm to thicken her flat flaxen colored hair. My rite of passage birthday will not come until my Sweet Sixteen and it will not include make-up. By then, Jayne and I will not be best friends.

The breaking of our relationship will be subtle. In high school band, we will continue to perform side by side but we will not share any classes because she has no need to exert herself academically; her life path is decided. I have every reason to. I will adorn myself in Black girl totems—pleather Africa medallions and bamboo earrings; a Nefertiti pendant and Reebok freestyles—to assert myself beyond the cataracted versions my classmates and teachers will assign me. Like in 4th grade, but by now with intention, I resist prescription. By 16, I will have learned how unsafe I am in my Black girl body and Jayne will just be discovering the power of her white one. She will secretly date a Black boy and he will allow himself to be her secret.

I am 16 the first time I am made aware of the offense of my breasts. My boyfriend that summer makes every attempt to disprove the notion, but he is not with me the day I am walking to the store in a crew neck shirt and Bermuda shorts when two white men attempt to call me to their car. They claim to want directions; I maintain my distance. I am not new to the untrustworthiness of white men and the lack of protection from them. As a pre-adolescent, my sisters and I are followed through downtown by "the man in the red car" on a few occasions. In his boldest move, he tries to lure us to his car. So we lure him to our house. When we arrive, we scream out for my father who bounds toward the car with cinder blocks to attack him. The man peels off. Miraculously my father, an impetuous and protective combat veteran, doesn't follow but decides to call the police before murder is the case. The local authorities are familiar with the man's behavior and identify his residence as a local public housing community full of children of color. They say there is nothing for them to do. So, on this day, at 16 I am leery and armed with history. It is when the men offer me "payment" that I roll my eyes and walk into the temporary safety of a store. They speed off and I am left to walk home aware that I am a 16-year-old Black girl and safety is not my birthright.

In my 16-year-old school picture, I choose a practiced grin instead of a smile. I slick my hair with Luster's pink lotion and wrap it under a scarf until the bus arrives that morning. In the photo, my gold chains frame the collar of my blouse and match the gold flat top frames of my glasses and my gold earrings. The picture is taken on the Monday after the Homecoming dance. I am sure I took longer than I needed to walk to the makeshift photo studio in the auditorium, to leave the auditorium, and to return to class. I am sure it was an advanced class and sure that my instructor did not notice my extended absence. I am sure I do not go to the lunchroom that day; I rarely do in this quarter when my best friends, Black girls: Tia, Tarnisha, and Adrienne, have different lunch periods. I spend the 45 minutes in the library where I may have written a letter to my boyfriend or maybe I read some magazines; I might have completed some of my homework so that I could have more time to talk on the phone after school.

I am 16 and I am certain of many things: the utility of Luster's pink lotion, my boyfriend's loyalty, and the imminence of my escape from the place that made me. I love to read, am good at geometry, and prefer to play the marimbas to the xylophones. In the years since 4th grade, I am learning how to fit into the whole of myself. There will be more years of tucking myself into my skin. But for now, I am at least aware that I am erased as often as I am absorbed; of the imposition of other eyes on me that would shrink me in their gaze. All Black girls are not—some of my friends choose lower-stakes classes and disloyal boyfriends to accommodate that gaze, privileging it over their own. They disembody and disembowel themselves in service to a gaze that never intended to see them or allow them to see themselves fully.

For those of us who have determined not to serve that gaze, our stories can disrupt and dismantle systems that deny Black girls opportunities to be visible and valued. That is why I have committed my art to telling mine.

References

Collins, P. H. (1986). Learning from the outsider within: The sociological significance of Black feminist thought. *Social Problems, 33*(6), 14–32.

hooks, b. (1981). *Ain't I a woman: Black women and feminism* (p. 63). South End Press.

Hunt, J. (1866). *The Negro's place in nature.* Van Evrie, Horton & Co.

King, M. C. (1973). The politics of sexual stereotypes. *Black Scholar, 4*(6/7), 12–23.

Morris, M. (2016). *Pushout: The criminalization of Black girls in schools* (p. 34). The New Press.

National Women's Law Center. (2018). *Dress coded: Black girls, bodies, and bias in D.C. schools.* National Women's Law Center. https://nwlc.org/wp-content/uploads/2018/04/web_Final_nwlc_DressCodeReport-1.pdf

Pilgrim, D. (2012). *The sapphire caricature.* The Jim Crow Museum. https://www.ferris.edu/HTMLS/news/jimcrow/antiblack/sapphire.htm

Simmons, L. M. (2015). *Crescent city girls: The lives of young Black women in segregated New Orleans.* University of North Carolina Press.

Thompson, M. K. (2022). Sexual exploitation and the adultified Black girl. *St. John's Law Review, 4*(94), 971–988.

2 The Project of Black Girlhood: Reimagining Interconnectivity and Indivisibility between Black Women and Girls

LOREN S. CAHILL AND NOOR JONES-BEY[2]

Introductions

I am Loren S. Cahill, a Black girl from Saint Louis, Missouri. I carry legacies of Black girls forced to Tennessee and Mississippi due to threats of poverty and sexual violence from white men. I am a descendant of midwives, sharecroppers, homemakers, nurses, federal judges, lawyers, and social workers. My family was always concerned with offering care for the Black community. Perhaps, it was my destiny that I followed suit. I became a youth community organizer at the age of 16 because I was deeply impacted by racism that permeated through my high school and I chose to document my experiences, and report them to the administration. My joy for service continued in college. While in Boston, I became a founding member of the school-community-university partnership which offered wraparound tutoring services to students in and after school. I was inspired by the work I accomplished but was somewhat discouraged by the limitations of only making interventions for youth in schools. I got my MSW to study youth-led organizing. I recognized through the process that agism constantly showed up and without translation and avid support from adults with influence that most concerns

---

2 This work would be impossible without the support of ordinary Black girls holding space with us including not limited to: The Colored Girls Museum, Our Mothers Kitchens, Black Quantum Futurism, Girls for Gender Equity, Berkeley Scholars to Cal, Fannie Lou Hamer Freedom High School, June Jordan School for Equity, Berkeley-Technology Academy, Scholar Sibs Writing Group.

were not heard from youth themselves. I decided that I wanted to study Youth Participatory Action Research (YPAR) to better arm youth with empirical data to mirror their lived experiences and shift power relations in their organizing campaigns. I obtained my PhD to learn this specialized expertise. While in New York, I did YPAR with several groups. One was an organizing collective composed of mainly formerly incarcerated young men. I loved this group, it was some of the most impactful organizing that I have ever been a part of but I was repeatedly discounted anytime I brought up concerns of sexism in and outside of our work. It was very confusing for me. Any time they brought up experiences of being incarcerated I believed them even though I had never encountered that level of violence personally but anytime I brought up examples of misogynoir I felt personally attacked, dismissed, or listened to momentarily and then disregarded. I slowly began to realize that we had built a whole campaign around healing justice but many of the girls in the collective, myself included, felt unsafe with our comrades. I eventually broke ties with the organization and pursued dissertation research to locate spaces and collectives where Black girls, trans, and femmes were loved and felt safe. I recognized those feelings that I had at previous institutions and movement spaces dissipated immediately without the concerns of racism and sexism plaguing me. I could alternatively reflect and create radical demonstrations of love with other Black girls. All of my most recent publications, studies, and creative work are centered around the axis of Black girlhood. While my work is centered around working with Black girls to understand how they remember, create rituals, and reimagine the world around them, it has forced me to ask myself the same questions. The project of Black girlhood is a freedom project. It has forced me to free my own inner Black girl to playfully create research and art that is meaningful, sustainable, and impacts others who share this identity.

I am Noor M. Jones-Bey, I was born in Wisconsin and was raised in the San Francisco Bay Area. I come from a long lineage of nurses, women named Gloria, care-takers, men who refused to be less than they are and were, grocery store clerks, writers, and domestic workers. I am the great-granddaughter of first-generation New Yorkers, Georgia sharecroppers, Bajan and Trinidadian and Jamaican migrants who left their countries and home states due to lack of opportunity and state-imposed violence. I learned about these worlds through nostalgic stories and experienced different models of mothering one born out of Jamaica and another from a German North Dakota which ultimately form the foundation for my practice of womanism today. I was regularly building imaginary lands, escape hatches, and bridges to leap betwixt and between the different and sometimes hella confusing household practices, rules, and accents, whether they be the gender expectations as a girl while practicing Islam and/or Christianity, or vegetarianism or meat-eating or how to spend summers. I was often moving through spaces that were not quite meant for me. It felt like wearing hand-me-down shoes worn to the shape of another's foot. There are always gaps. I was a target for people's confusion and questioning. I often felt pressure to teach people of all ages about my differences with patience and grace while also proving myself and battling interlocking gender, race and class stereotypes. School was tightrope and a carnival of sorts. Constant pressure, shifting acts, and costumes. Though I wouldn't know to call it literacies, I was often learning through alternative means whether it be music, art, discarded conversations, and silences made in the wake of what was demanded and the resulting run-off of what adults wouldn't make space for.

In college, I began volunteering for a women's group and almost every year since then I've created intergenerational women and girls groups to provide opportunities for mentorship across K-12 and university settings to create spaces for my students but also Black girls and women, like myself, to question, to be and express ourselves fully through creative dialogue, art, and writing. I have had many official roles, mentor, coordinator, afterschool tutor, college access director, classroom teacher, program director, and with each role, I have found myself searching for free space, for a portal. A place that is safe to be whole.

We came together through our mutual friend in a Black femme and gender-expansive folx scholarly support space. Our weekly conversations have helped us to understand that the project of Black Girlhood is never-ending. The scholarship, organizing, advocacy, and artistry made by Black women and girls are constantly inspiring us and unpacked more in the next section. We will introduce the Black femmes we view that our work is in conversation with and who have constantly invited us to return or project forward into our Black girl selves.

Literature Review as Portal

We recognize that Black women and girls are complex and always changing and thus, require an expansive grouping of Black voices, scholarship, organizing, art, and talk to foreground our work. We draw upon a catalog of resistance and re-imagine these works (Sharpe, 2016) a portal, a shoal (King, 2019), a space of futurity (McKittrick, 2013). In real-time these portals offer space to be, space to breathe, and space for which to re-imagine reality as a means to refashion self, community, and space. We reckon that this work of portal making is a necessary component of survival weaving past experiences while walking through a seemingly concrete present and attempts at remaking futures. This chapter would not be possible without conversations with and the study of/with many Black femmes and gender-expansive folx who we personally know and do not. We will deviate from the traditional literature review format and offer you our version of a portal that allows us to channel theory and praxis in a way that allows us to return to or project forward into our Black girl selves (Ewing, 2017; Boylorn 2012; Dominique Hill, 2018). Black womanist and feminist theorists have led in designing and constructing portals of possibility, resistance, and disruption by any means necessary (Shange, 2019; Hill-Collins, 2002; hooks, 1996; Butler, 2018).

The research reveals the many ways Black women and girls become misunderstood and misrecognized in the institutional, public and private settings by systems of power and everyday people (Morris, 2016; Cooper, 2018; Nash, 2018; Jordan-Zachery, 2017). They excavate the personal while simultaneously extracting the genius of Black girls (Gaunt, 2006). Genius made manifest by ordinary black girls (Vashti) Barbara Johns at the age of 16 leading a student strike for equal education at R.R. Moton High School in Farmville, Prince Edward County, Virginia (Kanefield, 2014), to Kakuya Shakur, at the age of 3, telling her mom to "break the bars" giving Assata Shakur the inspiration needed to plot her escape from prison (Shakur, 1987), to 11-year-old Naomi Wadler's gut-wrenching delivery of her speech at the Women's March in 2018 that discusses the violent death and daily oppression endured by Black girls. (Mathew, 2018), to Darnella Frazier at the age of 17, filming the murder of George Floyd providing the footage to lead to indictment and convictions of the police involved (Altschuler & Priscilla, 2020), there is abundant data that proves that Black girls routinely fight for our recognition and justice. The Black women and girls that we read, study, observe, break bread with, and pray to are portals that led us back to self-discovery and positioned us to be better equipped to witness the fullness of Black girls we may encounter in our scholarship, teaching, art, and organizing. In the next section, we will discuss our methodological approach for this chapter.

Methodology

In this chapter, we are using autoethnography to design a radical assemblage of our lives juxtaposed between our research experiences that have centered Black girls. We aimed to use this framework to answer the question of *What is the project of Black Girlhood?* by creatively and comprehensively bringing forth an aesthetically distinct alternative to reassess widely accepted notions of how knowledge production and acquisition should transpire in qualitative inquiry and analysis. We felt that autoethnography was the most generous method because it focuses on our analysis of how we have used our personal lived experiences to inform the political projects of our research, praxis, and ethics. Similar to the mosaic artform, womanist scholars reflectively frame together pieces of oppositional knowledge construction, dialogical voice, contextual multiplicity, theory, and praxis (Evans-Winters, 2019). Because our very existence as Black girls unfolds in a series of stages and beseeches collective wisdom and resourcefulness, we are materializing Black feminism/womanism in this inquiry as a mosaic through the resulting chapter.

This autoethnographic mosaic project aims to be narrow enough to provide answers and accessible enough to be useful. We have made the deliberate choice to write with our younger, present, and future Black girl selves by sketching vital lessons learned about trauma, freedom, love, care, and joy that we learned in and outside our research and fieldwork. We scaffold by recalling our personal experiences with these topics and then move to discuss how we have encountered these same topics in the field. We then theorize indivisibility against the backdrop of our own lived experiences. We believe that by doing so that we choose to make new visions of Black girlhood visible through this writing process. We are invested not only in telling our stories but also in making our stories useful and meaningful to Black girls. It is ethically very important to us that Black girls, in particular, find direct relevance in the stories we tell. When we were attempting to connect our relationship to self-reflection and scholarship, it felt critical for us to join Black feminists who have centered their experience and humanity in pursuit of freedom.

Indivisibility

Before we begin to sketch our autoethnographic analysis, we will explain some important theoretical tenants to help scaffold our avant-garde approach to the chapter. Indivisibility is a way of seeing Black women and girls which breaks the dominant conceptions of time and space as well as the understanding of singular selfhood. In reckoning with the complexity of Black women and girls, we offer this way of seeing self as multiple and spanning generations (in the past, present and future) as a route towards healing ourselves and the larger collective of Black femmes. We theorize Black women and girlhood as the process of remembering that is always in motion and in dialogue and therefore necessitating space for which to see ourselves more intricately and authentically. We draw upon African and Indigenous (Phillips & Matti, 2016; Silva, 2018; Trask, 1999) epistemologies to craft our assemblage of selves, experiences and ways of knowing that are rendered invisible and also separated in western notions of personhood. Through this lens we recognize Black woman and girlhood as deeply expansive, a space, a shoal of decolonial inquiry and care that bounds across space and time and also reveals our multiplicity, our multiple selves flowing inside each of us. Black women and girls' lives are inherently enmeshed given overlapping, reverberating and resonating points of contact with each other and the larger world. Thus, we draw upon the term indivisibility to underscore the ways Black women and girls are deeply connected, despite all that we were forced to forget or (dis)member intergenerationally.

As Black women scholars who love Black girls and who also have Black girls inside of them, there is a tenuous road we must tread to analyze the Black girls we are researching and care for our multiple selves that are both girls and women in the academy. We are both early-career scholars and quite new to this work but in the following section, we will unpack some of the vital lessons we have personally learned in our own lives juxtaposed with our fieldwork, teaching, and organizing experiences with Black girls.

Vital Lessons

In this section, we will traverse thematically the vital lessons about trauma, care, joy, freedom, and love that we have learned personally or professionally about Black girlhood and womanhood. We will describe how our personal experiences mirror one another by sketching throughlines between ourselves, research participants, and the community. We try quite earnestly to not collapse ourselves with others around us by naming the inherent differences and variances that exist between us and our Black girl interlocutors.

Trauma

In college, I (*Noor*) began as a volunteer with a women's group at an alternative high school with students who were identified as "dropouts" and "at-risk" and for the first time in my educational journey, I felt like I could breathe. I was called in to be a mentor and I quickly recognized how the definition of mentorship on my application was inaccurate, as the mentor and mentee relationship would shift with each new topic or question. I listened to young women speak with candid wisdom beyond their years and also spiral back into giggling little girls at the turn of a phrase. Each week I would bring new Black women from my college until the group grew off campus into exchanges, outings, and sleepovers. One night, Shayla, a talented and visionary student, was shot and killed at 16. The news told her story in stunted and deadening words which felt like an icy blow amid our immeasurable grief. The lifeless retelling muted her colorful yet shy presence into a jumble of statistics. On that night, I lost and gained one of the most powerful mentors in my educational work. Her life and death serve to remind me of the importance of recovering the lives and experiences of ordinary Black girls and women too often distorted, reduced, or rendered nameless by state-sanctioned violence.

While volunteering with SWV,[3] an organization that centered the intergenerational lives of Black women and girls with a healing justice lens, we held a circle and one young woman of about 15–16 shared that "Black girls don't have time to feel." I asked her "what do you mean by that?" Her response was heartbreaking and familiar at the same time. She immediately started sharing how difficult circumstances keep coming that she has to grapple with so there is no time to slow down and feel. Further, she shared how when she has taken the time to share her story it is often ignored or not listened to, so what's the point?" Her voice echoed that of Shaunice, both young women at similar ages distanced by time and space entered into dialogue. These young women wrote and spoke to free girls in the future as well as themselves. They taught me that our work is to name our pain and let it go and create new ways of defining and seeing ourselves. My work to make space for Black women and girls to be is dedicated to my slain students and to the moments of joy that bursts from girls playing in the hallway while late to class. It is within these liminal moments of learning, joy, and loss in schooling that I see the complexity of the critical nature of education, research, and practice to listen to Black women and girls.

Care

Similar to my first women's group in college, the Sisters With Voices[4] space, would transform into a sacred space at the start of each meeting. As young women would filter in, hands would curve about the chairs, bags would be placed to the side as the center space was decorated with strings of light, colorful cloth, ordinary objects, and important momentos. Everyone participated in shaping the circle. With a few guiding nudges by the older women, facilitators in the space, the meeting would begin. The young women and girls were co-creators as they moved to present questions and acute analysis which would steer the flow of the space. I now understand this space with words offered to me by womanist researchers, artists, and visionaries, as a

3 Pseudonym
4 Pseudonym

garden space, a shoal, or what we affectionately write as a portal where the lives of ordinary Black and Brown girls are remembered. In this portal, we could be without sanction. We could travel unfettered as we moved between the sacred and the profane with ease and curious attention. At times, care looks like a collective call and response, expanding the space to what was needed and shifting to honor what came up. Or in another moment, care looks like turning up a song that was requested, slowing to make more space after a question was posed. A halt to a stop when tears flow. A hand offering tissue and some chocolate or a raucous joke. We could say the things we were told to swallow. Honor the years, we spoke and no one turned to listen. A space to be in ways that felt good for us. A space to figure out what care looked like for each of us. We could ask questions of each other and learn alternative routes to what each of us dreamed as future freedom or for a bit of fun tomorrow.

Joy

I (*Noor*) created space for play, for research, for art, for community, based on memories of my girlhood and the depth of joy that always came out of these women's groups. I've learned to listen for Black girls across generations and make space for all ages. As a granddaughter, I learned how to listen to silence. My Grandmother, born in 1926, sits across from me. She leaps to a stand, pushing her cane aside, she bends her body and shifts her knees left to right in a slow timeless groove to show me how to do "the twist." I immediately know all of my attention is needed and that I will be tested shortly after. I am her granddaughter and know that my next moves are about legacy. I feel the same strict precision and attention to excellence in the small huddle of young Black girls practicing the latest dance at the corner of my classroom at a moment of transitioning between topics. I give them three tries before I call them back to the group. Over the years, I've grown to see lines of connection between these experiences of Black women and girls at play in allsorts of found spaces. The way their bodies, choices, belly laughter and flung words reveal stories and even more legacies of the Black women and girls before them. As a researcher, this listening to and holding space for—became a method, a way of knowing myself and other Black women and girls intergenerationally. What I now call a fete collage.

Beginning with an empty classroom, a loud speaker and some tasty snacks, we fill the chairs and push aside the trials of the day to speak and just be. We let it go in words, in body, in color on page, in throwing our heads back and singing with knowing smiles "You make me happy," hands outreached in dramatic stances to join Beyonce's soothing vocals in her remake of "Before I Let Go." We notice we've gone over time, the nighttime janitor, Jamal, wheels his supply cart by with a big smile and says, "take your time ladies!" We move, dance, clean, and also leave a heaping plate of delicious snacks for Jamal. We leave with journals filled with poetry, ancestor names, bits of wisdom and story, colorful half made collages, and most importantly a host of memories and connections alive within us. This intergenerational play space taught me the importance of making space for joy recognizing the cutting and immobilizing heaviness that comes with unbraiding silent stories that map out our ever reaching complexity.

Freedom
My gradual embrace of showing up differently than others around me has been a slow and laggard journey. I am not the best orator, fundraiser, or strategist. For a long time, I felt that my incapacity to do these things meant that I would never be able to contribute enough as an activist and organizer. I kept forcing myself to do things I was not well suited for and proceeded to become injured and harmed repeatedly in the process. So much so that I took a hiatus and thought about quitting completely. My ethnography for my dissertation helped me to understand that freedom projects can take form in a multitude of formats, roles, and practices. I wanted to ensure that I gave and did not just extract from the community partners, Our Mothers Kitchens, my volunteer service was supporting their annual summer camp for teen Black girls in Philadelphia. I was so amazed by how free they were picking collard greens, making jollof rice, doing creative writing, and reading in the grass. I thought about the lie that I had been led to believe that organizing was only successful when brought about system-level change. Offering strategies for Black women and girls to access freedom at any moment felt like a deeply radical intervention that had relational impacts for oneself and the community. Acknowledging and elevating culinary arts and creative writing as both essential strategies towards freedom building helped me to unleash creative processes inside of me and value not only my own contributions but those of the past and future matriarchs of my family. Your freedom project can look like the healthy, nutritious, food you grow and/or cook for your family. Or it can be the poem, book, journal article you write about your pursuit of freedom. Each engage in rituals, archive tradition, allow us to be in relationship with others and are each in their own unique way powerful examples of cultural work. My little sisters at OMK taught me that true freedom is always available to us and can be found in the littlest of things.

Love
I (Loren) had and still have really struggled with loving myself and others completely. I have spent the last five years really wrestling with what it means to change my own relationship to love. That self-love journey for me started with somatics, embodiment, and energy work. Interestingly enough,

one of my favorite research experiences happened concurrently during this period of love inquiry and innovation in my life. I am willing to wager that both processes were influencing one another. My therapist at the time suggested an opportunity to consult with a young women's group at Brownsville Community Justice Center. I learned that most of the young women were teen mothers, survivors or sexual assault and were quite close in age to me. Immediately traditional power dynamics were thrown out the window. I was a single unmarried nonmother PhD student just a few years older than most of the group members. I remember the first activity that I asked them to complete was a graffiti wall with the wildest dreams they had for themselves and their neighborhood. They struggled to complete the task. It felt so hard for them to imagine in that way. I scraped the curriculum I wrote and even my objective for us to get to product or organize a campaign. We began discussing easier things like our favorite food, music and hobbies and later discussed harder things like catcalling, surviving rape, pregnancy and rasing children. Those tough discussions that often included tears really changed my view on love. They taught me that self and collective love is a verb that emanates within and moves without. They taught me in that small little community center basement could became a space for ritual when you become a witness someone for someone who looks like you but maybe struggles differently than you. Those young women in Brownsville allowed me to love and be loved by them. That love was so palpable it forced me to embark on a journey of loving myself and others.

Conclusion

Researching and becoming in intergenerational women's and girl's spaces helped us to see from multiple perspectives to make deeper connections to our girlhood and womanhood. We write about Black women and girls as distinctly different, each holding a reservoir of distinct stories and experiences while also understanding the healing power of the collective to make connections across differences to heal and imagine futures. We both see our work as reflections and offerings for the communities that have helped us to recover parts of ourselves that have been hurt, targeted, or shunned in academic spaces, whether it be K-12 and/or the university system. The way we have worked together, centering the themes of this paper also serves as an intervention where we play while we write, remind each other to rest and take care, affirm and encourage each other is directly linked to the communities that we studied that are also ourselves. Our vision for this way of researching and writing is to make more space for our full humanity and our intergenerational selves in the writing and the research on Black girlhood studies.

References

Altschuler, S., & Priscilla, W. (2020). COVID-19 and the language of racism.
Altschuler, S., & Wald, P. (2021). COVID-19 and the Language of Racism. Signs: *Journal of Women in Culture and Society, 47*(1), 14–22.Blake, J. J., & Epstein, R. (2019). *Listening to Black women and girls: Lived experiences of adultification bias.* Georgetown Law Center on Poverty and Inequality, Initiative on Gender Justice & Opportunity.
Boylorn, R. (2017). *Sweetwater: Black women and narratives of resilience.* Peter Lang.
Brown, R. N. (2009). *Black girlhood celebration: Toward a hip-hop feminist pedagogy* (Vol. 5). Peter Lang.
Brown, A. A., & Outley, C. W. (2019). The role of leisure in the dehumanization of Black girlhood: Egypt's story. *Leisure Sciences,* 1–18.
Brown, A. A., & Outley, C. W. (2022). The role of leisure in the dehumanization of Black girlhood: Egypt's story. *Leisure Sciences, 44*(3), 305–322.Butler, T. T. (2018). Black girl cartography: Black girlhood and place-making in education research. *Review of Research in Education, 42*(1), 28–45.
Collins, P. H. (2002). *Black feminist thought: Knowledge, consciousness, and the politics of empowerment.* Routledge.
Cooper, B. (2018). *Eloquent rage: A Black feminist discovers her superpower.* St. Martin's Press.
Cox, A. M. (2015). *Shapeshifters: Black girls and the choreography of citizenship.* Duke University Press.
Dillard, C. B. (2000). The substance of things hoped for, the evidence of things not seen: Examining an endarkened feminist epistemology in educational research and leadership. *International Journal of Qualitative Studies in Education, 13*(6), 661–681.
Dubois, V. (2019). *About us.* Retrieved from https://www.thecoloredgirlsmuseum.com
Evans-Winters, V. E. (2019). *Black feminism in qualitative inquiry: A mosaic for writing our daughter's body.* Routledge.
Ewing, E. L. (2017). *Electric arches.* Haymarket Books.
Gaunt, K. D. (2006). *The games Black girls play: Learning the ropes from double-dutch to hip-hop.* New York University Press.
González, T. (2018). *From the classroom to the courtroom: The adultification of Black girls.* Fordham University.
Halliday, A. S. (Ed.). (2019). *The Black girlhood studies collection.* Canadian Scholars' Press.
hooks, b. (1996). *Bone Black: Memories of girlhood.* Macmillan.

Ife, F. (2017). Perhaps a Black girl rolls her eyes because it's one way she attempts to shift calcified pain throughout her body. *Occasional Paper Series, 2017*(38), 4.

Jordan-Zachery, J. S. (2017). Beyond the side eye: Black women's ancestral anger as a liberatory practice. *Journal of Black Sexuality and Relationships, 4*(1), 61–81.

Kanefield, T. (2014). *The girl from the tar paper school: Barbara Rose Johns and the advent of the civil rights movement*. Abrams.

King, T. L. (2019). *The Black shoals: Offshore formations of Black and native studies*. Durham: Duke University Press Books.

Mathew, A. (2018). The vocal memoir of Black girlhood. *Folklore Foundation*, India, *11*, 113.

McKittrick, K. (2006). *Demonic grounds: Black women and the cartographies of struggle* (1st ed.). University of Minnesota Press.

McKittrick, K. (2013). Plantation futures. *Small Axe: A Caribbean Journal of Criticism, 17*(3 (42)), 1–15.

Morris, M. W. (2019). *Sing a rhythm, dance a blues: Education for the liberation of Black and Brown girls*. The New Press.

Nash, J. C. (2018). *Black feminism reimagined*. Duke University Press.

Perszyk, D. R., Lei, R. F., Bodenhausen, G. V., Richeson, J. A., & Waxman, S. R. (2019). Bias at the intersection of race and gender: Evidence from preschool-aged children. *Developmental Science, 22*(3), e12788.

Phillips, R., & Matti, D. (2016). *Black quantum futurism: Space-time collapse I: From the Congo to the Carolinas*. The Afrofuturist Affair

Shakur, A. (1987). *Assata: An autobiography*. AK Press.

Shange, S. (2019). Black girl ordinary: Flesh, carcerality, and the refusal of ethnography. *Transforming Anthropology, 27*(1), 3–21. https://doi.org/10.1111/traa.12143.

Sharpe, C. (2016). *In the wake: On blackness and being* (Reprint edition). Durham: Duke University Press Books.

Silva, N. K. (2018). *The power of the steel-tipped pen: Reconstructing Native Hawaiian intellectual history*. Durham: Duke Press.

Smith-Purviance, A. L. (2021). Masked violence against black women and girls. *Feminist Studies, 47*(1), 175–200.

Toliver, S. R. (2019). Breaking binaries:# BlackGirlMagic and the Black ratchet imagination. *Journal of Language and Literacy Education, 15*(1), n1.

Trask, H. K. (1999). *From a native daughter: Colonialism and sovereignty in Hawai'i*. Honolulu. University of Hawai'i Press.

Tuck, E., & Yang, K. W. (2014). Unbecoming claims: Pedagogies of refusal in qualitative research. *Qualitative Inquiry, 20*(6), 811–818.

Winn, M. T. (2010). "Betwixt and between": Literacy, liminality, and the celling of Black girls. *Race Ethnicity and Education, 13*(4), 425–447.

3 Positioned to Listen

IMANI S. R. MINOR

I am not sure at what age I conceptually understood the weight of my identity as a Black girl. In my family, I was the only girl of five children. Hence, I considered differences between my four brothers and I based upon my girlhood, but not necessarily my Black girlhood. All my primary education was in predominantly Black schools in Georgia. I was keenly aware of the deeply embedded systemic racism within the public education system from a young age, despite little direct exposure to the dominant group. Thus, when I participated in county-wide events (i.e., Witzzle Pro in 3rd grade or band competitions), I attributed many of my racially heightened experiences to my Blackness, but not necessarily my Black girlhood.

In any case, I do know that when I began my undergraduate career at Northwestern University in 2017, I had the desire to be known as a "girl." This desire was two-fold. At this point, I had not yet understood the potency of my Black girlhood. However, I did understand the weight that the world placed on this marker of Black girlhood, hence my desire to disentwine the 'two' identities. Or more accurately, I understood the weight of my Blackness, given many of my experiences in Georgia attending predominantly Black schools amidst a predominantly White county. I did not want to be defined by my racial identity. I wanted to be seen as just a person, which for some reason meant only acknowledging my gender identity. Within a week of my time in Evanston, I witnessed an absurd conversation fraught with colorblindness that signaled to me the identity stripping and invisibilizing that can come with trying to ignore one's racial identity, particularly in a nation rooted in racism and patriarchy. I realized how deeply I wanted to be in community with Black people, thus quickly reuniting with the Black girlhood I tried to distance myself from.

I became reacquainted and more appreciative of my Black girlhood in a season where I was also becoming acquainted with my Black womanhood. As a then 18-year-old, and a now 23-year-old, I do not consider myself "grown" or an "adult adult" yet. Because of this, I have been contemplating the distinction between Black girlhood and Black womanhood. In this chapter, I explore the ways that valuing and listening to the voices of Black girls in my research has illuminated how I conceptualize my own Black girlhood and Black womanhood (Gilligan, 2015). Concurrently, I consider the unique positionality that I, as a young Black woman, bring into my work with Black girls (Rogers, Moffit, & Jones, 2021).

Coming to Understand My Positionality

I have conducted two data-driven thematic analyses that have placed the voices of Black girls at the fore (Minor, 2021; Rosario, Minor, & Rogers, 2021). The first of the two was during my second year at Northwestern, where I explored how Black adolescent girls within a predominantly Black, all girls high school navigated colorist ideology. I began this research when I was a nascent researcher. The primary investigator of my research lab, Dr. Onnie Rogers, had been collecting research data consisting of surveys, interviews, and focus groups, which asked the girls questions related to their self-concept. As I did focus group and interview verifications, I was particularly intrigued by sections regarding the girls' gender, racial, and intersectional (race x gender) identities. The ways in which some of the girls spoke about colorism stood out to me and prompted the exploration of my research project. In short, this project analyzed whether and how Black girls (n =59; M_{age} = 16.97), within a predominantly Black, all girls' high school spoke about colorist ideology. We used a mixed-methods approach. Analysis of survey data showed a strong positive correlation between rejection of colorism (as operationalized by Image Acceptance Measures; Plybon, Pegg, & Reed, 2003) and positive self-esteem (measured by Self-Esteem Scale; Rosenberg, 1965).

Using qualitative data, we explored whether girls mentioned colorism within their interviews, what aspects of colorism they described, and their response to mentions of colorist ideology. An important note was that colorism was not a question that the researcher asked about within the interviews or focus groups. Thus, 75% of the girls spontaneously mentioned colorism, in reference to their skin color, hair texture/style, attractiveness/femininity, and body type, as they spoke about their racial and intersectional identities showed the relevance of this construct to these Black girls. We then coded their references to colorism as accommodating colorist ideology in favor of approaching/desiring a closer proximity-to-whiteness or resisting colorist ideology in favor of affirming Afrocentric forms of beauty (Robinson & Ward, 1991). Notably, 74% of these references to colorism were resisting colorist ideology.

I am not sure that the relevance or resistance of colorism was particularly surprising to me or my team. I expected concepts related to colorism to show up within these girls' narratives, because of the permeation of whiteness throughout society. From an empirical standpoint, Janie Ward and Tracy Robinson-Wood are two phenomenal Black women who have been conducting research on Black girls and colorism for approximately thirty years, and they have documented Black girls' overwhelming resistance to colorism (Robinson & Ward, 1995). Thus, I was also expecting to hear some level of resistance within our Black girls' responses. Instead of feeling surprised at our findings, I felt a tremendous amount of pride and adoration for these Black girls whose voices I had listened to and whose words I read. Many of these girls spoke about their journey to self-acceptance and genuinely loving themselves and their Afrocentric features. I felt honored and privileged to be privy to their articulation of this journey.

As I attuned myself to these girls' narratives, I saw myself in many ways, which led me to many periods of identity reflection. My high school was predominantly Black, and I had perceived the ways that colorism and White supremacy had infiltrated our minds. I had been privy to light-skin versus dark-skin discourse. From a young age, I was already aware of which girls were perceived as prettiest—those with lighter skin, looser curls or straight hair, non-Brown eyes, etc... Thus, I often made intentional decisions about how I wished to wear my hair (i.e., opting to wear an afro and pompadour to prom my junior and senior years in high school instead of straightening my hair or getting a weave), because I believed myself to be pretty despite others' perception of beauty.

Although in many ways, I acted in defiance of these notions, this research illuminated areas in my own mind where I had internalized societal depictions of attractiveness and femininity. For example, I realized that although I wore my hair naturally and never had the desire to lighten my skin, I had grown to envy a particular curl pattern and wanted products that would make my curls very loose and wavy. Hearing the voices of these young Black girls demonstrated to me how a girl could accommodate colorism in one aspect but resist in another, hence *negotiating* the construct of colorism (Rogers & Way, 2018). Listening to the girls' negotiation made me better appreciate my own evolution and negotiation process as I was considering more deeply what it meant to be a Black girl/woman. I realized that I was still on the journey of self-acceptance myself.

This (now published) paper was the first time that I had experience writing a positionality statement (Rosario, Minor, & Rogers, 2021). As I collaborated on this project with my team and research lab, I became acutely aware of the lens that I brought to the table as a Black girl/woman less than two years removed from high school. It was my proximity to Black girlhood that enabled me to better hear the girls navigate this dimension of colorist ideology. In my positionality statement, I referred to myself as a Black girl/woman. I intentionally used the slash as an indication of me trying to piece together where I fell in the 'dichotomy' that I perceived between girlhood and womanhood. While I felt too old to consider myself a Black girl, I felt too young to consider myself a legitimate researcher. In my mind, researchers were adult adults, which again, I was not. Thus, I felt too young to consider myself a Black woman. Fortunately, I have been blessed to have Black women mentors throughout my life. Dr. Rogers was one such person. In an end of the year check-in, which happened after this colorism project had been completed and presented at an undergraduate expo, I jokingly (but seriously) told Dr. Rogers that I was not a real researcher like her. In response, she affirmed me, my intellectual capacity, and my Black womanhood.

A year or so later when Dr. Rogers asked me to be a part of an advisory board amongst other Black girls and Black women who were helping to create a curriculum designed for Black girls, I replied, "that's dope." However, upon being in the room of the advisory board with two high school girls, several Black professional women, and myself, a college undergraduate student, I once again was confronted with the in-between-ness that I occupied as not quite a Black girl and not quite a Black woman. I felt too old to be a Black girl, and too young (or rather, not advanced professionally enough) to be considered a Black woman. In the advisory board, I worked alongside the two high schoolers as they formulated their own research question, created and distributed a survey to other middle and high school girls, analyzed the data, then developed a brief presentation of the results which helped the advisory board understand how students were coping and learning in the midst of COVID. In doing so, we interacted on Facetime and via a group chat where we also began building a friendship. I was initially unsure of what I brought to the table, given the liminal space that I was occupying between girlhood and womanhood. However, as time progressed, I saw my liminality as an avenue for me to foster a deep level of supporting and uplifting these younger Black girls, simply by building a relationship with them.

Identifying as a Black girl *and* a Black woman—or rather, not quite a Black girl *or* a Black woman- has been a consistent musing of mine, particularly as I am now in a master's program at an historically Black college/university (HBCU). When I began school at Howard, many questions surfaced for me surrounding my age and not being qualified or good enough, not necessarily because of my Black girlhood but because of my age. My cohort consists of plenty Black women, many of whom are one to three times my age. This sort of imposter syndrome accentuated my ponderings about what separated Black girlhood and Black womanhood. As time has passed, I began to understand that some of my concerns were rooted in how society portrays adulthood, success, and individualism. Deconstructing societal notions of success and adulthood has been an ongoing process, that has been undergirded by my reflections on the distinctions between Black girlhood and Black womanhood.

Reflections on the Distinctions between Black Girlhood and Black Womanhood

With the wisdom that I have gleaned from listening to and interacting with young Black girls, I have spent a considerable amount of time these past few years growing, evolving, and considering more deeply what legitimately separates Black girlhood from Black womanhood, particularly in a society where young Black girls are subject to adultification bias. *Girlhood Interrupted: The Erasure of Black Girls' Childhood* and *Listening to Black Women and Girls: Lived Experiences of Adultification Bias* are two reports by Georgetown Law Center on Poverty and Inequality that show Black girls are more subject to adultification than White girls, and experience adultification in ways that are different than Black boys (Epstein, Blake, & Gonzalez, 2017; Blake & Epstein, 2019). Black girls are perceived and treated in ways that rob them of their innocence and childhood, inundated with more responsibilities at a young age, punished more frequently and with harsher sentences, and considered to need less protection than their peers (Morris, 2016; Morris & Perry, 2017). The pepper-spraying of a 9-year-old Black girl who was experiencing a mental breakdown while being told *not to act like a child* alongside the killing of 16-year-old Black girl Ma'Khia Bryant by law enforcement exemplify the harmful and potentially deadly consequences of the adultification bias.

A worthy distinction, then, is one that is based on the age and developmental stages that Black girls are in (Halliday, 2019). There are different needs that come along with these life stages, such that babies, young children, pre-pubescent children, adolescents, and adults have different emotional capacities that accompany their growth process. We should be concerned with protecting Black girls from the wiles of life by allowing them the room and space to grow, particularly as they come to understand who they are and their place in the world, societies, and in their communities. We should treat and interpret the behaviors of Black girls within their developmental phase of life (Blake & Epstein, 2019; Morris & Perry, 2017).

As I continued to dig deeper, I started to consider the unhealthy distinctions that I had typically assigned to childhood versus adulthood, and subsequently to Black girlhood versus Black womanhood. A common concept that I have been privy to is one that identifies women/men who treat others poorly or behave in emotionally immature ways as girls/boys. For example, if a man were to "run game" on a woman, many people would say, "that's not a grown man, that's a little boy" in explication of his actions and immaturity. Concurrently, I was hyper aware of the ways that I, and people around me, were engaging in emotionally immature ways, regressing to our childhood behaviors and feelings in various situations. Thus, one of my first inclinations was to reason Black *women* were healed/whole, thus equating Black girlhood with a lack of healing. However, equating Black girlhood with trauma and Black womanhood with healed wholeness is problematic for two primary reasons.

Firstly, this logic insinuates that young Black girls cannot begin a healing process at a young age. I believe that Black girls can be taught socioemotional skills that will be useful for them as they navigate pain, disappointments, loss, and other varying forms of trauma. My initial distinction marked Black girlhood as pain and hurt, missing the holistic nature, beauty, and resiliency of Black girlhood. Secondly, this reasoning also dismisses the reality that trauma is not a respecter of age. Black women also encounter pain and trauma. Moreover, this distinction negates the spectrum of wholeness and healthiness, such that we can always become more whole and healthier. There is thus beauty in accepting and loving ourselves in the present moment, while also practicing grace, kindness, and trust with ourselves as we address the past and look ahead to the future.

The crisis of connection framework is one formulated by Niobe Way and colleagues at NYU Steinhardt (Way et al., 2018). This framework explores the ways in which people, who inhabit a patriarchal, racist, and increasingly technologically dependent society, disconnect from genuine relationships with themselves and others. This framework guided my thesis as I explored how young girls are encouraged to disconnect psychologically (and physically) from themselves by way of self-silencing. Research has shown that self-silencing, particularly such that is in response to oppressive norms, is linked to poor mental health outcomes, such as anxiety, depression, emotional eating (Jack, 1991; Jack & Ali, 2010). Some of their research, which studies adolescent girls, examines how patterns formed in adolescence also affect girls as they grow into womanhood (Brown & Gilligan, 1992). I rest my point of curiosity between Black girlhood and Black womanhood here at the point of connection.

To continue, there is a very legitimate distinction between Black girlhood and Black womanhood, in relation to age and development. However, many of the emotional needs that young Black girls need are the same ones that they need as they mature into Black women (love, safety, security, belonging, etc.), although society would have us think differently. Moreover, the coping mechanisms that Black girls inherit [read: learn] and practice are likely the same ones that they carry into their Black womanhood. My ponderings on the nature of Black girlhood and Black womanhood began with an erroneous point of departure. I had initially believed that there would be a clear break between my Black girlhood and Black womanhood. However, I realize and understand that Black girlhood and Black womanhood are intricately connected at the depths of our beings. Thus, I personally believe that if we would choose to hear and connect with our younger Black girl selves, she would reveal to us the substance of our being.

Relatedly, our communities are composed of little Black girls and older Black women who teach us how to love, trust, care for, and show up for ourselves so that we would feel safe enough to be kind and free with ourselves. Young Black girls help to teach us lessons about the communal and spiritual nature of who we are when we engage in the communal and spiritual act of listening (Womack, 2013). As I continue to reflect on my work, I appreciate the unique lens that this between-ness offers me as I listen to Black girls, while also honoring the profound ways that these young Black girls have affected my own growth process as a young Black woman.

A Transformed Embodiment of Black Womanhood

Not only does my positionality influence how I come to understand myself as a young Black woman, but it also challenges me to consider how I choose to embody my young Black womanhood. The transformative task of critically assessing how I choose to show up in the world came about through the work that I conducted for my psychology honors thesis (Minor, 2021). For my thesis, I explored how adolescent Black girls, in comparison to Latina and White girls, describe patriarchal constraints in interpersonal contexts. My positionality as a young Black woman both served as the impetus of this exploration and influenced me as I listened to the stories of these girls. For context, this project began as an idea during the summer of 2020 amidst the heightened visibility of Black death. In this time, I was reflecting on what it meant to feel anger, grief, and hopelessness, while still somehow holding onto a semblance of hope. I began to really ponder stereotypes assigned to Black girl/womanhood (i.e., angry Black girl or strong Black woman), prompting me to question and want to systematically analyze Black adolescent girls' navigation of emotionality and emotion-laden stereotypes.

My thesis was an iterative, qualitative exploration based on interview data of 123 Black, Latina, and White 10th grade girls who were asked questions about their gender identity. Although I set out with the intention of studying emotional labor that the girls mentioned, this was a data-driven process. After becoming well acquainted with the interviews, I saw the ways that stereotypes surrounding emotionality were not directly about emotion(ality), but instead were rooted in power dynamics minimizing the assertion, vulnerability, and expression of girls by way of patriarchy. Thus, the research process itself, as well as how I conceptualized my vulnerability, was heavily influenced by the voices of the girls. My research questions thus shifted from focusing on emotionality to focusing on self-expression more broadly. I specifically examined the question: *How do girls talk about self-expression and self-presentation within the context of others' views and expectations of girls?* To do this, I, along with a coder who was a White woman, coded and conducted thematic analyses on two specific questions: "Do you ever feel there are expectations placed on you because you're a girl?; What do you think others think about girls?" Both questions implicate interpersonal pressures that girls may experience and that they perceive as a function of their girlhood.

My results showed that 72% of the girls (n = 88) spoke of patriarchal constraints on self-expression in relation to three primary categories: body (appearance and posture), voice (speaking one's thoughts), and emotions (how and when to emote). This project illuminated the ways that patriarchy functions to control the physical, sonic, and emotional space that girls *should* take up, while also illuminating how these categories relate to each other.

The most surprising category was the body constraints category, primarily because it was the largest category that girls mentioned, which was interesting given our expectation to largely find emotional constraints. However, the size of this category marked its relevance in considering the psychological and physical distinction that girls encounter, whereby girls are taught to disconnect not only mentally/emotionally, but also to devalue their bodies, which host their beings. The body constraints category was also notable because this was the only category where chi square tests indicated a racial distinction, with Black and Latina girls mentioning this category significantly more than White girls. Because our bodies are so intricately interwoven with the fabric of our existence, this was very telling, when considering not only how Black girls *should* show up in space, but also directly impacting their capacity to simply exist.

When the cops who killed Breonna Taylor were charged with wanton endangerment charges, I was in the process of 'nailing down' the topic/outline of my senior thesis. I felt restlessness in my bones as the realization sank in that, in practice, Breonna Taylor's body was appraised lower than walls. I went outside and began to walk and grieve. However, as I walked in Evanston, Illinois, I became increasingly aware that someone could hit me with a car without it mattering. I felt that, in relation to Breonna Taylor's Black woman embodiment, my body had no legitimate value to society. In these weeks of grief and restlessness, I was concurrently listening to the adolescent girls' interviews so that I could gain more knowledge of what I was researching. In this time, I could only listen to and verify the interview transcripts of Black girls. I honestly did not have the patience to listen to the White girls' interviews without frustration—not at the girls themselves, but at the racist system that is alive and well in our society today. The racist and patriarchal society that young Black girls are currently being reared in. However, listening to the interviews of Black girls served as a form of self-care for me.

Listening to these girls' interviews was powerful; I do not believe that someone can do such work without being transformed. As I listened to the girls describe various constraints that they felt, I resonated with them, and I felt a deep responsibility to allow the girls' interviews to speak for themselves without my own imposition. These girls' interviews illuminated the areas in my own life where I intentionally (and sometimes unintentionally) was engaging in self-deprecating behaviors within my relationships. In many of my close relationships, I donned the cloak of the Strong Black Woman. The strength in the "Strong Black Woman" narrative is often linked to lack of vulnerability, and is attached to negative outcomes, such as depression and anxiety (Abrams, Hill, & Maxwell, 2019; Donovan & West, 2015). As I realized the ways that I tried to distance myself from my emotions, using language like "I'm not a crier", or the ways I would adopt a savior complex in my relationships at the expense of my own needs and desires, I would think of some of the girls' quotes. I began to consider my healing process as a transformative and spiritual act that honored the Black girls' voices who I had the privilege of listening to and studying. In essence, the Black girls who lent their voices to these interviews helped me in my process of removing the ill-fitting cloak of Strong Black womanhood and exchanging it for a well-fitting, patterned, and textured coat of full personhood.

We were required to submit our senior theses at Northwestern's virtual undergraduate research expo. For our submissions, we had to upload a video describing our project, which I then disseminated (texted) to my family members. One of my aunts, who is in her early sixties, described feeling connected with my research and the quotes of the young girls. She recalled experiences from her childhood where she was told she was not feminine or girly because of the way she dressed and behaved. This conversation with my aunt was impactful because it demonstrated how listening to Black girls has the potential to speak to the lived experiences of the Black women who were once Black girls. Black girlhood studies honors the legacies of our pasts while also helping pave the way for future generations. Research on Black girlhood allows Black girls of today to feel seen, heard, valued, and free from societal norms and dominant ways of thinking that preclude or diminish the experiences of Black girls. I believe there is a sort of intergenerational healing and honoring as we study and respond to the hearts of Black girls. These Black girls will one day turn into Black women, who will either reinforce or resist the dominant culture's racist and patriarchal norms to Black girls they encounter.

As I study and interact with Black girls, in research and everyday life, I consider this communal nature of our beings that is perhaps overlooked. In listening to and honoring the plurality of Black girls' experiences and perspectives, I am transformed; I am called to listen to and honor myself. When I hear a girl speak about pressures to not be vulnerable, I consider how I do not practice vulnerability in my relationships. As I hear Black girls articulate experiences in a way indicating their evolving identity, I think about my own continually evolving identity. All these considerations funnel into me critically reflecting on my behaviors and thoughts, so that I will be a Black woman who fosters Black girls' resistance to dominant, oppressive standards and cultivates their capacity to simply ~be~ (Rogers & Way, 2021).

Conclusion

I proffer that intersectionality was not a word anywhere near my mind before Northwestern (Collins, 2009; Crenshaw, 2018). However, I consider how the conceptual nature of Black girlhood was operating in my life even before I was exposed to theoretical content and language that affirmed my own perspectives and experiences. As I reflect on myself as a little Black girl, I often discredit little Imani's capacity to really understand her Black girlhood at the time. The examples that opened this chapter reflected the times when

I considered my racial and gender identities as two separate entities, because they were at the fore of my mind and came quickest to my remembrance. However, in doing so, I missed the beautiful moments where I knew and found solace in being a Black girl surrounded by beautiful Black women. Here are a few examples of such moments:

1. In 3rd grade, I would have cartwheel races with my other Black girl friends. I would laugh as my beads and/or barrettes would clink against each other.
2. In 5th grade, at the Wax Museum, I chose to be Mae Jemison—the first Black woman to travel into space.
3. In 6th grade, I was one of the only girls at my school who was natural; I liked being natural. One day, out of genuine, childlike curiosity, I asked my momma why she was not natural like me. Shortly thereafter, she began the transition so I would not be alone in my hair journey.
4. In 12th grade, after being rudely disparaged by a White male administrator, I wrote out a spiel referencing my name, accomplishments, and next steps, so that I could tell him ~who~ I was. The following morning, I asked a Black woman administrator to come with me without providing any context of what had happened prior or what was to come. She stood there, with a look of awe, as I "talked my talked" to this man, then walked away. The presence of this Black woman provided me with solace and support.

Of course I knew that I was a Black girl from a young age. I loved to read, and I primarily consumed books from Black women such as Mildred D. Taylor, Sharon M. Draper, and Victoria Christopher Murray when I was young. I memorized the words to "Still I Rise" and "Phenomenal Woman", by my favorite poet—Maya Angelou at a young age. My momma was (and is) the most beautiful person in the world to me, and I recognized many aspects of that beauty as products of her Black womanhood.

When I think back on my childhood, I see how my soul was aware of my Black girlhood, even at times where I was not mentally cognizant of its role in my life. As I interact with Black girls, in research or in personal, everyday life, I am aware of their capacity to grasp onto their Black girlhood even if they may not always have the language to articulate the depth of its power. I knew that Black girlhood held weight, even as I had the inclination to distance myself from my Blackness upon entering undergrad, in the name of individuality. The beautiful thing about Black girlhood and Black womanhood is its connection to our being, and it's always open, welcoming embrace, no matter how far we may try to depart from it.

References

Abrams, J. A., Hill, A., & Maxwell, M. (2019). Underneath the mask of the strong Black woman schema: Disentangling influences of strength and self-silencing on depressive symptoms among US Black women. *Sex Roles, 80*(9), 517–526.

Blake, J., & Epstein, R. (2019). *Listening to Black women and girls: Lived experiences of adultification bias.* Georgetown Law Center on Poverty and Inequality.

Brown, L. M., & Gilligan, C. (1992). *Meeting at the crossroads: Women's psychology and girls' development.* Harvard University Press.

Collins, P. H. (2002). *Black feminist thought: Knowledge, consciousness, and the politics of empowerment.* Routledge.

Crenshaw, K. (2018). *Demarginalizing the intersection of race and sex: A Black feminist critique of antidiscrimination doctrine, feminist theory, and antiracist politics [1989]* (pp. 57–80). Routledge.

Donovan, R. A., & West, L. M. (2015). Stress and mental health: Moderating role of the strong Black woman stereotype. *Journal of Black Psychology, 41*(4), 384–396.

Epstein, R., Blake, J., & González, T. (2017). *Girlhood interrupted: The erasure of Black girls' childhood.* Georgetown Law Center on Poverty and Inequality. Available at SSRN 3000695.

Gilligan, C. (2015). The listening guide method of psychological inquiry [Editorial]. *Qualitative Psychology, 2*(1), 69–77. https://doi.org/10.1037/qup0000023.

Halliday, A. S. (2019). Introduction. In *The Black girlhood studies collection* (pp. 1–20). Women's Press.

Jack, D. C. (1991). *Silencing the self: Women and depression.* Harvard University Press.

Jack, D. C., & Ali, A. (Eds.). (2010). *Silencing the self across cultures: Depression and gender in the social world.* Oxford University Press.

McBride, H. L. (2021). *The wisdom of your body: Finding healing, wholeness, and connection through embodied living.* Harper Collins.

Minor, I. (2021). *An intersectional analysis on the patriarchal constraints of self-expression among adolescent girls.* Undergraduate Honors Thesis, Northwestern University, IL.

Morris, E. W., & Perry, B. L. (2017). Girls behaving badly? Race, gender, and subjective evaluation in the discipline of African American girls. *Sociology of Education, 90*(2), 127–148.

Morris, M. (2016). *Pushout: The criminalization of Black girls in schools.* The New Press.

Plybon, L. E., Pegg, P. O., & Reed, M. (2003, April). *The image acceptance measure: A validation study [Poster presentation].* Biannual Society for Research in Child Development, Tampa, FL.

Robinson, T., & Ward, J. V. (1991). "A belief in self far greater than anyone's disbelief": Cultivating resistance among African American female adolescents. *Women & Therapy, 11*(3–4), 87–103. https://doi.org/10.1300/J015V11N03_06.

Robinson, T. L., & Ward, J. V. (1995). African American adolescents and skin color. *Journal of Black Psychology, 21*(3), 256–274. https://doi.org/10.1177/00957984950213004.

Rogers, L. O., Moffitt, U., & Jones, C. M. (2021). Listening for culture: Using interviews to understand identity in context. https://doi.org/10.31219/osf.io/69h32.

Rogers, L. O., & Way, N. (2018). Reimagining social and emotional development: Accommodation and resistance to dominant ideologies in the identities and friendships of boys of color. *Human Development, 61*(2), 311–31. https://doi.org/10.1159/000493378.

Rogers, L. O., & Way, N. (2021). Child development in an ideological context: Through the lens of resistance and accommodation. *Child Development Perspectives, 15*(4), 242–248.

Rosario, R. J., Minor, I., & Rogers, L. O. (2021). "Oh, you're pretty for a dark-skinned girl": Black adolescent girls' Identities and resistance to colorism. *Journal of Adolescent Research, 36*(5), 501–534.

Rosenberg, M. (1965). Rosenberg self-esteem scale (RSE). *Acceptance and Commitment Therapy. Measures Package, 61*(52), 18.

Way, N., Ali, A., Gilligan, C., & Noguera, P. (2018). *The crisis of connection: Roots, consequences, and solutions.* New York University Press.

Womack, E. (2013). Chapter 7: Lessons in love, literacy, and listening: Reflections on learning with and from Black female youth. *Counterpoints, 454*, 174–190.

4 Seeing through Silence: The Memory of We

Stephanie Power-Carter

Women

They were women then— My mama's generation
Husky of voice—Stout of Step With fists as well as
Hands
How they battered down Doors
And ironed Starched white Shirts
How they led Armies
Headragged generals Across mined
Fields
Booby-trapped Ditches
To discover books Desks
A place for us
How they knew what we Must Know
Without knowing a page of it Themselves (Alice Walker, 1991).

In this chapter, I use memory and storytelling to trace my evolution as a Black woman scholar studying Black girls. I suggest that my experiences have led me to question the limitations of some current epistemological arguments on how we see Black young women and girls. Further, I suggest that the unique position of Black women scholars can help us better see and fully capture the experiences of Black young women and girls, particularly in schools and classrooms. It is also important to note that I intentionally engage in a meandering rhythm that moves from personal to academic to fully capture the tensions, intersections, and dualities of my identity as a Black woman Scholar studying Black young women and girls. I begin by exploring memories of the women from my community who shaped me and helped me see. Then, I share how memory helped me better capture and understand the experiences of Black young women in my scholarship. I conclude by arguing the importance of using Black women's logic of inquiry.

Memory Keepers: Reflection of Early Years

I cannot recall the moment I became conscious of my identity as a Black young woman, but I feel that I was aware of it at an early age. I credit my awareness to the Black women in the small Southern rural community where I grew up, especially my mother and grandmothers. Still today, Black women continue to play a tremendous role in my being and becoming; I use Walker's poem *Women* to pay homage to their contribution and illustrate their sacrifice. The poem captures how the Black women in my community purposefully carved out spaces for me and cultivated my Black "womanness." Walker's poem also captures the generational inheritance that Black women receive, the pressure, strain, and the constant push and pull that exists between memory, present, and future. Simply put, it captures what it means to be and become in a societal context that suffers from a psychosis of deep-rooted racial narcissism and arrogance grounded in whiteness, fear, and denial–a context where Black "girlness" and "womanness" are often viewed as trophies, commodities, or nothing at all.

As a young woman, my grandmothers, Matilda and Robbie, like many women in my community, taught me how to think critically and see myself beyond the limitations that others placed on me. They often used *thinking stories* to help me understand nuance and complexity within my lived experiences to juxtapose my present with a not-so-distant past. *Thinking stories* were grounded in historical knowledge about the Black experience and real people from my community. The goal of these stories was often to help make connections between past and present events within our community and the larger society, most of the stories explicitly or implicitly talked about race. These stories frequently invoked what Du Bois (1903) called double consciousness and often contained dilemmas. They also seemed convoluted and even a bit mind-blowing because simultaneously, they told of Black survival, peace, joy, and pain. These stories forced young women listeners like myself to grasp the magnitude of injustices Black people faced, injustices they continue to face, and their strength. One story that stuck with me was about *my uncle Robert's worth*. It went something like:

> It was summertime. You know, back then, chiren got out of school in the summer to help out in the fields. Us would use that money to buy shoes and clothes for the chiren. My chiren, your aunt and uncles, had two pair of shoes each-- one for school-- and one for church, and we bought winter coats for them too. Well every year, me and yo aunt and uncles would gather these peoples' crops in Bowman, Georgia. Your grandpa worked every day in the granite shed, so it was just me and the chiren. We worked in fields picking cotton Monday through Friday until the sun went down. We would get picked up at about 5:30 a.m.

and ride for about an hour on the back of an open back truck. My oldest chiren would work and one of the youngest would stay under a tree with the babies. Us worked for two families the Skeletons and the can't remember their names, but one day—I can't recall the name of that man—he asked me if he could buy your uncle Robert—showll did! Your uncle was about 9 or 10 at the time but that boy could pick some cotton! He picked about 300 pounds a day. One day, I am going to show you that spot where we picked cotton [which she did]. But I told that man that he was not for sale. We got paid $3.00 a hundred pound. Yes Lord, that time, back then was about family sticking together. They was some hard times but good times. We picked cotton until your three uncles Willie, Robert, and Leroy went off to Vietnam. (Robbie Hood)

I heard this story as a young girl of around 8 or 9 while in 2nd or 3rd grade. I had to grapple with the unimaginable truth that my uncle was literally considered property. It was terrorizing. Although painful and inconceivable, those types of realizations were critical to understanding my contexts. Equally important, my grandmother's *thinking stories* were about generational resilience and helped prepare me to breathe through tensions and uncertainty.

Although my grandmothers never went to college or graduated from high school, they never stopped teaching and preparing me for a life they never lived and a formal education they would never experience. When everyone else was fretting over the fact that I had not married in my mid-20s like other young women from my community, my grandmother encouraged me to ignore those pressures and pursue my education. My grandmothers and their *thinking stories* also helped prepare me for the callousness of our education system. Woodson (1933) argued that in the United States, schools are used to teach the "Negro" of his own inferiority: "When a Negro has finished his education in our schools, then, he has been equipped to begin the life of an Americanized or Europeanized white man" (p. 5). Early on, like Woodson, my grandmothers realized the inequities that I would experience. They somehow understood, even then, the limitations that an integrated public education system would have on me. An elusive system that seemed to switch its discourse to constantly pathologize Black people; a generation before, my uncle was property, now this generation, numbers and test scores. Even amid the horrific gaze of whiteness and discrimination, my grandmothers encouraged me to remember.

My grandmothers' *thinking stories* are akin to what Dillard calls cultural memories. "Such memories change our way of being (culture) and knowing (epistemology) in what we call the present" (pp. 11–12). Central to cultural memory is our ability to remember. Busia (1989) notes, "Remembering is being able to see again the fragments that make up the whole, not as isolated individual, and even redundant fragments, but as part of a creative and sustained whole" (p.4). My grandmothers equipped me to fearlessly see my little brown face in the gaze of another and not look away. To understand that my becoming was intricately tied to others, remembering was essential to navigating the silences and tensions that the gaze of whiteness would hold. However, remembering also nurtured and cultivated a sort of superpower that would sustain me when the weight of the gaze made my knees buckle.

As Black girls and women, our ability to remember is a sacred stream of consciousness that connects us to our sisters, ourselves, and tightly secures us to each other. My grandmothers understood that "to be whole," I must remember and bear witness. In that spirit, I became a teacher like my grandmothers who were community teachers and my mother who worked in a local child development center. Teaching and teachers were very much part of my scholarly journey.

Sista Guardians: My Teachers

As a former high school English teacher and educational researcher, education has always been central to memory. Five Black women teachers I encountered during my public-school experience are integral to my remembering:

- Ms. Shifflett, a teacher's aide in my half-day kindergarten.
- Ms. Sarah Willingham, my 2nd-grade teacher, dropped me off at my mom's job daily.
- Ms. Mattie Blackwell, my 3rd-grade teacher gave the best bear hugs and had a lovely smile.
- Ms. Thelma Shell, kindly reinforced discipline.
- Ms. Sarah Thornton, my inspiration for becoming an English teacher.

These Black women helped cultivate a consciousness that reinforced a strong foundation that reflected and ensured my emotional and mental safety in school as a Black girl. They taught me that I was intelligent, irreplaceable, and uniquely me. Strangely, bell hooks (2014) echoes a similar experience. She writes:

> Teachers worked with and for us to ensure that we would fulfill our intellectual destiny and by so doing uplift the race. My teachers were on a mission... effort and ability to learn were always contextualized within the framework of generational family experience. Certain behaviors, gestures, habits of being were traced back. (p. 3)

Interestingly, bell hooks, a prolific feminist scholar's description of her public-school teachers, is reminiscent of my own. I suggest that it is in the "tracing back" that I can capture meaning and cultural memory, the beautiful resilience and tenacity etched in our vaginas, breast, and brilliance and imbued with the desire to contribute and stay connected to something greater. It wasn't long after I became a high school teacher that I became increasingly aware of the gaze of whiteness that Black young women often navigated. Adisa, cited in bell hooks (1993) notes:

> Did you ever wonder why so many sisters look so angry? Why we walk like we've got bricks in our bags and will slash and curse you at the drop of a hat? It's because stress is hemmed into our dresses, pressed into our hair, mixed into our perfume and painted on our fingers... Much of this stress is caused by how the world outside us relates to us, at times we can change it but we can assert agency in our own lives so that the outside world cannot over determine our responses, cannot make our lives a dumping ground for stress. (p. 61)

I begin to see "them" in "me" and "we." I begin to remember. Remembering helped me understand Black "girlness" and "womanness" as unique positions that often provide a vantage point that others do not possess because Black women are often socialized to protect and serve (Harrison, 1997; Richardson, 2003; Ladner, 1971). The Black young women I encountered when I taught at Cedar Shoals high school were no different. I felt their pain and the weight of every misunderstood second, they experienced. Many Black young women found their way to me, often sharing the discrimination and disrespect they navigated. They were part of the reason that I went back to graduate school. In the same way, bell hooks (1991) writes:

> I came to theory desperate, wanting to comprehend-to grasp what was happening around and within me. Most importantly, I wanted to make the hurt go away. I saw in theory then a location for healing. (p. 1)

As bell hooks suggest, cultural memories and the process of remembering are often messy and complicated. While collective memories can be spackled with pain, scars, fissures, and even oozing wounds, they are also about belonging, community, personhood, creativity, and ingenuity (Muhammad, 2020; Power-Carter, Zakeri, & Kumasi, 2019). Morrison (1994) acknowledges the pressures Black women and girls often suffer in the *Bluest Eye*, but she also acknowledges their collective strength and resourcefulness. Morrison writes:

> Edging into life from the backdoor. Becoming. Everybody in the world was in a position to give him or her orders. White women said, "Do this." White children said, "Give me that." White men said, "Come here." Black men said, "Lay down." The only people they need not take orders from were black children and each other. But they took all of that and recreated it in their own image. (p. 138)

It is on the edge looking out that I have learned to embrace and listen to the silences that Black girls and women nurtured in me and each other. I have begun to cultivate my ability to succumb to remembering and understand that remembering is essential to my scholarship as a Black woman researcher.

Seem Invisible Sometimes

As I reflect on my work with Black girls, it was over 20 years ago that I met Pam and Natonya, two high school seniors. They participated in my ethnographic dissertation study. I served as a participant-observer in their British Literature classroom for five months and was in their school for approximately a year. My time with them allowed me to capture nuances of how Pam and Natonya navigated their school experiences. They will never fully understand how they inextricably changed how I see, and how integral they have been to my scholarship. Pam and Natonya were seniors and the only Black young women in the British Literature classroom. Pam described herself as speaking her mind, and Natonya described herself as quiet and shy. Although they had quite different personalities, they often worked together in the class. In my dissertation, I set out to better understand their experiences and capture how they were navigating whiteness.

Little did I know, Pam, Natonya, and my mother would fundamentally help me peel back and shift the gaze of whiteness and rethink silence. Two memories created an opening and shift that complicated my thinking about silence(s). The first is a distant memory of my mother, a polite, "dutiful" southern woman in a lively conversation with a friend (Power-Carter, 2022). The second memory is of my observation of Pam and Natonya while viewing a teacher-selected "good" example of a video debrief assignment of a student reflecting with a confederate flag draped across his bed in the background. After engaging in conversations with Pam and Natonya and examining video data, it became clear that they were not silent and like my mother, were strategically using non-verbal communication to communicate with each other. To further illustrate and capture Pam and Natonya's tensions, I pause to insert their words and pay homage to their experiences as they have significantly shaped my own scholarship and identity as a Black woman scholar. Due to page limitations, I share three short excerpts from larger follow-up interview conversations. It is important to note that the young women shared similar sentiments throughout the study. Excerpt 1 illustrates Pam's response to the teacher's good example of a video with the confederate flag, Excerpt 2, captures how Natonya values the importance of her and Pam *sticking* together. In Excerpt 3, Natonya shares how she feels *invisible* at times.

Seeing through Silence: The Memory of We

Excerpt 1
Pam:

> Actually, I was offended. I looked, I said okay yea, confederate flag. I you know, I found that shoot, actually I was offended. You know I mean cause usually when somebody, especially a White person with a confederate flag, you know that brings you back to segregation and um discrimination between Blacks and Whites, you know.

Excerpt 2
Natonya:

> Um without that [sticking together], I feel like closed, you know what I am saying, into my own thoughts, with nobody else feeling, you know what I am saying, what I'm feeling or thinking the same way that I am. And another reason is I'd be the only Black girl in there you know what I am saying? The only Black yea, the only Black girl in there and usually, Black girls some Black girls, I'm not going to say all, but some Black girls, when they see something, you know that you've been through or or you know what I am saying what they're offended by or what not, they know somebody next to them feel the same way. And so by that me and Pam we can relate to a lot of things you know what I mean. It's- It's something different about being a Black girl, not just because you're Black, you know what I'm saying. Because a lot of Black people don't go through the same things other Black people go through.

Excerpt 3
Natonya:

> I can say that since me and Pam the only two Black girls, *we seem invisible sometimes.*

In retrospect, I have come to view my experiences with Pam and Natonya as transformative; not only because their experience collided with the memory of my mother, but also because they summoned memories of my grandmother's *thinking stories*—Stories that prepared me to live in a world that would not value my uniqueness. Although Pam and Natonya were generations beyond mine and my grandmothers', they were still strategically responding to whiteness.

Fortunately, they didn't allow it to hold their futures hostage and were able to complete the course and graduate from high school.

Pam, Natonya, my mom, and the Black women from my community were critical in me shifting the gaze of whiteness and theorizing silence(s) as more than just an empty space. Pam and Natonya, as well as the memory of me observing my mother, brought me to a realization that silence might function differently for Black women in different contexts. Silence(s) was more complex than I had initially realized (Carter, 2000, 2007). Moreover, my work with Pam and Natonya also suggested that shifting the gaze and decentering whiteness can make visible rich and generative spaces that Black young women and girls create for themselves in oppressive contexts. As I sit and write, it is not lost on me that there are probably countless examples of Black women strategically and purposefully using and embodying silence to make a difference in the lives of others (e.g., Harriet Tubman).

"Continuing": Translating the Work and Shifting the Register

My work with Black young women and girls has inspired me, much like Dr. Maya Angelou's (2016) poem "Continue." As a Black woman scholar, mother of a Black son, sister, auntie, cousin, friend, and a Black feminist, whiteness, and discourse analysis scholar, remembering is essential to my scholarship. Dillard (2006) notes that remembering requires vulnerability–"A reaching down inside oneself and across others to a place that may break your heart" (p. 11). Unfortunately, all too often in US institutions of higher education, vulnerability is not necessarily supported or valued. Thus, we as Black women scholars are often placed in situations where we must tuck in and tightly secure our memories within academic girdles. Girdles that seek to keep our knowledge and ways of being and seeing hidden under the guise of objectivity. Over the years, I have personally grappled with the stress of trying to loosen or rid myself of such academic girdles. As a young scholar, the rejections, denial, and erasure felt like life was being sucked out of me. It was over 20 years ago that I attempted to publish interdisciplinary work in an educational journal using a Black feminist lens to capture the experiences of Black girls in education; the cycle of rejection and endless resubmissions was overwhelming. Reviewers felt my work was too subjective, not empirical enough, or both. They liked it but could not fully grasp the intersections of my scholarship with my memories or how my memories with my grandmothers and mother were instrumental to me capturing and understanding the nuance and complexities within my scholarship. I was caught in an endless cycle of revise and resubmit. I eventually withdrew that work because I couldn't theorize without remembering and acknowledging my mother and grandmothers. They were integral to helping me complicate silence. Just like the women in Alice Walker's poem, they gave me a tremendous gift, and I couldn't deny their role in my understanding of silence and whiteness. In retrospect, I realize now that it was crucial because part of cultural memory is bearing witness and often a critical part of the scholarship of Black women scholars who research Black young women and girls. Our memories are who we are and denying and girdling them up will not make them go away. Further, when we do, we suffer tremendously. Williams (1988) notes:

> There are moments in my life when I feel as though a part of me is missing. There are days when I feel so invisible that I can't remember what day of the week it is, when I feel so manipulated that I can't remember my own name, when I feel lost and angry that I can speak a civil word to people who love me best. There are times when I catch sight of my reflection in store windows and see a whole person looking back... I have to close my eyes at times and remember myself, draw an internal pattern to smooth this world. (p. 17)

The above quote is important as it challenges us, Black women scholars, doing work with Black young women and girls, to ponder, what happens in the absence of our memories? Similarly, Patel (2015) asks, "What kinds of logics and relationships are being created through educational research? What types of practices are made legitimate?" (p. 32). I extend her question and ask, how are those logics and relationships in academic research consequential to the lived experiences of Black women scholars? Particularly for those of us who study Black young women and girls, how do logics of inquiry that the field of education and other areas of study traditionally use limit knowledge as well as how we see Black young women and girls in our research? or how we see each other? These are not necessarily new questions. They echo the work of Woodson (1933), and others (e.g., Collins, 1990; Crenshaw, 1990; Carter, 2007; Evans-Winters, 2011; Fordham, 1993; Haddix et al., 2016; Henry, 1994; Ladner, 1971; Lorde, 1984; Morris, 2016/2019; Perlow et al., 2018; Richardson, 2003; Seely-Ruiz, 2011; Truth, 1851) who have argued that America and its education system centers whiteness. For those from historically marginalized communities, the outcome is often to erase "existing knowledge and replace [it] with European epistemologies and practices" (Dillard, 2016, p. 38), rather than use their knowledge in ways that shape practice. Although more than two decades later, the field of education has begun to embrace topics on young Black women and girls, much work is still needed to include our logics of inquiry and our meaning-making.

To facilitate shifts in practice, pedagogy, and policy, as Black women scholars, especially those who study Black young women and girls, we must unapologetically use our cultural memories to document our own logics of inquiry (Haddix et al., 2016). Our cultural memories are often the North star that leads us to theorize and give us epiphanies and insights. These insights and epiphanies often lead us to seeing more fully, and making sense of ourselves in tenacious and powerful ways. Who is better prepared to theorize and capture the experiences of Black young women and girls? (bell hooks, 1994).

Advancing Black Women's Logics of Inquiry

Logics of inquiry is a model utilized in research to make visible questions and issues in education. It asks scholars to move from traditional paradigms to make sense of what is happening for whom, how, and within which contexts? Further, logics of inquiry also acknowledges how the limitations of epistemological arguments can mask conceptual or ontological ways of understanding and being in the world (Green & Lee, 2006; Bloome et al., 2006). Given that Black women scholars are often uniquely positioned to see and theorize in their work with Black young women and girls in ways that others may not (Perlow, 2018), a logic of inquiry model might be helpful in better understanding their lived experiences, particularly since traditional research paradigms often limit who they can be and become in educational contexts.

Thus, I suggest that Black women scholars' theorizing is not just about epistemology and the study of knowledge but can also center ontology—our being in the world. Foregrounding ontology that acknowledges memory helps capture Black women's ways of being and becoming as crucial to understanding the experiences of Black young women and girls. In my own experience and scholarship, I have been acutely aware of the gaze of whiteness, how it functions, and its consequential nature on the lived experiences of the communities with whom I work.

However, an ontological approach that centers cultural memory, can help shift the gaze of whiteness (e.g., Pam and Natonya) beyond simplistic, pathological, helpless, and "damaged-centered" ways (Tuck, 2009). As I have illustrated from my own experience, drawing from cultural memories help to see Pam, Natonya, and my mother in ways that capture their tenacity, strength, intellect, and passion. Without such a lens, nuance and complexity might have otherwise been hidden or obscured.

Conclusion

Fundamentally, Pam, Natonya, and my mom have been the catalyst to change how I see and have been impactful in other studies that I have conducted. They have also led me to contemplate what it means to do research and the boundaries of doing research. My own journey as a Black woman interdisciplinary scholar that uses a Black feminist, micro ethnographic discourse analysis lens and engages scholarship with Black young women and girls in educational contexts has suggested that doing research is not immaterial and disconnected from the researcher's personal experiences. If a researcher's cultural memory is suppressed or "girdled up," it can be quite consequential for the researcher and participants, particularly scholars of color or those from historically marginalized communities that do research in communities that they are from (Pellet & Nelson, 1997; Ladson-Billings, 2005).

I suggest that righteous objectivity and rigidity in some fields of study have helped whiteness elude us. In some ways, it has held Black and Brown youth captive by reproducing the same pathologies and narratives in academic journals, while seldom acknowledging that it is how we, as scholars and researchers are seeing, and what we see through (e.g., theories and our experiences) that can make us complicit in this cycle (Fine, 1991, 2018). My journey has taught me that our work is contextualized and loaded with meaning; whether we acknowledge it or not, whether we see it or not, and regardless of our good intentions meaning is always there (Bloome et al., 2022). More importantly, our scholarship can be consequential to the lived experiences of everyday people. It is important that we use approaches that help us better capture and understand the experiences of Black women and youth and stop holding them hostage in paradigms that were not designed to fully see or value them.

In closing, while many who have had an imprint on my scholarship have passed away, and I have fallen out of touch with Pam and Natonya, in the spirit of remembering, in this chapter, I have sought to pay homage to their imprint on my scholarship. They provided great insights and have given me an imagination of sight, a level of consciousness that means "to be present with and fully free" (Bishop, 2006). As Black women, we must continue to acknowledge the uniqueness of our We. It is in the beautiful cacophony and resilience of We that our silences can be better captured and understood, and that We "be" liberated by remembering, remembering "that which we have learned to forget" (Dillard, 2016).

The Power of We

By: Stephanie Power-Carter

They fought, my grandmothers' mothers' mothers whose memories sashayed across oceans and played on the sands of Africa
Africa to
America—a stolen land—A land of freedom and justice For Some

Still One
By one they fought Hands ripped Body contorted
Carrying the weight of the future Back breaking wait
Day after day Still
One

By one they fought Planting
Protecting Nurturing
Seeds of perseverance, wisdom, and hope
Building bridges linked around time One
by one they fought For
ME YOU
Past to Present to Future One
by one they fought

Past to Present to Future We Fight

References

Angelou, M. (2016). *Continue*. https://www.nspirement.com/2021/05/28/continue-maya-angelou.html

Bahktin, M. (1935). *The dialogic imagination*. University of Texas Press. (Trans. 1981).

bell hooks. (1989). *Talking back: Thinking feminist, thinking Black*. South End Press. bell hooks. (1991). Theory as liberatory practice. *Yale JL & Feminism*, 4(1).

bell hooks. (1993). *Sisters of the yam*. South End Press.

bell-hooks. (1994). *Teaching to transgress*. Routledge.

Bloome, D., Carter, S. P., Christian, B. M., Otto, S., & Shuart-Faris, N. (2004). *Discourse analysis and the study of classroom language and literacy events: A microethnographic perspective*. Routledge.

Bloome, D., Power-Carter, S., Baker, D., Castanheira, L., Minjeong, K., & Rowe, L. (2022). *Discourse analysis of languaging and literacy events in educational settings: A microethnographic perspective*. Routledge.

Busia, A. (1989). What is your nation?: Reconnecting Africa and her diaspora through Paule Marshall's praisesong for the widow. In C. A. Wall (Ed.), *Changing our words: Essays on criticism, theory, and writing by Black women* (pp. 196–212). Rutgers University Press.

Carter, S. P. (2001). *The possibilities of silence: African-American female cultural identity and secondary English classrooms*. Peabody College for Teachers of Vanderbilt University.

Carter, S. P. (2007). "Reading all that white crazy stuff": Black young women unpacking whiteness in a high school British literature classroom. *The Journal of Classroom Interaction*, 41(2), 42–54.

Collins, P. H. (1990). *Black feminist thought: Knowledge, consciousness, and the politics of empowerment*. Unwin Hyman.

Crenshaw, K. (1990). Mapping the margins: Intersectionality, identity politics, and violence against women of color. *Stanford Law Review, 43*, 1241.

Dillard, C. (2006). *On spiritual strivings*. State University of New York Press.

Dillard, C. B. (2016). Learning to remember the things we've learned to forget: Endarkened feminisms and the sacred nature of research. In Qualitative Inquiry—Past, Present, and Future (pp. 288–305). Routledge.

Du Bois, W. B. (1903). *The souls of Black folks*. A. C. McClurg.

Fine, M. (1991). *Framing dropouts: Notes on the politics of an urban high school*. State University of New York Press.

Fine, M. (2018). *Just research in contentious times: Widening the methodological imagination*. Teachers College Press.

Fordham, S. (1993). Those loud Black girls: (Black) women, silence, and gender "passing" in the academy. *Anthropology Quarterly, 24*(1), 3–32.

Green, J. L., & Lee, C. D. (2006). Making visible the invisible logic of inquiry: Uncovering multiple challenges. *Reading Research Quarterly (41)*1, 140–150.

Harrison, J. (1997). Lisa's quiet fight: School structure and adolescent females. In K. Lomotey (Ed.), *Sailing against the wind: African American and women in U.S. education* (pp. 45–53). State University of New York Press.

Henry, A. (1994). There are no safe places: Pedagogy as powerful and dangerous terrain. *Action in Teacher Education, 15*(4), 1–4.

Ladner, J. (1971). *Tomorrow's tomorrow: The Black woman*. Doubleday.

Ladson-Billings, G. (2005). *Beyond the big house: African American educators on teacher education*. Teacher College Press.

Lorde, A. (1984). *Sister outsider: Essays and speeches*. Crossing Press.

Morrisson, T. (1993). *Nobel Prize lecture*. [Online]. http://www.nobel.se/literature/laureates/1993/Morrisson-lecture.html

Morrisson, T. (1994). *The bluest eye*. First Plumb.

Muhammad, G. (2020). *Cultivating genius: An equity framework for culturally and historically responsive literacy*. Scholastic Incorporated.

Paris, D., & Winn, M. T. (Eds.). (2013). *Humanizing research: Decolonizing qualitative inquiry with youth and communities*. Sage Publications.

Patel, L. (2015). *Decolonizing educational research: From ownership to answerability*. Routledge.

Pellet, G. (Producer), & Nelson, S. (Director). (1997). *Shattering the silences: The case of minority faculty* [Video file]. https://vimeo.com/ondemand/shatteringthesilences

Power-Carter, S. (2020). Re-theorizing silence (s). *Trabalhos em Linguística Aplicada, 59*(1), 99–128.

Power-Carter, S. (2020). Re-theorizing silence (s). Trabalhos em Linguística Aplicada, 59, 99–128.

Power-Carter, S., Zakeri, B., & Kumasi, K. (2019). Theorizing and languaging Blackness: Using the African philosophy of Ubuntu and the concept of Sawubona. In R. Beach & D. Bloome (Eds.), *Languaging relations for transforming the literacy and language arts classroom* (pp. 195–215). Routledge.

Richardson, E. B. (2003). *African American literacies*. Psychology Press.

Truth, S. (1851). *Aint I a woman*. https://www.nps.gov/articles/sojourner-truth.htm

Tuck, E. (2009). Suspending damage: A letter to communities. *Harvard Educational Review, 79*(3), 409–428.

Walker, A. (1991). *Women*. https://www.pngisd.org/cms/lib/TX02205731/Centricity/Domain/2205/women.pdf

Williams, P. J. (1988). On being the object of property. *Signs: Journal of Women in Culture and Society, 14*(1), 5–24.

Willis, A. I. (2008). *On critically conscious research: Approaches to language and literacy research*. Teachers College Press.

Woodson, C. (1933). *The miseducation of the Negro*. The Associated Publishers.

Part II Revelations: What I've Learned or Unlearned from Studying Black Girls

The contributors in this section explain what they've learned and unlearned from their work with Black girls. They offer important insight into the lived experiences of Black girls and acknowledge ways this knowledge has impacted them personally and/or as a scholar of Black girls.

5 Setting the Trend: What Black Girls Taught Me about Showing Up and Dancing with Complexity

CHARLENE M. BROWN

As a former Black girl who had a *lot* of questions about everything around me, I came through the academy learning how to widen that lens. Since my Work (with a capital W) in the world has to do with letting Black girls and women know how their unique brand of awesome is needed in this world, I have found myself in numerous intentional places and spaces that have allowed me to work with Black girls. As an adult, I wonder, with all that is thrown at Black girls today, are they okay? While completing my doctoral work, I got to ask just this question to a few girls and their mothers. What follows here is my understanding and experience of Black girls and myself, both from my formal academic work, as well as my broader experiences working with Black girls.

Among the things this Work has taught me over the years are that: Black girls surely know about more than I and probably most adults would think to ask them about; social media is far more pervasive than I thought, as a veritable extension of their identity; and sex and sexual scripting may come from adults more than teen girls themselves. Further, girls today, Black girls today, have much more complex lives and stimuli than was true for girls of previous generations, and this impacts what girls do and how, and who they think they are at many levels and layers of their being. Their families and family dynamics also play a huge role in who the girls are and how they operate in the world. And Beyoncé! Beyoncé is truly Queen Bey for many Black girls (and women!), and her impact is undeniable. Finally, I learned that respectability politics always requires context.

As I explore these topics in the remainder of this chapter, a few stylistic notes to keep in mind: I generally capitalize Black, but also will use the original author's denotation when citing material. Unless otherwise noted, I am usually referring to Black people in the United States, and girls and women will usually denote Black girls and women. I completed my dissertation as a multiple case study of how Black girls felt about themselves, and I use the two girls from my study as named examples (pseudonyms, in accordance with ethical research practices with minors). And while I am using my doctoral study to hold the container and frame this discussion, and because I gathered the *thick, rich data* for which qualitative research is known, I use my participants as representative of the many other conversations and interactions I have had over the years with Black girls and Black women—Black mothers among them—noting the differences when relevant. Using my dissertation participants as examples also allows me to personalize them for the reader.

Academic Framing of Black Girls

Academia, based in science and the scientific method, often purports to be able to study things as a singular aspect, unobstructed from every other aspect, and is often framed through a lens of pathology. While conducting my dissertation research, I was greatly dismayed at the lack of formal academic writing and studying done about Black girls. And as is true for many disciplines, much of the literature that included Black girls was in comparison to white-girls-as-default. Rarely were academics studying Black girls as compared to themselves as default.

During my dissertation process, I amassed about 500 articles and other literature. Of them, only 26 (~5%) pertained specifically to Black high school aged girls (the focus of my study). Of the 26 included studies, 12 were dissertations, and 9 discussed sexuality either directly or indirectly. In my own dissertation (Brown, 2018), I dissect these numbers more thoroughly, but my main point is that in working through academic framing, there is a dearth of information regarding the intersectional, real-world lived experiences of Black girls. Furthermore, many of the questions researchers are taught to ask serve to maintain the same pathological and sexual scripting that psychological literature relies on more generally, including with the presumed promiscuity of Black girls; this sexual framing of girls was overrepresented in academic literature. While more research *is* being conducted with and about Black girls, research is a slow process.

Additionally, I have come to understand that in too many cases, there is a lack of wanting to be held accountable by many of the institutions that are supposed to support girls (e.g., K-12 schools). And there is sometimes major push-back from academic institutions that do not benefit from widening the lens of what is understood about Black girls. Essentially, this means that the barriers to working with Black girls as their full intersectional selves begin at the level of the very structure of academia, where the (mostly) Black women who are attempting to depict Black girls wholly, are already having to jump through extra hoops just to get permission and or funding to conduct this research, and then often having to do so within the predetermined scope of what academia considers "good" (i.e., non-intersectional) research practices. It is no wonder we, collectively and broadly, know so "little" about Black girls. Thankfully, there are still a great and growing number of adults who are working to change this, who are spending time and resources (even if outside the confines of academia) and getting to know what's really going on with Black girls. Indeed, Black girls themselves are also joining this pursuit and publishing their own material about what it means to be a Black girl, such as Olivia Clarke, who, at 16 years old, recently published an anthology called *Black Girl, White School: Thriving, Surviving, and 'No, You Can't Touch My Hair'* (Clarke, 2020). Despite the slow speed of the academy, real measurable progress *is* being made.

Family Dynamics

Most of the girls I've connected with over the years have had known families and generally lived within the context of their family home/s. These girls relied heavily on their families for their sense of identity. For the few girls that I was aware were either unhoused and or didn't live with their families, they tended to rely mostly on themselves, maintaining a hyper-self-reliant perspective on how they moved in the world. While an important topic, the latter were a very small number of the girls I've interacted with, and thus, the focus of this section is on the former.

In the 1990s, scholars began earnestly studying African American family dynamics as distinct from Euro-centric American families. As noted in a seminal overview by Littlejohn-Blake and Darling (1993), the strengths-based approach to African American families provides a deeper understanding of the families within their greater social contexts. In brief, Littlejohn-Blake and Darling (1993) found that some assets of African American families include a sense of spirituality, extended kin networks, a strong sense of self, and a sense of "ethnic" identity.

The girls I've been connected to largely adhere to these norms and values. From my doctoral study, the two girls I interviewed, Kayla and Aria, very much mirrored their mothers, whom I also interviewed (Brown, 2018). After spending time with and interviewing my participants, I felt that both of their family units, respectively, were relatively closed ecosystems. In my work with youth, I've found that regardless of how they feel about their relationship with their mothers, girls tend to emulate their mothers to some extent. The mother-daughter dynamic was deeply related to how girls moved out in the world beyond their households, and daughters listen to their mothers, perhaps especially when the daughter seems *not* to be listening. The advice from their mothers that the daughters were likely rolling their eyes at, was the very same advice the girls were giving to their girlfriends. In fact, many of the girls I've known enjoyed seeming "wise" based on giving this advice in their friend-groups. And girls admired their mothers too: no matter the clashing that happened between them, girls were watching their mothers closely.

In my observation from the girls with whom I've worked, family units often include a religious component, or distinct lack thereof. Teen girls I've known tend to generally mirror the religious contexts of their households. In informal contexts, especially those outside of a prescribed religious context, the specifics of religious beliefs are not usually regular discussion fodder. For Kayla and Aria, their relationships with religion were very much part of the context of what they do as a part of their specific families. However, within the context of a girl's household, at least from my experiences with them, the entirety of the family dynamics is always at play, and though it is not often named in the dialectics of daily family life, it is intrinsically understood, including the family's relative religiosity.

An additional complex component of Black families is a daughter's relationship with the various people parenting her. A daughter's household parental relationships could include any mix of parents, grandparents/other family caregivers, and stepparents; the relationships and level of bondedness that girls have with each; as well as the location or proximity of each person parenting the girl. For example, I once worked with a girl who had a young child, and lived with her best friend's family, while her own biological family was 2500 miles away. Her relationship with her best friend and best friend's mother and uncle was as complex if not more so than her relationship with her biological mother.

From my dissertation study, Kayla lived with both of her biological parents and was bonded to both, though each served a different set of functions in her life. For instance, she talked to her mother about very different things than she talked to her father about. Aria, on the other hand, lived with her mother and stepfather, while her birth father lived in a different state. She was securely bonded with her mother, wanted to be bonded with her father, and barely mentioned her stepfather at all—in fact, she seemed to be completely unbonded to him, though she had lived with him since she was four. The father relationship, or its prevalent lack, was a point of ongoing challenge for Aria. For other girls I've worked with, they tended to be bonded tightly with at least one of their parents (I use parents here to denote the people raising the girls, and generally in whose house the girl lived or spent extended periods of time). I also have noticed the distinct demarcation between "Dad" and "Daddy", with girls having a closer relationship with those they referred to as "Daddy", and a more distant, and sometimes complicated and resentful relationship with "Dad." Further complexifying matters, the "stepfather" title may be given to a man who is actually the boyfriend/partner of a girl's mother and often living in the same household; however, the stepfather may change over time. From my experience, mothers, almost exclusively, do the gatekeeping of which men are present in a daughter's life, no matter what his title may be. I've also observed that the most complex relationships between daughters and the people parenting them tend to come from trauma-based relationships, whether from violence, substance abuse, sexual abuse, poverty, and or any combination thereof (collectively termed Adverse Childhood Experiences, or ACEs).

Additionally, sibling relationships provided even more variables, including how many (if any), how close in age, where in the sibling-chain a girl was, if she lived with her sibling/s, and her family's socioeconomic status, which all played a part in how a girl expressed her thoughts and feelings about being a sibling. A note here, in many Black American families, distinctions between full-siblings and half-siblings, and sometimes even cousins, is not usually made, and "siblings" is generally referring to the kids in the household. Finally, for the girls I've worked with, awareness of her Blackness usually also plays a definitive role in her experience of herself in the world, as does her perceptions related to her Black *femaleness*, though these identifications are not always explicitly tied to family dynamics. And while I would classify many Black girls I've known as confident and ambitious, many of them also struggle/d with self-worth; in other words, they believed in their own capabilities, but did not necessarily operate as if they were worthy of other people *wanting* them, whether through friendship, getting a coveted opportunity, or through romantic love relationships. Here again, while this was not necessarily a direct offshoot of her experiences *at home*, these dynamics eventually played into how a girl might behave in her household and vice versa.

Social Media and Beyoncé as Icon

Social media was quite a surprise to me in how intrinsically personal it is for girls. I have an anecdotal theory about younger generations: that their sense of self is no longer intrinsic, and their core-self is now external. With the explosion of social media and its numerous platforms, and many people feeling like they must cultivate a certain presence and persona on each, I'm not sure that younger people know who they are when they aren't performing for a camera.

The girls in my dissertation study taught me how important their social media presence is to them. It was a veritable extension of their identities, in the way that I might think about my arm or my leg. Furthermore, social media, specifically, adds additional complexities relating to trust factors, and thus resilience or lack thereof. From my study, Kayla relayed to me that social media contributed to distrust of her peers, especially if someone "exposed" someone else, when they were supposed to be friends. For example, if Kayla texted something personal to someone she considered a friend, and that person, not only didn't keep it between them, but posted it on the internet to "expose" her, Kayla's sense of who she can and cannot trust has potentially been completely eroded by this single interaction. Further, now, this exchange is on the forever-internet, where anyone can not only find it, but laugh at and ridicule Kayla *into perpetuity*. One bad day never goes away. In fact, it lasts forever, where each time it dies down, it is simply bound to flare up again. In this way, this one bad day and the perpetual torment it may cause, can be world-shattering, especially if the person involved doesn't have an internal sense of self. Where I might have been teased for my bad day when I was an adolescent, today's girls might consider (and enact) suicide because of this same bad day that now continues forever. It is no wonder that the anxiety, depression, and suicide rates for younger generations are so astronomical. And while, of course this may not be true for every Black girl in younger generations, Kayla, Aria, and the many other girls I've worked with over the years showed me in a very visceral way how mental health, wellness, and social media are linked in extraordinarily complex ways.

Additionally, within the subtext of social media, Aria told me that having a "Twitter beef" (or any other platform) was a real thing. There was also a sense that, for Aria and Kayla, at least, the ways they presented themselves on social media needed to be at least a little bit "woke"—meaning up to date on current social justice issues—and that this self-perceived wokeness played prominently into their cultivated personas on the various platforms. In our conversations, Aria described herself as "sometimes preachy"—on social media channels and in real life—in her quest "to inform and educate" her peers about the social justice topics of the day. Kayla expressed that it was necessary to have an idea about some of these social justice issues, but used her social media to cultivate non-social-justice-related aspects of her personality. I'm often left wondering, how much nuance and subtext is lost without having disagreements face-to-face, as in the case of Aria's Twitter beef? As perhaps an unintended result of social media channels more broadly, younger people don't know how to take constructive feedback, and seem to have an overinflated sense of self, without having real-world skills or experience to back that up.

Enter Queen Beyoncé. While interviewing Black girls who could *sang* and their Black mothers, Beyoncé surely came up! Before I had to write my dissertation, and for reasons that no longer matter, I was not a fan of Beyoncé, for some of the same reasons bell hooks articulates in her critique of Beyoncé's *Lemonade* (e.g.,. performative capitalism, performative feminism, and performative stereotypes) [hooks, n.d.]. In having to give Beyoncé a fair chance and understand her as a cultural icon, I had to come to a deeper understanding of why she was so important to the Bey-hive in the first place, and more specifically, her place in the Queendom as it relates to Black girls.

First, her name is Beyoncé, accent and all! Consciously or unconsciously, this gave every Black person with a creatively spelled name or a name that defies Anglicized norms permission to be full in their expression of themselves. Second, the sheer range of songs that Bey has allows her to find a relatable bridge to many different kinds of women, as agentic themselves, and also in relation to men, their children, their parents, and self as sexual woman, brass-knuckled woman, sister, sweet woman, woman who makes her own choices and sets her own rules, Boss woman! In short, as Icon!

In forgiving the image of Beyoncé from my earlier contempt and allowing the space for her as a true icon to Black women and girls everywhere, I get it now. Black girls of younger generations clearly see that what older generations are doing, and the way we are doing it, is not going to work for them. Of course, this is not true for every Black girl everywhere, but I have noticed an underlying distrust for what older generations are doing from Black girls across at least eight U.S. states and several countries around the world, and the similarity of the sentiment was striking. Beyoncé, in her myriad facets, provides a way out, a possibility of what *could be* for everywoman, everygirl. In a similar way that many Black boys in the 1980s and 1990s thought they were going to be basketball stars because of the likes of Michael Jordan and his peers, Beyoncé provides an avenue away from current circumstances to become larger than life! And if we remember, life for Black girls in the 2020s, has a lot of complexity on and in platforms that the girls have no control over; Beyoncé has control over just about every aspect of her life! Why wouldn't girls see that and say, I want *that* kind of agency over my own life too. Aria, certainly did, as have many of the other girls I've worked with in the past two decades!

While perhaps not in the lexicon of teenagers, Beyoncé embodies political and Afro-centric attributes in a way no one else does. Whether her feminist presentations, such as using Chimamanda Adiche's words in her music (Knight, 2015), or Afro-cultural ones, such as presenting Yoruba Orisha Osun in her 2017 Grammy's performance (Ehrlich & Horvitz, 2017), Beyoncé has the unencumbered ability to embody a great many aspects of womanhood, in all its layered complexity. Queen Bey also projects femininity, power, and sexuality, in which many of the young women I connected with found a powerful, empowered representation of their *super-selves*. Furthermore, Bey undisputedly has agency over herself, her sexuality, and her work. Within the context of the scope of Beyoncé's influence, I have a much deeper understanding of and respect for all the implicit cultural elements she has brought to the mainstream, and how she has done so in extraordinarily digestible ways, whether or not I agree with them. This understanding was further enhanced by the connections between my somewhat academic study of "Why Beyonce!?", coupled deeply with the near ubiquity of her reign through the thoughts, admiration, and emulation of her by so many of the Black girls I have encountered over the years.

Respectability Politics

In academia, as a theory, *respectability politics* is well-defined and historically understood to mean the policing of what Black women and girls can and cannot do, especially in a public sphere (Higginbotham, 1992). And it is often regarded as a negative, unwanted thing. The main piece I understood from my dissertation was that respectability politics always required context. Because the relatively closed ecosystem of families was largely at play regarding the complexities of respectability politics, in this section, I focus equally on the mothers of the girls in my study as on the girls themselves.

From Kayla, Aria, and each of their mothers came words, phrases, and expected choices that would fall heavily into the ideas of respectability politics—what, whom, and with whom the girls could do or not do certain things, especially in public. Kayla, in particular, often talked about underlying things that would be considered "appropriate" for her to do or not do. The mothers told me similar things, though none of my participants named it respectability politics [A note here that the mothers from my study were both highly educated and would likely have a nuanced understanding of respectability politics as an academic theory].

What I also know from working with kids for almost 25 years, is that they appreciate when their adults have standards for them to meet. Most teens won't say this outright to their adults, but it shows up instead in the emulation of the adults' character traits. In this case, Black girls do not differ so much from their non-Black counterparts. As I think back on my many interactions with Black girls and their parents, the framing of "trying to protect my daughter" is most prevalent, even if the words and actions to do so would fall under the academic umbrella of respectability politics.

However, there is also crossover into more nuanced and emerging ideas about respectability politics, such as those proffered by Brittany Cooper (2017), who invites readers "to reimagine Black women's political and activist work as work rooted deeply in a set of shared intellectual concerns about Black humanity and personhood, … about putting together strong Black families, and about notions of community and unity" (pp. 144–145; In this volume, Cooper also explores other sites of contextualization regarding how respectability politics has historically shown up in what she calls the Race Women, which frames the current discussion at the meta-level, but of which the specifics are outside the scope). The mothers in my study, for example, both said their daughters were a little too cocky for their liking some of the time, but that they both made conscious efforts not to psychologically knock their daughters down, and let the confidence remain true. Renee (Kayla's mother) and Theresa (Aria's mother) certainly also wanted to instill in their daughters the ideas about Black female intellectual personhood.

And, as I've observed more widely in my work specifically with Black girls, the ideas that Black mothers are passing along to their Black daughters have much more to do with the reality of wanting to set the girls up for success in the world as it exists (or is perceived to exist) rather than based solely within the confines of an academic theory's trajectory. In other words, from my experience, Black mothers are trying to pass on what they think is best for their Black daughters to maximize the chances that the daughters will reach adulthood with the abilities and skills to thrive. What academia calls respectability politics, in the real world, was about ensuring survival based on lived experiences, which further muddled the compounded nuances of addressing respectability politics without proper contextualization. It was a very complex topic and necessitates deeper understanding, as Cooper (2017) elucidated.

Violence

Equally complex was the naming and not naming of violence. As it relates to the Black girls and women of all ages whom I've encountered, I found that there is a lot of what I would call cultural conditioning around what is and is not called violence. From the numerous, often candid conversations I've had with girls over the years, this lack of naming violence was quite pervasive and, frankly, perplexing. In part, I think this is due to my own framing—my master's degree is in women's spirituality with a strong feminist lens, which means I spent a good deal of my studies learning about the nuances of violence and how omnipresent it is, showing up in language, entertainment, working structures, home structures, and just about every other facet of society. Both in my doctoral study and in my experiences more broadly, I think most people understand or define *violence* as overt physical harm caused by one person to another. In my study, Aria was the only one of my five participants who explicitly provided a definition, but in looking at my numerous interactions with Black girls (and their mothers) as a whole, I can see how anything absent this physical-based definition might not present as "violence."

In large part, I find what Kimberlé Crenshaw (1991) said, when she introduced intersectionality to the world at large, to still be true 30 years later: "Women of color are differently situated in the economic, social, and political worlds. When reform efforts undertaken on behalf of women neglect this fact, women of color are less likely to have their needs met than women who are racially privileged" (p. 1250). Professor Crenshaw was referring to the systemic supports supposedly in place to help protect women from such things as intimate partner violence. In engaging with both Black girls and women about violence, it was very interesting to see the many ways that their definitions and examples differed from my own. In addition to the lack of naming it, there is also an underlying normalization of violence against Black women and girls, what Patton and Ward (2016) described as a "politics of disposability" erasing Black women and girls and the violence enacted against them.

From my dissertation participants, Kayla's mother, Renee, named several instances where Kayla was being infringed upon by a male—instances that I would surely call violence, but neither Kayla nor Renee characterized it as being violent. Aria also provided several examples of episodes that I would consider violence, and yet, she and her mother, Theresa, were both reluctant to use that word either. My participants' framing versus my own more nuanced framing has been an important site for continued learning as I have and continue to be present for Black Girls as a trusted adult, where they get to name their experiences what they want, without my projection.

What was less nuanced was the near-universal experience of what's now termed "street harassment." Many of the Black girls I have connected with over the years have told me about some form of street harassment, where a male, often an older-than-her male, is calling out to her, telling her to smile, and sometimes even grabbing her physically, as she is moving about her day. While there is sometimes a feeling of sexiness and power for some girls I have known, often this street harassment is outright uncomfortable for the girls and women who have experienced it. And while in the moment, many don't know what to do about it. As with the politics of disposability, most of the Black girls that I've worked with, have a vague, often unnamed understanding that if something bad were to happen to them, there would be very little if any attention brought to helping them, or seeking justice on their behalf, at least on a widespread scale; in essence, they understood that Black women and girls are not cared for by the media and therefore the society at large. And again, while not named with that sort of clarity, it is intrinsically understood by many of the Black girls I regularly encounter/ed.

Though adolescence today is much more complex than it was even 20 years ago, many Black girls still cope by armoring—changing their behavior or thoughts as a coping mechanism to deal with their interactions with the world around them. For Aria and Kayla, their armoring tended to pull them in opposite directions, with Aria tending to speak up and out, and Kayla withdrawing inward; these actions were further enacted on their social media platforms as well, respectively.

Seemingly paradoxically, there is also a sense of more boldly engaging with harassers and or more expressly removing herself from a nasty situation for some of the Black girls of current younger generations. When I was the teen coordinator at a community center, some years back, I remember in one conversation with my girls (who were mostly Black, with a few Latinas), that I was sharing an example of when a man was being sexually inappropriate in a public space. I was a teen when the incident happened and was with my childhood best friend. Both of us were extremely uncomfortable but remained where we were without knowing what to do. When I relayed this experience to my girls, one of my Black girls asked if I spoke up or did anything about it. She was upset when I said no. She then detailed all the ways she would have acted in that situation. While, of course, we don't know what she would have actually done had she been in that position, many of the young women I've worked with over the years do have a boldness to them, that makes them more likely to value their own well-being over socially expected conventions, which I appreciate in my role as a youth-worker. Unfortunately, however, I think the societal sentiment remains, that violence and dehumanization, especially toward Black women and girls, is so pervasive in United States and global societies, that the average person doesn't even notice it when it occurs, much less know what to do about it while it's happening.

Conclusion

Adolescence has changed exponentially in a short period of time. I began my doctoral process wondering if Black girls were okay. And while they are dealing with a great many different things than I dealt with as a girl, they are valuing their mental health, their time, their space, and their peace in unprecedented ways. There are still so many things about them that I don't quite understand, especially as it relates to tying their identities so inextricably with social media, and I think that is going to have repercussions long into the future. However, the Black girls that I know seem to be making a way for themselves, even through the complexities. They are so smart in so many different ways. And they want to be valued for their unique contributions—which is true for most of us generally, but with the crux of modern-day Black girls having grown up with everything personalized just for them. For example, phone apps that collect their habits and personal rhythms, such as tracking their periods or telling them they've been sitting sedentary for too long; games where they can build customized worlds, houses, levels, rooms, or outfits that may reflect a mood or want/need of the moment; the explosion of availability of design options for items such as personal cell phone cases or jewelry, as well as the ability to 3-D print items near instantaneously; and even completely differentiated instruction that some schools offer (and may find ideal); all of these speak to a level of personalization that was foreign to me as a girl. In a way, I wonder if this personalization exacerbates the sense of self being so externalized and needing external validation.

I think girls today also have more social agency and value having their opinions being heard, including in difficult sexual situations. For many of the girls I've worked with over the years, they seem to be more likely to say NO to an uncomfortable sexual situation, and then get out of dodge to avoid any complications to their no. I think this may translate to a greater sense of agency for girls present and future. They are less accepting of the things that girls-past have had to endure, especially as it relates to limits, boundaries, or prescribed roles that women and girls must adhere to; today's girls are not interested in being told what they can't do. In my experience with mothers of Black girls, this sense of limitlessness is often intentional: the mothers sometimes find their daughters a little too boundary-pushing for the mother's taste, but the mother often consciously does not dampen that confidence in her daughter. This seems to have socioeconomic dimensions as well, and may be more likely in middle-class households than lower socioeconomic classes, at least as I have noticed these differences. And, to be sure, many of the conversations I mention here are skewed toward those girls and or families who are actively trying to support the girls, as many of my interactions have been in the context of specific programs (e.g., afterschool programs, college readiness programs, etc.).

Finally, I am so glad that girls today get a much more reflective experience than I had as a girl, and that great strides have been made in representation, though of course, there is still a mighty long way to go. While I don't recall that my lack of representational reflection bothered me so much as a child, or even as a teenager, I am grateful that girls of today get to see themselves, in all their glorious diversity and melanin-richness, in an everyday way that can't be ignored or dampened. As Kayla said of Black women and girls, "we set the trend."

References

Brown, C. M. (2018). *Strong and confident: How Black adolescent girls define their identities using a multiple case study approach* (Publication No. 10814170). [Doctoral dissertation, California Institute of Integral Studies]. ProQuest Dissertations and Theses.

Clarke, O. V. G. (Ed.). (2020). *Black girl, White school: Thriving, surviving, and 'No, you can't touch my hair'*. LifeSlice Media.

Cooper, B. (2017). *Beyond respectability: The intellectual thought of Race Women*. University of Illinois Press. https://illinois.universitypressscholarship.com/view/10.5406/illinois/9780252040993.001.0001/upso-9780252040993

Crenshaw, K. (1991). Mapping the margins: Intersectionality, identity politics, and violence against women of color. *Stanford Law Review, 43*(6), 1241–1299. https://doi.org/10.2307/1229039

Ehrlich, K. (Executive Producer), & Horvitz, L. J. (Director). (2017, February 12). *59th Grammy Awards* [Awards Show]. United States: Recording Academy.

Higginbotham, E. B. (1992). African-American women's history and the metalanguage of race. *Signs, 17*(Winter), 251–274. https://doi.org/10.1086/494730

hooks, b. (n.d.). *Moving beyond pain*. Bell Hooks Books. https://bellhooksbooks.com/moving-beyond-pain/

Knight, H. (2015, April 15). *Why Beyoncé speaks for a generation*. Retrieved from http://www.bbc.com/culture/story/20150415-beyonc-voice-of-a-generation

Littlejohn-Blake, S. M., & Darling, C. A. (1993). Understanding the strengths of African American families. *Journal of Black Studies 23*(4), 460–471. https://doi.org/10.1177/002193479302300402

Patton, L. D., & Ward, L. W. (2016). Missing Black undergraduate women and the politics of disposability: A critical race feminist perspective. *The Journal of Negro Education, 85*(3), 330–349. https://doi.org/10.7709/jnegroeducation.85.3.0330

6 Revelations: What I've Learned from Black Girls

JANINE JONES

Learning from Scratch

Introduction: A Blackgirl Testifies

In the fall of 2016, I sat in a classroom with a group of Blackgirls in an alternative school in Greensboro, North Carolina, where children are sent when suspended from the schools they regularly attend. I ran a focus groups in preparation for an upcoming African American Policy Forum Town Hall (AAPF). Focus groups were recommended by the AAPF as a way of engaging Blackgirls and encouraging them to give testimony regarding problems Blackgirls face. During one session, I, along with about eight Blackgirls, sat and listened to 14-year-old, Taniesha, who stood in front of the class, and gave an account of her arrest by the police at the school she previously attended. Taniesha began, "I tried to break up a fight between a white dude and a black dude. The police came and arrested me and the black boy. They didn't do anything to the white boy. They put me and the black boy in the back of a squad car. They put the handcuffs on tighter than usual. (Tighter *than usual*, I thought.) They kept me in jail the whole week-end."[5]

The AAPF publication "Black Girls Matter: Pushed Out, OverPoliced, and UnderProtected," which reported the 2011–2012 Department of Education findings regarding punitive disparities with respect to race and gender, confirmed that "the national pattern of racial disparity in the distribution of punitive discipline against Black students prevails in New York

---

5 None of the statements in this paper are verbatim. Statements have been reconstructed from recordings and memory, the latter fallible. Quotation marks indicate speech only. Further, names of people and institutions are not given.

and in Boston" (AAPF, p. 19). Monique Morris observed in *Pushout: The Criminalization of Black Girls in Schools*:

> A 2007 study found that teachers often perceived Black girls as being "loud, defiant, and precocious" and that Black girls were more likely than their White or Latina peers to be reprimanded for being "unladylike." Other research has found that the issuance of summonses and/or arrests appear to be justified by students' display of "irate," "insubordinate," "disrespectful," "uncooperative," or "uncontrollable" behavior. These labels underscore the use of discipline, punishment, and the juvenile justice system to regulate identity and social status. They also reflect a consciousness that refuses to honor the critical thinking and leadership skills of Black girls, casting them as social deviants rather than critical respondents to oppression—perceived and concrete. (Morris, 2016, Loc. 222)

Looking directly at me, Taniesha interrupted her own narrative. "But this is not what we need to be talking about." "Oh?" I asked. "What do we need to be talking about?" "What's going on right now, here in this school," she replied.

This paper recounts and provides an analysis of some of the things I learned from Blackgirls in an alternative school. The first section describes methods and methodologies used; the next section continues Taniesha's narrative and narrates *the scratch* that occurred when Blackgirls and I attempted to co-improvise an intervention against *the order of things* in the school. Finally, this chapter concludes by describing one central thing I learned by being in Blackgirls' worlds.[6]

Methodology and Methods

The methodology I used—the overall research strategy that guided my work with Blackgirls—resembled *Participatory Action Research* (PAR). PAR "assumes interdependence between action and research knowledge" (Johnson & Guzmán, 2013, p. 406) and "emphasizes the idea that the knowledge produced should be meaningful and relevant to the people involved in the research and the contexts in which it is being produced" (p. 406). Further,

---

6 Blackgirl worlds refers to contexts in which I have and will be working with Blackgirls. These include preparing Blackgirls to present at the DIVAS conference, held at Elon College in October 2016 (https://sites.google.com/site/drdivas/2016-divas-conference/call-for-proposals) to working with Blackgirls in Stronger Together (ST), an intergenerational group of concerned students, families, educators, and other community members fighting against anti-Black racism in Cobb County (GA) Schools, and, finally, to being with Blackgirls for *Constructing a Cosmic Curriculum*, a community-based summer enrichment series, designed by ST.

Revelations: What I've Learned from Black Girls

PAR methodology understands that "research is not for producing knowledge alone but for promoting research praxis that contributes to issues of social justice" (p. 406). PAR requires that "participants acquire an active and creative role, participate in defining problems and generating transformation strategies, and provide local and experiential knowledge about issues being addressed" (p. 406). "At the same time, the researcher is required to move from the position of an outsider to an involved participant such that the research becomes a collaborative process between researchers and members of the community or social group" (p. 406).

Focus groups were the main tool or method I used. I conducted weekly focus groups with Blackgirls in different schools—primarily non-alternative—over approximately a 4-month period. I had two visits with a girl in a juvenile detention center whom, I knew from the beginning, could not be a testifier at the AAPF Town Hall. That didn't matter, since *my* personal goal had never been simply to find testifiers. I wanted to hear what Blackgirls in alternative schools in North Carolina were talking about. I desired to share with the girls I met an undefinable something that we might co-create during our meetings. Dominique Hill's (2019) concept of *grooves* corresponds with "Black feminisms deployment of embodied understanding as well as Black Girlhood Studies centering and homage to *living from the body*" (Hill, 2019, p. 276, emphasis added). This concept of *grooves* may best describe how our focus groups—where the focus on living in the present foregrounded "process over rules and unwavering instructions" (Hill, 2019, p. 276)—played out. Grooving together, we co-created a situational *scratch* as accidental but perhaps as inevitable and transformational as the scratch that made a noise when Grandmaster Flash stopped his record with his hand to hear what his mother was shouting to him and heard the scratch for music. "Grandmaster Flash discovered that by touching the actual vinyl—considered a taboo practice—he could better manipulate the record and avoid disjointed mixing, allowing partygoers to dance uninterrupted. This record manipulation effectively transformed the turntable into an instrument, introducing the advent of scratching, a fundamental technology of hip-hop music" (Lozenski, 2022, p. 1).

Focus groups provided a way of allowing the Blackgirls I worked with to decide whether they wanted to testify at the Town Hall. For the most part, future testifiers made their decision during the first two weeks of our encounter. There was a great deal of flexibility in how I ran a focus group, having realized early on that flexibility was my friend. Sometimes I had only two girls. At other times, just one girl. Hill wrote "One is the Magic Number" (Hill, 2019, p. 278). Indeed, it was. Two was a charm. I was not collecting data, so numbers didn't matter. From my perspective, the girls who actively participated seemed to enjoy the greater degree of captive Blackgirlwoman attention that the *magic number* or even the charmed number afforded *them*.[7]

The explicit aim of focus groups was to reveal Blackgirls' problems in particular areas of interest to the AAPF, such as school as a pipeline to or pre-packaging for prison or dress code. These were the types of problems that commissioners at a Town Hall could address as future action items. I had to find a way not to impose an *area of interest*—including that of the AAPF—on the girls. Such imposition is not *my way*. If we think of the focus group as my primary tool of engagement, tools within it included anything that could provide a frame capacious enough for eliciting the kind of stories desired by the AAPF, as well as for prompting Blackgirls to discover stories that they desired to tell. Sometimes the two desires came together, as is the case of the story presented in this paper. Often, they did not. For instance, a dominant testimonial theme, across schools, was colorism. Colorism was not, at the time I conducted focus groups, an AAPF-designated topic for Town Halls, perhaps because it is unclear how commissioner-directed action could emerge from such a problem. The same might be true of another prominent topic. Some girls wanted to talk about their very strong dislike for their mothers. I barely had to say a word, let alone provide a frame, for that topic to get off and running. School pushout over problems pertaining to Blackgirls and dress-code was ubiquitous as a desired topic of conversation for Blackgirls in all the schools I visited and for the AAPF. The ways in which dress code rules penalize Blackgirls and their bodies provided an incontrovertible point of agreement between the AAPF and the Blackgirls as far as possible topics for testimony were concerned. In the story presented in this paper, this topic would underpin the creation of *the scratch*.

Framing tools included pocket documentaries,[8] and pictures or stories—excerpts from fiction or non-fiction—used to open a discussion. For instance, I used a cover of Octavia Butler's *Fledgling*, which depicted little brown feet appearing from underneath a long white dress, the suggestion of a body, a shrouded face. I asked a group of Blackgirls what they thought the story was about, just going by the cover.[9] Quite excitedly, some girls exclaimed "A Black girl"!" Others cried, "An African American girl!" I told them it might be about neither, or about both, and proceeded to read the opening pages. "I awoke to darkness. I was hungry—starving!—and I was in pain. There was

---

7 I borrow the term "Blackgirlwoman" from D. Hill. See Hill, D. T., 2019, p. 278).
8 Pocket documentaries use computer technology (phones, androids, *iPad*, sound and image banks) to capture data for montage using an app., such as *iMovie*.
9 See Figure 1 below.

nothing in my world but hunger and pain, no other people, no other time, no other feelings" (Butler, 2005, p. 7). They were mesmerized. Some said "I want *that* book!" Through such openings, they were able to give voice to other things they wanted to talk about.

I continued reading a bit more of *Fledgling*, with the heroine, Shori, describing her fear as she heard someone approaching. Was it an animal that approached? Shori seized it, killed it, and gorged herself on its flesh. Shori's kill-and-feast created an opening for asking, "If the feet on the cover belong to Shori, the person telling the story about herself, do you still think it's an African American girl, or a Black girl?" They were quiet. But no one said "No."

One tool critical to grooving with the girls, to locating testifiers (or to Blackgirls discovering that they wanted to be testifiers), and to learning *explicitly* from Blackgirls about the problems they faced and what was needed to resolve them was an AAPF video of Blackgirls and Blackwomen testifying in an AAPF Town Hall, *Breaking the Silence* (2014). Another critical tool was Monique Morris's *Pushout*. I read excerpted selections of Blackgirls narratives. I then asked questions such as, "Do you know what this girl is talking about?" At the alternative school, one girl with whom I used this technique invariably saw herself in a situation like that of a girl in *Pushout*. She sometimes offered excellent solutions to the problem as it arose in her *specific* situation: solutions that invariably require resources. For instance, she needed a counselor to greet her at the door before entering the classroom to check on her state of mind. Having *to mother* her younger sisters—one a baby—every morning before school, she arrived most days fighting mad.

Breaking the Silence broke ground in every situation in which I showed it to Blackgirls. Its use in the alternative school is particularly memorable. I offered a brief description of AAPF Town Halls and the idea of Blackgirls telling their stories before presenting it. The girls seemed more or less interested, except for one girl, who turned her back to the screen. A White woman—either a teacher or an administrator—entered the room. The woman asked me, indicating the seemingly disinterested girl, "Is she paying attention?" This woman must have slipped by the Blackwoman counselor, Ms. Greenlee, who welcomed me warmly into the school. She kept White women, who would have been constantly interfering with me and the girls if left to their own devices, out of our way. I responded: "She's fine," and watched the woman leave the classroom. The girls and I continued watching the video. Dantze, whose back had been to the screen, turned around a few minutes later. By the end of the video, some of the children were crying. Others comforted their classmates—their arms around them, holding them, stroking them. One student, Karla, still crying, said "I want to be a testifier. I want to help Blackgirls." Dantze left the room.

The following week, I told the girls that we would begin doing pocket documentaries to help them think about their stories. Although the school had some computers we, unfortunately, were never given enough time. (I had to steal time from their activity-filled schedules. I couldn't convince anyone to let me be with the girls more than an hour, once a week.) This meant that we could not do pocket documentaries as they were intended to be done. That is, with each girl collecting her pictures (with a phone), selecting her sounds (from a sound app), narrating her story and recording it, and mounting and editing everything on an app, such as *iMovie*. So, I asked them to bring me pictures, sounds (that they could record on their phone and transfer to mine), and a few words explaining why their chosen pictures were meaningful to them. Some brought me pictures. No one brought me sounds, except for Karla, the girl who wanted to be a Town Hall testifier. She brought me the sound of her own voice, telling me a story about some pictures. One of the pictures depicted a swimming pool she had frequented when she was younger. "It's not a big deal or anything," she said, speaking in a voice which, to my ear, sought to feign indifference. She would see!

I had to inject myself into their pictures, find sounds, music, and a sequence for the pictures that would create an image that Karla would not deny. I did not add a word to what Karla said in the video about the pictures: for instance, about the swimming pool where so many girls allowed one girl to make them all miserable, with a statement or a look; or about the science center where her father, imprisoned and awaiting deportation to Jamaica, used to take her.

The following week, Karla was nervous before the presentation of her pocket documentary. I had to reassure her that it would be all right to show it. I watched Karla's tight face open up into a mode of receptivity, as she watched her story unfold—and as she received what she must have already known—more or less—through a new light. She wanted to make another pocket documentary. Other girls promised to bring their pictures and statements about them (That doesn't mean that they all kept or could keep their promise.). Dantze had wandered in, before the viewing began. Throughout it, she remained in one position—her chin on a stretched-out arm: eyes on the screen. Over the next few weeks, I would be told by a young Blackwoman intern that some people in the school thought that I presented the girls with material that was too hard for them to handle. But I had also been told by Ms. Greenlee, the counselor who continued to welcome me warmly, that after *Breaking the Silence*, Dantze had come to the office and told a counselor about things that had happened to her. Because of Dantze's testimony, the school was able to demand that the state pay for therapy she badly needed. Without her testimony (or someone's testimony) they had not been able to make an argument on her behalf.

Breaking the Silence had helped Dantze see Blackgirls, such as herself, breaking their silence to help themselves and to help other Blackgirls. Her response gave me a certain courage to continue helping Blackgirls see themselves and to see other Blackgirls like themselves. An important way of understanding Dantze's action is to see her as having re-created the idea and the reality of the Town Hall and deploying it as a self-liberating act. She re-created, re-imagined the Town Hall as something hybrid. It could be presented virtually and extended into her *here and now* through her guidance and what she selected to help her. *I* wasn't a commissioner. Dantze knew that. What could I do? I had done what I could do. But she knew the kind of thing that counselors did. Their range of action was different from mine.

Dantze found a counselor who could serve the function of commissioner: a counselor-commissioner who could intervene for her in an explicitly material way. Through Dantze's initiative, the process and the goal of the AAPF was enacted right then and there in an alternative school space. Without formality, fanfare, or performativity, Dantze had reimagined and re-created the Town Hall. She recomposed the Town Hall when and where it was needed: then and there, where she was.

What's Going on Right Now, Here in This School?

Taniesha had interrupted her own narrative about a weekend in a detention center to discuss what was going on right then and there in her school: an unjust rule that targeted the bodies of certain Blackgirls needed to be broken. Showing skill in considering the school's side of the story Taniesha led with the following idea. "I get why they want us to wear uniforms. Some kids have more money than others. They can dress better than other kids. If everyone's wearing a uniform no one gets teased about their clothes. I don't have a problem with that. But then I saw some kids wearing whatever they wanted to. So, I said to myself, 'If *they* gonna wear what they wanna wear, so am I. But I got in trouble.'"

Some girls remained quiet. Other girls spoke up, confirming Taniesha's conclusion: some girls could wear what they desired, while others had to wear the uniform. "What kind of trouble do you get in?" I asked. One girl who, as it turned out was being punished *as we spoke*, explained. "You can either keep on the clothes you wore and sit by yourself all day, and miss your classes, or you can wear the clothes they give you." At that moment, Elaina was wearing clothes they had given her. "See these pants…" She sat back slightly, revealing a tight waist band. I got a better view of her legs. "These pants are so tight they are cutting off my circulation. They give you clothes that are either too big or way too small." "Why didn't you choose the larger ones?" I asked. "How would you like to wear big ole clothes that make you look like a man!" I bet Elaina's response would be categorized as loud, as disruptive, as insubordinate, and as in need of correction and punishment, instead of voicing a concern about being masculinized or miscategorized as a man, both of which happen to Blackgirls and Blackwomen.[10] She was already in an alternative school. What would have been the next alternative?

Taniesha intervened again. "I want to speak with the principal." "I do too," Elaina said. I agreed that we could go see the principal together. I headed down the hall with Elaina and another girl, Sheree, who had had a few words to say. Taniesha, as it turned out, had to be somewhere else. We ran into Ms. Greenlee, who greeted us with a big smile and invited us into her office space. "Where are y'all headed?" I guess we looked as though we were on a mission or something. "We're going to see the principal," I said. "What's going on?" Mrs. Greenlee asked.

There in Ms. Greenlee's space, Elaina began her statement of the problem, which was pretty much the account that Taniesha had given. There was a rule about uniforms. Some girls could break it. Other girls, like her, were punished if they did. She showed Ms. Greenlee how tight her pants were. It was impossible not to see that the pants were cutting off her circulation. A man—a Blackman—entered the space. Space was tight. It was shared. Anyone could enter almost any space at any time, uninvited, it seemed to me from my outsider's perspective. From my point of view this man had *broken* into our conversation with "There are other pants. You can choose the larger pants." Ms. Greenlee confirmed his statement. Elaina replied "All those other pants are too big. Some girls wear leggings to school, and nobody says anything to them. How would you feel having to wear big clothes that make you look like a man?" she asked, desperation pushing up against her voice and her face. Ms. Greenlee turned to me, still smiling. "But you know how it is," she said. "Some girls can wear leggings. Other girls can't. Some of them don't look decent." Ms. Greenlee's words created the conditions for the scratch. They constituted the edge of the scratch.

---

10 See Goff, P. A., Thomas, M. A., & Jackson, M. C. (2008). " Ain't I a woman?" : Towards an intersectional approach to person perception and group-based harms. *Sex Roles: A Journal of Research*, 59(5– 6), 392–403. https://doi.org/10.1007/s11199-008-9505-4

I do not remember what I looked or sounded like in that moment. The girls and I had often talked about breathing. Taniesha's cousin had died, bleeding in her arms. A shooting. He now visits Taniesha as her guardian angel, she told us in one session. Her guardian angel's name was Knowledge. "He tells me to breathe. Remember to breathe". We talked about the advice Knowledge had given her, which was particularly pertinent in the context of fights—something most of the girls knew about. Some of the girls, Taniesha, amongst them, said that when they got to fighting, they came back to themselves only after the fight was over. They would get the sense that they had temporarily lost themselves. On hindsight, that's what must have happened to me when I responded to Ms. Greenlee.

"I had one of those indecent bodies," I said.

I'll never know whether it was the general force-field emanating from my body that brought tears slipping down Ms. Greenlee's beautiful brown face, and these words whispered from her lips: "I had one of those bodies too."

Perhaps if Taniesha had been present, she would have seen me melting and said something to alert me to the fact "This fight ain't over yet." The man had long since been eclipsed in this discussion. I have no idea where he was. We—Elaina, Ms. Greenlee, Sheree, and I—had all changed positions. We were no longer seated. We were standing, Elaina closest to the door. Sheree hadn't had her say. She found her words at this moment. "Ms. Greenlee when I don't wear my uniform it's because it's not clean. My grandmother puts clothes on me that are clean."

Ms. Greenlee reminded Sheree "We have told your grandmother that if she needed something she has only to let us know it. If she needs money for laundry, she can let us know." Sheree's eyes narrowed. Her face hardened. Then Ms. Greenlee said, "The rule is not going to change." She said it more than once. It began to sound like a refrain in a song to me.

Elaina left the room and didn't look back. Beloved Ms. Greenlee—and she was loved by the girls– ran down the hall after her, calling her name. No one could accuse Elaina of being a Loudie (see E. W. Morris's "Blackgirls, Ladies or Loudies," 2007) through such a swift, nonverbal move, which enacted the last *real* spoken word of the encounter. But Sheree had formed an idea about what she and I could do in that moment. Two *was* a charm! "Take my testimony," she said. "Okay." We went together into a contiguous room. Sheree sat in a chair, and I prepared my cellphone. "Ready?"

Sheree looked directly into my eyes. She spoke clearly and resolutely. "I love my father to pieces. He physically abuses me. It has got to stop."

Perhaps Sheree had been prescient. She had never brought pictures for a pocket documentary nor testified in the classroom, as other girls had. If she sensed that this was her last chance with me, she had sensed right.

I was let go. There was no process of conflict resolution within the process of conflict resolution set in motion by a Blackgirl, Taniesha, who had used her words to approach and elucidate a situation of social injustice against Blackgirls, and express a reasoned, affective, incontrovertible position. There was no process of conflict resolution within the process of conflict resolution followed by another Blackgirl, Elaina, who had used her words to repudiate a system bent on denigrating her body and spirit and that of other Blackgirls' bodies and spirits in the name of a masked, then unmasked, respectability politics named "decency."

I did see the girls one last time, however. Ms. Greenlee, the woman who did indeed love those girls, made our last meeting possible. Somehow it was also made possible that the White woman who had tried to surveil my meetings with Blackgirls was sent to monitor us. I brought roses and packets of seeds for the girls to plant. We listened to Aretha Franklin's *A Rose Is Still a Rose*. Some girls didn't want a rose, or at least not one from me. That was just fine: giving and taking in this groove had nothing to do with force. Taniesha wanted more than one rose. She wanted to share them with girls in the place where she lived, she said. I assumed that the girls knew that I would not be returning. They expressed their surprise when I mentioned that this would be our last time together. Surprise was followed by a small chorus of "We know why!"

Normally, I would have asked them "Why?" That was our MO. But I figured that they had heard about *the scratch*. I wasn't about to expose their spoken word about *the scratch* and its aftermath to the surveillance officer in the room. Therefore, I gave them all, including, the officer on duty, a short lecture on how, in the United States, since Black enslavement, Blackgirls and Blackwomen had been denied the norms of femininity and the protections they *purport* to provide. These were reserved for White women, especially of the middle class. I invited the girls to think about ways in which past is present. (Some of them may have surmised that present is future.) Several times the surveillance officer lowered her head. I looked at the top of her head, my eyes saying "Look up! Look up! You came in here to see and to hear. To watch us. What! You thought that your presence would make us the *subjects* and the *objects* of your observation?" The girls behaved as though she wasn't even there.

What I Learned from My Engagement with Blackgirls

"Take our differences and make them our strengths—the poet's intention recalls the black feminist position as trouble. For it refuses to disappear into the general categories of otherness or objecthood, that is, blackness and womanhood, and refuses to comply with formulations of racial and gender-sexual emancipatory projects these categories guide. (Ferreira da Silva, 2018, p. 20)

In focus groups with Blackgirls, I learned about some of the ways they refuse to comply with controlling images of Black womanhood *and* Blackgirlhood that reflect "the dominant group's interest in maintaining Black [girls'] and women's subordination" (Collins, 266 girls' added). Because Blackwomanhood and Blackgirlhood have merged in White hegemonic space, when Black people look at themselves *and feel themselves*, and look at each other and feel each other *through the eyes of others*, Black people often look at Blackgirls through versions of the same controlling images through which Blackwomen are seen and felt. This merger, which sometimes results in adultification of Blackgirls, can lead to a perception of Blackgirls as "aggressively feminine" (Epstein, Blake, & González, 2017, p. 11) and cause them to be "punished more harshly than their peers for the same behaviors when referred to the disciplinary office" (Epstein, Blake, & González, 2017, 9). However, the merger may indicate the deployment of a politics of respectability and dissemblance that seeks to protect Blackgirls[11] even as it is deployed through a White hegemonic gaze embodied in a Blackwoman, as it was in the case of Ms. Greenlee. Thusly deployed, protection is a Blackgirls' punishment, which stabilizes or reinforces White hegemonic space. A Blackwoman who administers this type of loving, caring treatment might be a version of a Captive Maternal, a gender-neutral function, based on my understanding of the concept.[12] If most Black people love and care for other Black people—their children, their sisters and brothers, etc.—in global White hegemonic space, then Ms. Greenlee is not the exception. She is the rule.

Blackgirls refuse. But I learned that Blackgirls' approach might sometimes best be described as an "I can" rather than as a refusal. The stance that Olympic champion Simone Biles took against the International Gymnastics Federation (FIG) exemplifies the embodiment of an "I can" approach. Simone Biles was not properly awarded for some of the difficulty she performed. Recognizing the unfairness leveled at her in judging ("They don't

---

11 See Brittney T. Cooper. (2017). *Beyond respectability: The intellectual thought of race women*. University of Illinois.
12 See Joy James (2016). The womb of western theory: Trauma, time theft, and the captive maternal. *Challenging the punitive society: Carceral notebooks*, Vol. 12.

want the field to be too far apart. And that's just something that's on them" (Abad-Santos, 2021) Biles said that she would continue doing what she was doing. When asked why, she replied, "Because I can."

> "I have seen what a Town Hall is and what it is for. I'll put one into motion right here to get what I need. I reimagine it. I re-create it. Because I can."
>
> I can love my father to pieces and demand that he not be allowed to abuse me. Because I can!"
>
> "I will tell this woman what we should be talking about: the dress code used against us. I tell her because I can."

Like Simone Biles, the Blackgirls I communed with can see the difference between when a rule is applied fairly and when it is not.[13] Before the *refusal*, which comes in the form of noncompliance with the rule, Blackgirls' actions seem to speak "I *can say* when the rule is unfairly applied, and so I will say it! Because it is unfairly applied, I can ignore the unfair rule!"

Living *in focus* with Blackgirls, I learned what it's like to live in a world of beings who exemplify an enactivist theory of cognition which, at its most basic, understands perception in terms of "the 'I can' (i.e., the idea that I see objects in terms of what 'I can' do with them)" (Gallagher, 2017, p. 42), and in terms of a "pragmatic orientation towards the environment, which is not just physical, but also social and cultural…" (Gallagher, 2017, p. 42), and where "social cognition is an attunement process that allows me to perceive the other as someone *to whom I can respond or with whom I can interact* (Gallagher, 2017, p. 12). I learned that some Blackgirls will seek to perceive themselves and each other through certain frameworks that make them perceivable and recognizeable to each other. They will often speak up for themselves and each other, perhaps because seeing themselves in each other provides a necessary condition for them to know "I can."

And so, they do.

Thus, I learned that *within the logic structuring many a Blackwoman-refusal is a prior Blackgirl-perceiving-"I can."* If we want to learn with and from Blackgirls and help them to navigate social spaces, we must notice and encourage what they can do rather than construct worlds in which "I cannot" becomes their *modus operandi*. But perhaps for this we must rediscover in ourselves the little Blackgirls that could by helping each other to navigate and create spaces and times in which our "I can" is not overcome or overshadowed by necessary refusals, or by the "I cannot." Doing so may be

---

13 Interestingly, or not!, the difference in rule application has to do with differences in bodies.

a component of care that can be leveraged, in some instances, against the enactment of a respectability-politics protection plan.

References

Abad-Santos, A. (2021, July 24). *The Simone Biles controversy explained.* Retrieved from https://www.vox.com/22575301/simone-biles-olympics-scoring-explained-gymnastics-yurchenko-double-pike

Butler, O. (2005). *Fledgling.* Seven Stories Press.

Collins, P. (2009). Controlling images and Black women's oppression. In J. Macionis & N. Benokraitis (Eds.), *Seeing ourselves: Classic, contemporary, and cross-cultural readings in sociology* (8th ed.). Pearson.

Crenshaw, K. W., Ocen, P., & Nanda, Jyoti. (2015). Black girls matter: Pushed out, over-policed and underprotected. *African American Policy Forum.* https://www.aapf.org/_files/ugd/62e126_4011b574b92145e383234513a24ad15a.pdf

Epstein, R., Blake, J., & González, T. (2017). *Girlhood interrupted: The erasure of Black girls' childhood.* National Institute of Corrections.

Ferreira da Silva, D. (Winter, 2018). Hacking the subject: Black feminism and refusal beyond the limits of critique. *philoSOPHIA, 8*(1), 19–41. https://doi.org/10.1353/phi.2018.0001.

Gallagher, S. (2017). *Enactivist interventions: Rethinking the mind.* Oxford University Press.

Hill, D. C. (2019). Blackgirl, one word: Necessary transgressions in the name of imagining black girlhood. *Cultural Studies ↔ Critical Methodologies, 19*(4), 275–283. https://doi.org/10.1.1177/1532708616674994.

Johnson, T., & Guzmán, A. M. (2013). Rethinking concepts in participatory action research and their potential for social transformation: Post-structuralist informed methodological reflections from LGBT and trans-collective projects. *Journal of Community & Applied Social Psychology, 23,* 405–419. https://doi.org/10:1002/casp.2134.

Lozenski, B. (2022). *My emancipation don't fit your equation: Critical enactments of Black education in the U.S.* Brill.

Morris, E. W. (2007). "Ladies: or "loudies"?: Perceptions and experiences of Black girls in classrooms. *Youth & Society 38*(4), 490–515. https://doi.org/10.1177/0044118X06296778

Morris, M. W. (2016). *Pushout: The criminalization of Black girls in schools.* The New York Press.

7 *The Road So Far:* My Unlearning and Relearning about Black Girls in Educational Spaces

LATEASHA MEYERS

Author Vignette: I enter a room filled with mostly white educators and white presenters while at a conference in Houston. This particular session that I attend focuses on student and teacher voice. This session has great attendance with barely any seating left once the presentations begin. An African American woman's presentation sticks out to me because it focuses on how to change disciplinary policies while including students' voices, particularly Black girls' voices. When it came time to answer questions, A middle-aged African American male who is an administrator of a school district asks something to the extent of, "at what point are we just giving Black girls an excuse to be disruptive in addition to providing them a crutch?" This question throws me by surprise a little bit especially, given the statistics displayed about Black girls being disproportionately pushed out of school spaces and the presenters' own work-related experiences she discussed. At this moment, I could feel an intense sense of anger. The administrator's use of words such as, "disruptive" and "crutch" did not sit well with me and it was evident that others in the room were disappointed by his question, too. Furthermore, the question reinforced the idea that school educators tend to see Black girls through a deficit lens (Watson, 2016).

Before I could chime in about why his language and outlook were problematic, there was a host of educators in the room that gently let him know his outlook was perhaps misplaced. Additionally, the presenter's response to the question emphasized the importance of relationship building and understanding for Black girls instead of seeing them through a deficit lens. Perhaps Morris (2019) gives this administrator some of the best advice about his student's behavior when she explained, "our challenge is not to mediate student misbehavior, but rather to better understand that this misbehavior is almost always associated with a student's perception of, and reaction to, harm" (p. 26). In the case of the administrator, I wonder what the students he was referring to might be perceiving or reacting to. At that moment, I reflected on how deeply race, gender, and age influence the educational experiences of children of color. I thought about how visual representation of race, gender, and age specifically influences the way we, as a society, see one another. I wondered what Black girls might say if they were there to represent themselves in response to this question.

As a Black woman who studies Black girls, doing this work has revealed to me the attitudes and deep-rooted beliefs some educators tend to have about Black girls, like the administrator in the above vignette. However, this work has also revealed to me the asset-based ways scholars and community members are working to provide nuanced and diverse ways to understand Black girls' experiences in school spaces. The purpose of this chapter is to reflect on what I have learned and unlearned researching on/with Black girls in schooling spaces.

As a part of my unlearning and relearning, I begin with memory work on my experiences as a Black girl in childhood in educational spaces. Dillard (2012) asked,

> what do such memories mean for the teacher/scholar of color (and those embodying critical consciousness) and how might we more explicitly and systematically engage them, (re)member what we have forgot as a way toward healing not just ourselves those who we teach and do research? (p. 11).

There are memories of my girlhood I learned to forget while there were others that seemed too painful to remember, but these memories contributed to my narratives about Black girls. Remembering has allowed me to bring my whole self into my research while navigating through how research can be used as a tool for healing for the Black girls I work with. Unlearning has meant reflecting on the biases I had against my images of Black girls. It has also meant deeply reflecting on where some of my deep held beliefs came from. Relearning has meant inviting in new narratives and continuing to reflect on my position as an educator and researcher in the academy.

Silence in Black Girls' Voices

Author vignette: I was in the second grade; I remember it like it was yesterday. My grandfather had just passed away and I missed a week of school to grieve. Upon my return, my reading teacher was visually upset. Before I could say why I was absent for so long she went on a rant about how behind I was in reading and how much work she would have to do to catch me up. Somewhere between her rant, I was tired and emotionally exhausted and blurted out, my grandpa just died ok. After yelling this at the top of my lungs, she looked horrified. I am not sure if it was the lack of care and empathy I was shown or if it was that I just yelled at the top of my lungs. Either way, that day, my Black girl pain was not taken into consideration until the damage was done.

I tell this story because this was one of the first times in my life I could remember when my Black girl voice was silenced, and my pain was not taken seriously until the damage was already done. These messages continued to get reinforced especially in schooling spaces in a variety of experiences later on in life. In learning more about how to be intentional about my reflections on my Black girlhood while also listening to the experiences of the Black girls I worked with, I saw a continual cycle of how their voices become deliberately silenced. According to Brown (2013), Black girls are often "taught to be unseen and unheard, their silence may be self-imposed or sanctioned. Silent Black girls have a lot to say; however, without time, good relationships, and patience, their voices remain a backdrop to conversations about them" (p. 184). Unfortunately, as much as I never wanted anyone to feel the way I felt that day as a child. I sometimes perpetuated this narrative I was taught early on in childhood—Black girls needed to be silenced and their voices should not be taken seriously. This contradiction and the deeply entrenched beliefs I had been taught about Black girls through my childhood led me to want to examine more deeply my relationship with my Black girlhood by learning more about Black girls.

The Beginning of My Scholarship on Black Girls

A year after starting my doctoral program in 2016, I remember hearing an increase of stories about Black girls being mistreated, ignored, or silenced in educational spaces. This brought me back to my girlhood and reminded me how ideas about who Black girls are "supposed" to be, tend to get reinforced as a single-story narrative. One story that is by now familiar to many, stuck out to me; however, I did not hear about it until the aftermath. In 2015, in Columbia South Carolina, at Spring Valley High school, a Black girl was videotaped being put in a chokehold and flipped out of her desk by a police officer. Her name is Shakara and she was 16 years old when this took place. Her teacher called the school's administrator who then escalated to calling the school's resource officer because she did not put her phone away "fast enough". According to her classmates, Shakara was not on the phone, she just had the phone out. Regardless of the situation, no child deserves to be treated like Shakara was treated. To add insult to injury, Shakara's classmate, 18-year-old Niya was also arrested for protesting the injustice Shakara was facing at the hands of the school's adults (Jarvie, 2015). Both girls were eventually charged with being disruptive in school. However, sometime after this incident, there was an uproar in organizations, advocates, and political organizers calling for charges to be dropped. Eventually, they were, but the resource officer and the other school personnel involved were never charged for the harm and damage they created. The trauma from this event could not be undone.

Sometime after this incident, I kept reading about other Black girls who were being disciplined for subjective things like their hair choice. Whether it was wearing an afro, hair extensions, or having braided patterns, their hair was being treated like an object for examination and ridicule amongst the public. The incident with Shakara and the ongoing harassment of Black girls' hair led me to want to examine how Black girls experience educational spaces. I wanted to understand more about this phenomenon of Black girls being harshly treated. More importantly, I wanted to better understand their experiences from their perspectives, not just secondhand narratives written about them. I remember as a Black girl child, I often wore hair extensions and braids. I also was expressive and let school figures know if I did not feel like something was fair. These events reminded me how easily these things could have happened to me in my Black girlhood. They also reminded me how committed our society is in controlling the Black girl body and making sure her body is "compliant" to all authority under a white supremacist gaze. This further led me to think about images, both literal and figurative that we create about Black girls. Furthermore, I became more curious about the images Black girls create about themselves and their understanding of the conditions in our current society. My reflections, the injustices Black girls were facing, my positioning in the academy, and my intellectual curiosity led me to my work and research with Black girls.

Setting the Stage with Research

This chapter is a reflection heavily situated in work I completed with Black girls in an after-school space known as Girls Purpose Squad (GPS). GPS is an after-school space located in the midwest Rust Belt. The space is particularly located in a mostly African American community. In terms of participation

The Road So Far: My Unlearning and Relearning

in GPS, there were at any given time upwards of twelve girls in the space; however, five girls in total participated in the study related to the current reflection. The girls who participated were Kayla, Phooj, Lil Ken, Blai, and Jale. The girl's ages ranged from 13 to 15. For the particular study and girls I worked with, I wanted to understand their experiences through their words and photos. I particularly wanted to gauge how race, gender, and age construct their educational experiences through their eyes. Photovoice was used to engage in this work. Photovoice is a participatory method that has three goals. These include, (1) allowing people to represent their lives through their eyes (2) engage & promote critical dialogue about strengths and concerns of the community (3) reach policy makers and other people in power (Wang, 2006, p. 148). In regard to the girls I worked with, photovoice provided a space for them to discuss and represent their experiences in educational space through photography. Through their pictures and working with them in the after-school space of GPS, I came to gain insights into how we have all been and largely continue to be miseducated about Black girls through "controlling images" (Collins, 2000). Working directly with the girls, I learned and unlearned a lot more than anticipated. For the purposes of this chapter, I will focus on the top three things I learned, unlearned, and how my scholarship has been impacted by these new insights.

Locating Their Voices

My work with Black girls has been and continues to be centered on understanding. I wanted to understand how they navigated their educational worlds. I wanted to locate their narratives in spaces where their narratives are often excluded, education. Not only through words, but also through visuals, I wanted to understand the "oppositional gaze[14]" Black girls tend to develop in a society that largely adultifies them, stereotypes them, and discriminates against them. hooks (1992) explains, "the "gaze" has been and is a site of resistance for colonized black people globally" (p. 116). That is, Black folks, in our ploy towards justice, have developed a particular lens through which we resist. Further reflecting on this oppositional stance as knowledge, Collins (2000) states that oppositional knowledge is "a type of knowledge developed by, for, and/ or in defense of an oppressed groups interest. Ideally, it fosters the groups self-definition and self-determination" (p. 299). Later

---

14 Patricia Hill Collins (1990/2000) defined oppositional knowledge as, "a type of knowledge developed by, for, and/ or in defense of an oppressed groups interest. Ideally, it fosters the groups self-definition and self-determination" (p. 299).

in this chapter, I will show how Black girls use Black Girlhood as Visual Oppositional Knowledge (Meyers, 2020). For now, it is important to have some understanding of the work I previously did with Black girls.

Unlearning Societal Messages about Black Girls

It might sound like a cliché, but one of the first things I learned in entering the after school space and researching with Black girls was that I had a lot of unlearning to do specifically with how controlling images shaped the ways in which I engaged with Black girls especially when it came to conducting the research. Growing up as a Black girl in the late 1990s and early 2000s I was well aware of the negative images and labels we put on some Black girls in addition to the generational differences that might exist. Even with these differences, I found similar labels that were placed on Black girls in the 1990s continued to be put onto Black girls in 2017. For example, the terms *she is fast, a little woman and, disruptive* are stereotypes society has put onto Black girls (Meadows-Fernandez, 2020; Thomas, 2021). The Black girls I worked with taught me about the importance of accepting them for who they are rather then put them into a box or only accept those who align with respectability politics. Without even knowing it, the girls in GPS allowed me to further explore my undoing of societal expectations as a Black woman who is situated in academic spaces. They challenged me to thoroughly examine the previous labels I mentioned while further interrogating where these labels stem from. Several scholars have examined how stereotypes from the slavery era in the U.S. are directly connected to stereotypes we continue to have about Black girls and women (Davis, 1981; hooks, 1992; Collins 2000; Harris-Perry, 2011). When we are not reflective, we continue to put these labels on Black girls. I went about unlearning by going deeper into the scholarship and most importantly, by listening to the girls I worked with. There were days when I barely talked during my time with the girls in GPS; instead I chose to intentionally listen to the girls' experiences and how they were understanding the world. As an adult in the space and a researcher in the academy, this was no easy task. Being trained in academia to ask the questions and be the "expert," it is difficult navigating these expectations while also balancing intentional listening. A part of my unlearning was knowing I was not the expert on the girls' lives; however, they are the experts on their own lives, and it was a gift that they shared their experiences with me.

Secondly, I learned there are ways in which our society and our community (the Black community) tend to force Black girls into growing up too fast. The girls I worked with reinforced for me the significance of understanding the importance of allowing and providing children the space to experience their childhood. When Black children are responsible for doing adult expectations such as caretaking duties and working to help support the household it can send a message that they are already adults. Adultification bias is when adults treat Black girls as more mature for their age in comparison to their white peers (Epstein, Blake, & Gonzalez, 2017). This bias has consequences for how Black girls tend to experience childhood. Furthermore, it tends to eliminate giving Black girls the benefit of the doubt for doing age appropriate behaviors. This bias can be a double-edged sword for parents raising Black girls. Meadows-Fernandez (2020) asks a good question, "How can I preserve my daughter's childhood while preparing her for a world that may judge her prematurely?" (para.7). Those who care about Black children are faced with a dual reality. We must prepare them for the reality of the world while also trying to preserve their childhoods. This is a difficult and delicate balance to foster. However, as much as it is important to prepare our children for the injustices of the world, it is also important to allow them space to be children.

Finally, although there were times in the after school space when there was immense pain, hurt, and misunderstanding, there were mostly times of pure Black girl joy, which often gets lost and silenced amongst the controlling images that exist to delegitimize Black girls' childhood and joy. This is important because especially in educational spaces, joy can often be left in the background or forgotten. I am reminded of a picture that Blai asked me to take of the girls in GPS. The girls were in a circle talking with one another, exchanging conversations about their day, and laughing while joking with one another. This experience and picture stood out to me because, at that moment, you could feel the joy coming from the girls in a very simple exchange. Furthermore, when this picture was showcased at a community exhibition, I reflected on the importance of the ways in which Black girlhood narratives and scholarship need to be complicated beyond the good and bad narratives. We also need to understand the joys of Black girlhood in everyday moments. While also understanding how Black girls are navigating their educational worlds. Black girlhood needs to be celebrated in all its authenticity. These three things I learned from working with Black girls in GPA also encouraged me to rethink beliefs I previously held about the girls I work with and my Black girl childhood.

Rethinking Beliefs about Black Girlhood

In the first half of her chapter, *The Mis-Education of Black Girls: Learning in a White System,* Jones (2015) discusses the consequences Black girls face from being socialized in a white supremacist education system. She explains that Black girls are taught to be apologetic about their being because they are educated in a white system that tries to define, "Black girl's body images, culture beliefs systems, perception of self, and various meanings of success for her (Jones, 2015, p. 270). If we think about this not only in education, but in the larger society, a lot of us have been duped by the stereotypical narratives, misrepresentations, and images that have been constructed about Black girls in a white supremacist society. In other words, we have all been miseducated about what it means to be a Black girl. This miseducation should cause alarm for concern. As it continues to affect and influence the ways in which we work with and see Black girlhood. We tend to miss the nuances and diversity within Black girl childhood. I am no different, and this reality became more apparent to me as I spent more time in the field learning with and about Black girls. As a Black woman working with Black girls, I was encouraged from the girls' experiences to rethink some of the ideas I held. I especially had to challenge my beliefs about their experiences in educational environments. I realized that we often hold beliefs about how and why Black girls should change themselves without examining the inequalities Black girls often face in a variety of institutions such as the schooling environment. In an interview with Phooj, I was reminded of this when she explained,

> So my educational experiences are just how the white teachers would always single Black kids out like, how we said uhm…even like the dress code situation [referring to a conversation we had earlier]. Like….long pause.
>
> She continues to elaborate,
>
> Like, if the Black girls had on shorts that some of the white girls had on, we would get dress coded and the white girl wouldn't and in class, like, they'll always call more on the white kids more than the Black kids that I've seen, that I've noticed (Interview 5/2019).

Phooj is not only noting how in her school Black girls and white girls are treated differently based on the way they dress, but she is also pointing out a larger belief within our society, Black girls need to change. This belief is reinforced in several ways throughout our society. Going back to my first vignette in this chapter, the school administrator felt Black girls were provided a crutch and if we did not provide them with this imaginary "crutch" their behavior would improve. However, this belief does not acknowledge the larger systematic barriers Black girls contend with. Continuing to work with and read about Black girls in educational spaces has moved me to contemplate this belief in more depth. As I continue to do this work, I continue to think about the ways in which I can challenge this belief by being a more intentional scholar and writer.

Discoveries through the Scholarship and the Impact

The final section of this chapter is a discussion on what I have discovered through working with Black girls and how it has impacted the academic work I continue to do. Through being in conversation with Black girls and reading more scholarship, there are several discoveries I have reflected on which will continue to impact the work I do moving forward.

A large discovery that seems obvious, but is lacking in our society is, Black girls are important, and they should be valued by our society. There are several ways we intentionally try to silence Black girls' experiences. One of which is by assuming they all are the same without considering their diverse experiences. With that, we need to listen to the voices, images, and experiences of Black girls. If we listen, and I mean really listen to their voices, Black girls have important knowledge to contribute to our world and our understandings of our world. For example, researching with the girls in GPS, I found that Black girls create *Black Girlhood as Visual Oppositional Knowledge (BGVOK)(Meyers, 2020)*. That is, they use images and words to create knowledge that allow them to self-define and determine what they want to share. This discovery has implications for my scholarship as I am still developing this framework and understanding about Black girls (Meyers, 2020).

Final Thoughts on Black Girl Scholarship and Programming

When I think about the knowledge I have gained from scholarship on Black girls and working with Black girls, I am reminded of how impactful this work could be. I am also reminded; it is simply not enough just to include Black girls in a society that maintains a status quo. To further elaborate this, hooks (1995) explains, "inclusion without any disruption of the status quo, usually reinscribes, in a different form, the very patterns of domination that have been critiqued and interrogated to make an opening (p. 104). Therefore, simply producing more scholarship, building more programs, organizations, and rites of passage programs are not enough if we are not interrogating the dominant narratives and images about Black girlhood. In other words, it is not enough to have good intentions but continue to replicate respectability politics. A Nyachae and Ohito (2021) analysis of extracurricular programming displayed how these spaces, although with good intention, often reinforce, there is an incorrect and correct way of displaying Black femininity. This has impacted my scholarship the most. I continue to reflect on ways in which I continue to perpetuate this narrative, but also ways in which I am working to break this narrative. Moving forward for the study of Black girls, my hope is we continue to learn from, listen to, and complicate the Black girlhood work we do as scholars, writers, and community activists. I plan on continuing to learn from Black girls and how their educational experiences are shaped by their race, gender, and age. Learning from them provides tools to understand how we can better develop programs and spaces for them. Moreover, when developing programs and spaces for Black girls, we must be reflective and ask "what works for whom- as opposed to simply what works- to create ECPs (Extracurricular Programs) that respect that diversities of girlhoods existence among Black girls (Nyachae & Ohito, 2019, p. 23).

References

Brown, R. N. (2013). Hear our truths: The creative potential of Black girlhood. University of Illinois Press.

Collins, P. H. (1990/2000). *Black feminist thought: Knowledge, consciousness, and the politics of empowerment* (2nd ed.). Routledge.

Davis, A. Y. (1981). *Women, race, & class*. New York City, NY: Random House Inc.

Dillard, C. B. (2012). *Learning to (re) member the things we've learned to forget: Endarkened feminisms, spirituality, and the sacred nature of research and teaching*. New York, NY: Peter Lang.

Epstein, R., Blake, J., & González, T. (2017). *Girlhood interrupted: The erasure of Black girls' childhood*. Georgetown Law Center on Poverty and Inequality.

Harris-Perry, M. V. (2011). *Sister citizen: Shame, stereotypes, and Black women in America*. New Haven, CT: Yale University Press.

hooks, b. (1992). *Black looks: Race and representation*. Boston, MA: South End Press.

hooks, b. (1995). *Art on my mind: Visual politics*. New York: New Press.

Jarvie, J. (2015, October 29). Girl thrown from desk didn't obey because the punishment was unfair, attorney says. *Los Angeles Times*. https://www.latimes.com/nation/la-na-girl-thrown- punishment-unfair-20151029-story.html.

Jones, J. J. (2015). The mis-education of Black girls: Learning in a White system. In C. F. Collins (Ed.), *Black girls and adolescents: Facing the challenges* (pp. 269–286). Santa Barbara, CA: ABC-CLIO.

Meadows-Fernandez, A. R. (2020, April 17). Why won't society let Black girls be children. *The New York Times*. https://parenting.nytimes.com/preschooler/adultification-black-girls

Meyers, L. N. (2020). *Seeing education through a Black girls' lens: A qualitative photovoice study through their eyes* [Doctoral dissertation, Miami University]. OhioLINK

Electronic Theses and Dissertations Center. http://rave.ohiolink.edu/etdc/view?acc_num=miami1586263706742763

Morris, M. W. (2019). *Sing a rhythm, dance a blues: Education for the liberation of Black and Brown girls.* New York: The New Press.

Nyachae, T. M., & Ohito, E. O. (2019). No disrespect: A womanist critique of respectability discourses in extracurricular programming for Black girls. *Urban Education, 58*(2), 1–31.

Thomas, A. (2020). Out of the box. Strong Black girls: Reclaiming schools in their own image. In A. Apugo, L. Mawhinney, & A. Mbilishaka (Eds.), *Strong Black girl* (pp. 9–19). New York, NY: Teachers College Press.

Wang, C. C. (2006). Youth participation in photovoice as a strategy for community change. *Journal of Community Practice, 14*(1–2), 147–161.

Watson, T. N. (2016). "Talking Back": The perceptions and experiences of Black girls who attend City High School. *The Journal of Negro Education, 85*(3), 239–249.

Part III Being a Scholar of Black Girls and Black Girlhood

Contributors in this section elucidate what it means to be a scholar of Black girls and Black girlhood, including the inspiration behind their work, the impact of their work, and the ways their work has shaped their academic careers.

8 But Some of Us Are Brave: Exploring How Black Girlhood Origin Stories Shape Sister Scholarship

DANIELLE K. WRIGHT AND RASHIDA GOVAN

Everyone has an origin story. Origin stories are not reserved for superheroes and villains. Each of us has a unique life course with pivotal moments and experiences that shape us. To know your origin story is to know your "why." For those of us who work with girls, our origin stories are important to acknowledge because they inform how we pursue our work, they impact the quality of our relationships, and they are the motivation behind our efforts. In our work with the women who work with girls, we frequently discuss the importance of reflecting on our origin story as a necessary step in delivering the healing-centered practice that is so essential to our relationships with the girls we serve. Here is our origin story, our reason "why" we do what we do, and the paths that brought us into this sacred sisterhood.

This chapter explores the question "What inspires us to do this work?" Here we share our unique stories on how we began this work, the key lessons we have learned that emerged from our work with girls, and how prioritizing healing is essential in our practice. We hope that our stories resonate with you and give you some "food for thought' as you consider the ways in which you support Black girls and women.

Inspiration Part I—Dr. Wright's Story

It's been over two decades since I experienced my very first encounter with shame, as the result of a dress code violation. I still remember the experience as clearly today as I did over two decades ago. At the time of the incident, I was a middle school student at a local New Orleans public school. Earlier in the school year and prior to the incident occurring, a White Art teacher held an assembly for all the girls, to discuss the dress code. She explained that Black girls would need to wear their shorts, skirts and dresses a little longer than their White counterparts because according to her, we had bigger butts. I remember thinking, at that moment, that I would need to avoid contact with this particular teacher for the remainder of the year. I did a great job of doing just that, until I was assigned Art as an elective in the fourth quarter of the academic year. I remember that upon entering her class, I would feel overwhelmingly nervous that I would be sent home because of my attire. I also remember observing White girls wearing very short shorts, confidently entering the class and navigating their way around school with ease and freedom. On the other hand, I was trying to cover up my shorts by tying a jacket around my waist, and hiding behind other students as I walked in the class, and even running to my seat to avoid being noticed. I spent more time and energy trying to avoid the art teacher, than actually learning art.

One day, what felt like the inevitable, finally happened…the "rip the band-aid off" moment where I walked in the class and she yelled across the room that my shorts were too short and I needed to go to the office to call my mom to pick me up. I was horrified, ashamed, and embarrassed. I ran out of the trailer, where art class was held, and walked to the office. I was nervous. Would I get into more trouble with the school disciplinarian? Were there other consequences besides calling my mom and being sent home?

Once I made it to the office, the Assistant Principal, Brenda Blakely, a Black woman, whom I admired greatly, greeted me. She was always so professional, so very kind and perfectly polished and well put together, like the kind of put together where there was never a hair out of place. She greeted me with warmth, and I immediately began to calm down. I explained to her why I had been sent to the office. She responded with a look of disapproval and said, "I'll walk you back to class." In that moment I realized that the look of disapproval was not towards me, but it was in fact, towards the art teacher's decision to put me out of the class.

Ms. Blakely and I entered the class together, and the art teacher began yelling that I needed to be sent home because my shorts were too short. Ms. Blakely calmly stated, "she'll be staying." Ms. Blakely instructed me to have a seat, and I did just that.

In that moment, Ms. Blakely provided me with a healing interaction that served as an antidote to the "flight or fight" response that my body experienced from the shame and horror of being put out of class, because of a dress code violation (Burke, 2018). Ms. Blakely made me feel safe and protected. This experience was incredibly transformative for me.

Unfortunately, for many black girls, these experiences of adultification bias in the absence of healing interactions, such as the one that Ms. Blakely provided for me over two decades ago, are far too prevalent. Adultifcation bias against Black girls is an age compression in which historically negative stereotypes of Black women are mapped on to Black girls (Epstein, Black, & Gonzalez, 2017). Interactions between racism and sexism cause Black girls to experience hyper-vulnerability to adultification bias. In my experience, the historically negative stereotype of a "Jezebel" was being mapped on to me, where my body was being hypersexualized.

Dress code violations continue to be biased against Black girls. For example, in 2018, a New Orleans Black girl, Faith Fennidy, made national news when she was sent home, from a Catholic School, for violating a hair policy that prohibited her from wearing her braided hairstyle (Padgett, 2018). Discriminatory policies and practices in schools continue to create dehumanizing experiences for Black girls that prohibit them from the freedom of behaving in ways that represent normative development.

I now recognize that what Ms. Blakely did for me, over two decades ago, when I was a New Orleans Black girl, like Faith Fennidy, was far more than protecting me from a biased dress code violation. She taught me the value of being an advocate for justice. She planted the seed for the work that I currently do to advance justice for Black girls.

As a licensed clinical social worker, I work to advance justice for Black girls across all the systems with which Black girls interface. I develop and implement programming that focuses on cultivating the social and emotional development of adolescent Black girls. I work with Head Start centers to provide parental attachment therapeutic services to Black moms/caretakers and their babies. I also develop and facilitate trainings that seek to expand the capacity of educators, school based mental health professionals and school leaders to transform schools into healing spaces for Black girls. The data gathered from the aforementioned clinical services is utilized to generate policy briefs and reports that seek to expand the knowledge of the community-at-large, as it relates to the lived experiences of Black girls and the ways in which we can better meet the needs of our girls. I feel so incredibly fortunate to be doing the work of centering Black girls and subsequently growing the seed that Ms. Blakely planted over two decades ago.

Inspiration Part II—Dr. Govan's Story

My origin story takes me back to 2006 when I was working in student affairs at a community college in Baltimore, Maryland. My work in the community frequently involved me working with Black women and girls through the facilitation of workshops on a variety of topics like self-esteem, healthy decision-making and relationships, to talks at programs geared at preparing sisters for the college experience. I rather enjoyed that work and found it to be somewhat therapeutic for me. I found that I had something to offer to help sisters build the dynamic relationships with each other that would help them navigate the trials that they would face as Black women, and it brought me a lot of satisfaction to be able to draw on my own experiences (good, bad and in between) to help young girls and women develop an ethic of love and care for self that can serve as a foundation for their wellness. At the same time, I was at a crossroads personally and professionally. I had experienced some measure of success in my career but was beginning to desire more. I had no idea what was next for me personally or professionally, but I knew there was something I was being called to do.

One day a sorority sister of mine reached out to me, as she had in the past, to come to the high school she founded to facilitate a workshop with her girls. I was already mentoring a girl at the school through a program at the school, and frequently volunteered in that space. I decided to facilitate a vision board workshop with them as I had just learned about the concept from a book I was reading, while I was engaged in my own personal journey to discover and manifest the things my heart desired. I thought the process sounded like a valuable tool to help us get clear and excited about the life we wanted to create for ourselves. It seemed especially suitable for the girls because our work with them was heavily focused on preparing them for a bright future. For me, the process was a necessary step in my internal work to discover my "calling."

The night before the workshop I began to work on my own vision board. I reflected on the experiences that fulfilled me and I prayed to attract more. As I began to look through my magazines to clip pictures for my board, I came across an article that was maybe two years old that profiled a woman named Niambi Jaha Echols. She wrote a curriculum that helps Black girls to navigate their transition from adolescence to adulthood and started a companion program called Camp Butterfly that would bring girls of African descent from across the US to engage in art, yoga, meditation and a variety of culturally-centered experiences that would help them through this important stage of development. As I peered at the picture of Mama Niambi's regal pose, I decided to post the picture and description in the center of my vision board. The work she was doing was precisely what I wanted to do. That was the moment I discovered and declared that my passion for supporting Black girls and women was indeed part of my purpose.

I realized that creating these safe spaces for girls to grow and heal was necessary in our journeys as Black women and I wanted to give a measure of what I had been given throughout my life to other Black girls and women so we could collectively thrive. My desires were further solidified the next day when I facilitated the visioning workshop for the high school girls. Their vision boards depicted them in what I would consider stable, middle class lives. They desired houses, cars, travel and the basic niceties and comforts afforded many people in the middle class, but that escaped them in their current economic situations. Yet they also included images of athletes and entertainers with whom they believed were necessary to align with in order to access those comforts and stability. Our discussions confirmed their perspective and I commenced to work with them to realize that their visions were attainable on their own. I worked with them for several weeks to help them discover that they had the capacity to create the life they wanted for themselves on their terms. At the same time, I was affirming this lesson for myself.

Two weeks after the session I was at my desk in my Baltimore office when an email came through my inbox with the subject line "Camp Butterfly needs your help!" I recognized the name from my vision board process and reached out to see if it was the same program. When I called the number (with the Chicago area code), a woman answered and I inquired if the camp in question was the one featured in Essence Magazine. The woman confirmed and I began to babble on in excitement about my vision board and my desire to do this work with girls. The woman stopped me to share that she was on another line (I was a bit embarrassed) and I apologized and agreed to a later call. Before I hung up I asked with whom I was speaking, and it was Niambi Jaha Echols, the woman featured in the magazine. When I hung up I was overwhelmed by the moment. I had manifested this connection that would (unbeknownst to me) thrust me into my calling. And I have never looked back.

That summer I attended Camp Butterfly as a counselor, and would do so the next few summers. I was trained in their facilitation strategy, learned the curriculum, and continued to support the organization for years. When I moved to New Orleans in 2008 to pursue my doctorate, I continued my work with girls, launching an offshoot of Camp Butterfly with high school girls in the city. In January of 2009 Project Butterfly New Orleans was founded and we have since worked with nearly 400 girls across New Orleans through our culturally-rooted, rites of passage program for girls of African descent.

Visibility: The Experience of Being Seen and Understood

As a Black woman who works with Black girls, when I think about my work, I tend to think about its impact on the Black girls that I have served, and the ways in which I have supported their healing journey. I tend not to highlight the ways in which being a healing practitioner or a facilitator of healing for Black girls has supported my own healing. As Black women working with Black girls, we enter this work with the same vulnerabilities cultivated by racism and sexism, that the girls that we work with encounter. We, too, are on a healing journey. I love to share and reflect on my experiences working with Black girls, and particularly those that specifically support my success as a practitioner, like the moments where my positive interactions with Black girls have helped them to feel seen and understood. However, the moments where I have healed and grown most, as a practitioner, have been during times where I was forced to face my own acceptance of racist and sexist ideas, which were, in fact, inhibiting the freedom of the Black girls I sought to support. Confronting this did not feel good, but was essential to expanding my capacity to do this work.

One of my favorite stories to share about the importance of Black women working with Black girls is when I worked as a school social worker at a local, public high-school in New Orleans. During that time, I was doing a lot of clinical group work with adolescent Black girls. I had taken one of the girls' groups on a field trip. New Orleans humidity is notorious for disrupting whatever your intentions are for your hair. I'm pretty sure that New Orleans is ranked as the American city with the highest relative humidity. As far back as I can remember, New Orleans humidity has caused my hair to swell in ways that left my original hairstyle unrecognizable. As an adult, I'd grown to accept my incredibly frizzy and thick hair, and I also learned to always keep a ponytail holder in my purse.

On this particular day, the humidity had caused my hair to swell, and I forgot to bring a ponytail holder to work. The girls and I were entering the school, returning back from our field trip, and I overheard some of the girls commenting on how "big" Arianne's hair had gotten from the humidity. She looked mortified. Our eyes met and I calmly said, "Arianne, you have hair like me. Look at my hair, it looks exactly like yours." She smiled, and for the remainder of the school year she referred to herself as having "hair like Ms. Danielle." I also noticed that the other girls would comment about Arianne having "pretty hair, like Ms. Danielle." Arianne and I expanded their group's ideas about beauty by including frizzy hair in the ways in which we define "pretty hair."

This is an adorable example of the importance of Black women affirming Black girls. It's a story that typically makes those listening feel warm and fuzzy. However, it does not represent the full breadth of my experience working with Black girls. It represents the stories that we love to elevate during qualitative interviews for evaluations. But it does not capture the breadth and depth of the healing that happens for Black women, doing this work. It does not capture the hard stuff.

Also, while working as a school social worker at a local high-school in New Orleans, I was confronted with conflicting beliefs about the way I saw myself and the way that I was responding to a Black girl. Next door to the school where I was working, was an abandoned apartment complex. It had been said that students would sneak into the abandoned apartments to have sex. On one particular day, rumors were swirling amongst the student population about a Black girl, Alyssa, and three Black boys, Joe, Rob and Melvin. It had been alleged that Alyssa, Joe, Rob and Melvin, checked themselves out of school early, and went to the abandoned apartments to have sex. The adults in the building were made aware of the incident, because the significant others of the boys in question were upset, as they felt betrayed by their boyfriends. And their emotional distress was disrupting their ability to learn. I was called in by the assistant principal to provide assistance with mitigating the emotional distress, being experienced by the girls.

By the time I was called in, Alyssa, Joe, Rob and Melvin had already received their disciplinary action. They had all been suspended and were potentially up for expulsion. I advocated for mental health services for Alyssa. I explained that I felt strongly that there was an underlying issue that led to her to having sex with the three boys in the abandoned building. I wanted to have a mental health assessment done and have her referred for services.

I met with Alyssa. I explained to her that I thought a mental health screening would be helpful in accelerating the process of getting her the proper support needed. She looked at me and asked. "Ms. Danielle, are you screening the boys for mental health support? If you think something is wrong with me for having sex with them, why don't you think something is wrong the three of them?"

Her question rocked me to my core. I had to accept that at that moment, I was operating from racist and sexist ideas. I normalized the experience for the boys, but decided that it was pathological for Alyssa. I was treating Alyssa unfairly. My actions made Alyssa feel unseen and misunderstood. This was very difficult for me to accept. At the time, I considered myself to be an ardent advocate for Black girls in schools, and believed strongly that my work advanced justice for Black girls in schools. I was experiencing cognitive dissonance between the way I saw myself and the information that Alyssa presented to me.

I spent a lot of time practicing self-awareness to better understand why it never occurred to me, to refer Joe, Rob and Melvin for mental health services, for the same incident that I referred Alyssa out for mental health services. I deeply contemplated why I only thought to make the referral for Alyssa and not the boys. And even today, many years later, I still spend time contemplating that decision.

It is interesting that my middle school experience of Ms. Blakely saving me from a teacher who was mapping the historically negative archetype of the hypersexual Jezebel onto me, was such a defining moment in my life. I've come to understand the connection between that experience and my unfair treatment toward Alyssa.

My colleague Dr. Rashida Govan, and I, co-created a training in the area of adultification bias against Black girls, and we present those trainings to teachers, school leaders, school based mental health professionals and school discipline staff throughout the city of New Orleans. There is an important part of the training called, "If you spot it, you got it" (a phrase Govan adopted from Niambi Echols, Founder of Camp Butterfly). During this time, we ask professionals to reflect on the behaviors that children exhibit, that really get under their skin. In doing so, professionals recognize that the behaviors that get under their skin always trigger some unhealed parts of themselves. That's what Alyssa did for me. She triggered an unhealed 12-year-old who had been unfairly treated because of racism, sexism and body shaming. In an attempt to protect Alyssa from being labeled as hypersexual, I pathologized her behavior. Any attempt to protect Black girls, in the absence of self-awareness and self-reflection, can cause harm. We are not protecting Black girls when they are not being given the opportunity to feel seen and understood. I understand that now, and Alyssa, by far, has been one of my greatest teachers in this work.

Visibility: Shared Experiences

Storytelling is a valuable tool for facilitating learning and healing (Chioneso et al., 2020; Humes, 2016). It is also a valuable mechanism through which to surface the shared experiences of Black girls and women in an effort to normalize these experiences, to provide empathy and support to Black girls and often, to share pathways to healing and resolution. The *Mama Monologues* is one of Project Butterfly New Orleans' signature programs in which mentors employ the use of storytelling through the performance of monologues to give visibility to some of the common experiences and challenges faced by girls of African descent. The mentors write monologues that reflect their experiences as teenagers with self-esteem, body image, familial relationships, sexual violence, mental health challenges, sex, and other common issues faced by Black girls and women. The Monologues give space for mentors to be vulnerable and transparent with girls, and allows them to connect with the audience by performing these pieces from their vantage point as teenagers. This helps the audience gain an intimate view of the turmoil, challenges and joys experienced by girls of African descent. An open dialogue with the audience and cast is held after the performances.

The Mama Monologues was a dream of mine for some time. For a long time I held space for girls and women to process their trauma and I could see commonalities in the experiences of both the girls and women with whom I worked. Moreover, I saw so much of myself in the testimonies and trials of the Black women and girls within my community. Often, the deep trauma that I helped women and girls process was done privately. So many sisters, including me, were suffering silently, in many cases, feeling alone and isolated. I knew that by creating this space for Black women and girls to tell their stories out loud and to name the experiences they were having on their terms, we all could begin to heal.

The first time we hosted a *Mama Monologues* performance was at a retreat for our butterflies-in-training (participants in our program). The mamas and aunties (mentors) had a few hours of silence to prepare their monologues to perform that evening as a surprise for our girls. I remember feeling petrified as I wrote my piece chronicling my bouts with low self-esteem and sexual violence. In order to deliver something that was impactful, I was going to have to expose a truth I had buried deep within. Everything in my monologue was antithetical to the confident manner in which I present myself most of the time. The girls and the mamas and aunties (mentors) were about to see another side of me. But I was not alone in this process, as all the other mentors were going through the exact same thing. We created a situation where we trusted the process, because none of us knew what we would hear in these monologues.

When it was time for our performances, we lined up our chairs in a row and one by one we told our stories. One of the mentors talked about losing a loved one. One mentor talked about her experience going to prom. Another monologue was about a first date. Another mama told the story about an experience with revenge porn, while an auntie talked about an experience with sexual violence. One by one, we heard stories that resonated with us on some level. As each woman told their story, they gave visibility to their experiences and their feelings, giving visibility to the rest of us. With each story told, I felt seen (and so did our girls). I was not alone in my experiences of self-doubt. I was not the only one who experienced fear and uncertainty about my future, or who was struggling with relationships with my family. And I was not the only one who had experienced sexual violence.

When it was my time to perform I told the story of an experience I had with sexual harassment and assault by an adult working at my school. I returned to the memory of that traumatic experience to surface the emotions I felt in order to properly convey and reveal the impact that experience had on me at that time. I expressed the fear I felt beneath the false bravado I felt compelled to put forth to get through the situation. I remembered the way I felt this disgusting feeling like bugs were crawling on my skin on the parts of my body he touched without my consent. I performed what it was like to experience that creepy, awful feeling associated with that sort of betrayal and violation. Somehow, through the cover of jokes and light pop culture references in my performance, the girls and women saw all of me. They could see right past the bravado and the quips and they could see the vulnerable and scared little girl in me. The safety of that space, the shared vulnerability and the courage of the women in that room allowed me a moment of healing. The way our girls held the room for us, sitting attentively, reacting with empathy and care, and the way we expressed our love and appreciation for the generosity of each person in the room was transformative. Our bonds were made stronger. Our voices were more powerful and the weight of what we carried slowly rolled off of us. This is a story of healing.

Fundamentally, the work Black women do with Black girls to center their experiences and prioritize their well-being is work that requires a level of honesty, transparency and vulnerability to do it well. Although, I am clear that boundaries and intentionality are critical in what we choose to share and how we show up with the girls we support, our role as healers in this work requires us to also engage in our own personal healing work. Ultimately, Black women who are dedicated to supporting Black girls must constantly pursue their own wellness so as not to project their unhealed wounds onto the girls they serve during their interactions. At the same time, our personal healing journeys are a lifelong process. We must demonstrate that truth through our transparency, and we must model for Black girls that the work of healing is worth it. We are worth it.

Healing Centered Work through Shared Identity and Shared Experiences

In the Spring of 2020, during the global uprisings, punctuated by the murders of Breonna Taylor and George Floyd, many of the leaders of organizations that serve African-American girls, in New Orleans, had growing concerns about how the anti-police brutality and anti-racism protests were impacting Black girls' emotional well-being. This country had not seen protests and civic unrest at this magnitude, since the assassination of Martin Luther King, Jr. The pandemic had illuminated racial disparities across wealth, health and economics, and the carceral violence was like gasoline thrown on the fire of racial inequalities. We led several conversations with Black women working with Black girls, to explore how to heal from the collective trauma we were all experiencing. We decided to co-facilitate a virtual healing circle for the program participants of five organizations that serve African-American girls. The organizations make up a collaborative called the Collaborative for African-American Girls and Women (CAAGW).

CAAGW is a consortium of community-based organizations/projects that support African-American girls in the city of New Orleans. CAAGW works to address the ascending disparities in education, health and economics that African-American girls face. CAAGW utilizes a collective impact framework to evaluate the impact of programming across the partnering organizations that serve African-American girls in the city of New Orleans. CAAGW leads small-scale research initiatives to examine the experiences of African American girls and young women that can be brought to scale to better support a landscape that advances equity for African-American girls and women.

The virtual healing circle sought to hold space for Black girls' healing. We used prompts to explore how the girls were feeling. We created a virtual space to learn more about what the girls were experiencing, and what they felt they needed to heal both themselves and one another. There were five themes that emerged from the healing circle. The themes were as follows: (1) Erasure of Black Women as Victims of State-Sanctioned Violence, (2) Vulnerability and Fear of Violence, (3) Stereotypes of Black Women and Girls Flatten Complexities and (4) Collective Support from Black Women (Navigate Nola, 2020).

The healing circle illuminated what we, as co-facilitators, already knew from both conventional wisdom and lived experiences. Black girls and women in New Orleans experience feelings of erasure when there is little mention or no notice of their experiences with state sanctioned violence. Black girls in New Orleans express a fear of violence and feelings of vulnerability linked to violence against girls and women. Black girls and women report that stereotypes of Black girls and women make people less likely to see them as victims, minimizing the response and concerns of the community regarding their well-being (Navigate Nola, 2020).

As co-facilitators of the healing circle, we felt seen and understood listening to the girls elevate their experiences. We also felt deeply saddened and burdened by the idea that, even as young adolescent and teenage girls, they understood that we (Black women and Black girls) are collectively fighting for the right to full citizenship and dignity that we are entitled to by the 14th Amendment of the Constitution.

> *The erasure is frustrating because...Black women carried this country on their back, and it's like we can't even get the recognition that we deserve when we die* (Navigate Nola, 2020).
>
> *I feel scared as a Black woman to know that I'm going off to college at a PWI. How will people feel about me? How will they react, especially because of the Black Lives Matter movement* (Navigate Nola, 2020)?
>
> *I feel like Black girls shouldn't have to...confine to stereotypes that we have, because I feel like a lot of people don't want to see us necessarily succeed. I think we should be able to express ourselves and have a space where we feel comfortable to do so* (Navigate Nola, 2020).
>
> *People always see Black women as strong, and so our stories get swept under the rug because people think oh, they're gonna get over it anyway* (Navigate Nola, 2020).
>
> *We support each other and lift up our stories. I know if something happened to me, I know y'all are going to lift it up, I know y'all are going to fight for me, I know it. So, I'm grateful for the sisters in this room and I'm grateful that we have each other, but I really am going to demand that people respect our humanity as we move forward in this world* (Navigate Nola, 2020).

These shared experiences and our shared identity helped us to begin the healing process (Ginwright, 2018). We also saw this as an opportunity to both heal through activism and to elevate the voices of Black girls' by sharing vignettes from the healing circle, with the community-at-large, in the form of a report. We presented the report through a virtual report release, moderated by the President of 100 Black Men of Metro New Orleans.

We used the report findings to generate a Call to Action, outlining strategies and recommendations generated by Black girls and women for schools and communities to cultivate, inclusive and healing spaces for Black girls. The Call to Actions was divided into four categories: (1) Professional Development and Training. (2) Direct Services/School Support, (3) Philanthropy, and (4) Policy. We continue to carry out this work, across the aforementioned categories, to address the interlocking systems of oppression that Black girls face across the systems with which they interface (Navigate Nola, 2020).

Closing

The public commonly views Black girls through a prism that is narrowly informed by historically negative archetypes of Black women. This prism gives rise to adultification bias. It is through the work that we have discussed in the chapter, that we begin to expand the prism through which the public views Black girls. It is also through this work that we expand the prism through which we see ourselves, as Black women. Centering the voices of Black girls, shifts us toward a better understanding of their lived experiences, and subsequently informs the way we create healing spaces that allow Black girls the freedom needed to process their identities.

This chapter traces back our histories as Black women who work with Black girls. The stories we have shared illuminate the important role of supporting and loving Black women in our lives who helped us through challenging times, and the ways in which this work is for some of us a Divine calling. The lessons we learned through the decades we have engaged in this work have helped us to become better healing practitioners and also better (and well) women. Finally, we posit that Black women who work with Black girls have an obligation to do our best to model the importance of personal healing work throughout our life journey. In sum, when Black women and girls are in community together, our love and support can lead to healing and transformation for all of us.

References

Burke, H. N. (2018). The deepest well: Healing the long-term effects of childhood adversity. Houghton Mifflin Harcourt

Chioneso, N. A., Hunter, C. D., Gobin, R. L., McNeil Smith, S., Mendenhall, R., & Neville, H. A. (2020). Community healing and resistance through storytelling: A framework to address racial trauma in Africana communities. *Journal of Black Psychology*, 46(2–3), 95–121. https://doi.org/10.1177/0095798420929468

Epstein, R., Black, J. J., & Gonzalez, T. (2017). *Girlhood interrupted: The erasure of Black girls' childhood.* Center on Poverty and Inequality – Georgetown Law. Retrieved from http://dx.doi.org/10.2139/ssrn.3000695

Ginwright, S. (2018). *The future of healing: Shifting from trauma informed care to healing centered engagement.* Retrieved from https://medium.com/@ginwright/the-future-of-healing-shifting-fromtrauma-informed-care-to-healing-centered-engagement-63

Humes, L. H. (2016). *African American storytelling: A vehicle for providing culturally relevant education in urban public schools in the United States.* [Doctoral dissertation]. Retrieved from https://fisherpub.sjfc.edu/education_etd/264

Navigate Nola. (2020). *#SayHerName: Vignettes from a healing circle held by The Collaborative for African-American Girls and Women.* https://www.flipsnack.com/navigatenola/healing-circle-report.html

Padgett, L. (2018). African-American girl brought to tears after school told her to leave because of braids, Family says. *Fox 23 News.* https://www.fox23.com/news/trending-now/africanamerican-girl-brought-to-tears-after-school-told-her-to-leave-because-of-braids-family-says/819109150/

9 (Re)membering Black Girlhood: My Journey to Working with and for Black Girls

MISHA N. INNISS-THOMPSON

As the daughter of an unapologetically Black woman educator, I learned who and what I surrounded myself with was central to my upbringing. While I was raised by a mom who cultivated Black communities and environments for me, my upbringing was also filled with feelings of disconnection and anti-Black girl violence. After navigating many oppressive spaces and places, I realized I wanted to be in spaces where I felt affirmed and listened to. I sought to bolster my imagination by reading and building community with other Black women and girls. Back then, I did not imagine my personal experiences would lay the foundation for me to become a Black woman whose life's work is being a Black girlhood scholar. Now, I recognize that in centering Black girls, I (re)member the little Black girl in me who was taught of her inherent worth.

My research is focused on the impact of families, communities, and schools in shaping Black girls' mental health and wellness using a cultural-assets perspective. I am passionate about centering Black girls' voices in the research process through methodological approaches such as photovoice and youth participatory action research. So much of my research is concerned with answering long-standing queries that animated my Black girlhood. For instance, I use qualitative approaches to explore: (1) how social contexts (e.g., schools, peers) shape Black adolescent girls' mental health and wellness; and (2) what can be gained by creating epistemological and physical spaces and places that support Black girls' development. In this chapter, I reflect on the central role that storytelling has played in my life and how it has propelled me into being a Black girlhood researcher.

My love of storytelling began when I started playing with Barbie dolls as a girl. I would spend hours imagining worlds for my Barbies to navigate and create stories to animate the drama of their day-to-day lives. By the time I was four years old, I eagerly anticipated any opportunity to add a new doll to my collection. My mom and I regularly visited KB Toys on the weekends, going up and down the aisles to find the right Barbie to bring home with me.

One shopping trip is particularly etched in my memory. I had my eye set on the 1998-themed graduation Barbie. Her blond hair and blue eyes reminded me of Barbies I had played with at my cousin's house. I was used to getting what I wanted and expected that my mom would purchase this new doll if I only asked. However, to my surprise, my mom told me that I could not have the Barbie. I was shocked, enraged, and livid as I cried loudly throughout the store. At first, I could not fathom why I could not have the Barbie. Then, as I walked through the store, I realized that while I had played with white Barbies at other folks' houses, Black Barbies were the only ones allowed in my household. With that revelation in mind, I screamed: "Are you not going to buy this Barbie for me because she's White!?" Despite her embarrassment, my mom ultimately explained that I would have to wait until the Black graduation Barbie became available. From that moment onward, I realized my mom wanted me to value having figures in my life that looked like me. Only years later would I learn how influences such as Toni Morrison's *The Bluest Eye* and the "doll test" of the *Brown v. Board* era impacted her conscious decision to celebrate Blackness and to teach me to celebrate mine.

This memory is one of many that shaped my understanding that who and what I surrounded myself with as a girl significantly impacted how I made space to imagine a Black girlhood filled with celebration and imaginative storytelling. As a developmental community psychologist, I believe Black girlhood is shaped by the (1) spaces we traverse and resist and (2) stories we create and consume. This chapter offers a critical reflection on the spaces and stories that inspired my decision to unapologetically center Black girls' ways of knowing and wellness in my research.

Traversing Sites of Oppression

> I feel most colored when I am thrown against a sharp white background… Among the thousand white persons, I am a dark rock surged upon, and over-swept, but through it all, I remain myself. When covered by the waters, I am; and the ebb but reveals me again. (Hurston, 1928 [2020], p. 153)

My mom was committed to ensuring I was surrounded by people and toys that looked like me. Nevertheless, in addition to my mom's consciously pro-Black racial socialization, I was tasked with navigating physical places like schools where I was often the only or one of few Black girls in the room. Both physical and imaginative geographies were foundational to how I understood myself and the world around me. Whereas physical geographies encompass elements of the built environment, such as configurations, landscapes, and architectures, imaginative geographies emphasize how our ability to dream and create metaphysical spaces enables Black people to survive amid daily exposure to anti-Black racist violence (McKittrick, 2006). Despite isolating experiences in school, I created imaginative geographies that allowed me to dream of spaces wherein I could feel safe, free, and cared for.

Reflecting on my Black girlhood, I recognize that high school was one of the most salient physical places that shaped my understanding of the world around me. I am the daughter of a Black American woman educator who instilled in me that education (both within and outside of formal schooling) is a lever for social transformation. My mom taught me to value the privilege of having access to high-quality education. However, once I entered high school, I realized that not all transformations within formal education were positive.

High school was an incredibly taxing four-year period for me. From the moment I walked into my high school, I was an outcast. I was a Black girl (read: the only Black girl in a graduating class of 117 students) in a white, wealthy independent school. My high school experience was a constant journey of trying to be enough. I thought that perhaps if I always ensured my hair was straight and my clothes were fashionable, my elite peers would validate me. I continuously sought recognition that I belonged there from an intellectual and social perspective.

One incident remains etched in my memory. On a fall day during my sophomore year of high school, I sat in my advisory group composed of nine other students, five of whom were Asian international students. One of my peers, a Korean international student, began discussing how he enjoyed watching *The Boondocks* because it was a chance to see how "foolish Black people act." What astonished me was that I was sitting right next to him as he had this conversation, yet he had no regard for my presence. A flurry of emotions took over at that moment: I was angry that he could make such a racist comment so flippantly while also being sad that no one in that space said anything to challenge his thinking. Yet, my peers carried on as if that were a usual comment. I left the advisory group that morning, seeking a space to process what had just happened with people who would understand my righteous rage about the situation.

That incident prompted me to seek tools to create spaces where Black girls like me could process the regular impact of navigating systems rife with anti-Blackness. In the days and months that followed, I leaned on the few Black faculty in the school to help me begin reflecting on how I felt and considering ways I could contribute to future generations of Black students at the school in feeling more seen, supported, and respected. One mentor, the Director of Multicultural Affairs at the school, offered books to build up my knowledge about racism and the need for Black students to have affinity spaces. At his suggestion, I began reading books such as Beverly Tatum's *Why Are All the Black Kids Sitting Together in the Cafeteria*. Tatum's work reminded me of the power of being in affinity groups with other Black students navigating similar experiences. I sought places where I felt like my experiences and personhood were affirmed. I learned about the Student Diversity Leadership Conference (SDLC), which gathers students from various independent schools nationwide to learn about the complexity of diversity and its implications in our everyday lives. I heard the stories and struggles of other Black girls who attended independent schools. I recognized that across geographic regions and schools, Black girls experience gendered anti-Blackness. Participating in SDLC left me eager to find spaces where conversations centered on Black girls' experiences were prioritized. That desire for Black girl space would remain a driving force as I considered navigating college and graduate school.

So much of my high school journey was a process of losing myself in a sea of white people, norms, and values. To this day, I am still recovering from the damage that such negative feelings had on my sense of self. Upon graduating from high school, I became eager to learn how to disrupt my feelings of isolation and inferiority. Not only did I want to heal myself, but I also began to hope that I could somehow become the person who could help other Black girls feel like they belonged. My experience navigating white academic spaces taught me to seek and make spaces in service of Black girls.

Imagining a Space for Black Girls

> The act of making the space of Black girlhood exists outside the linear and Eurocentric understandings and practices of time. (R. N. Brown, 2013, p. 51)

Colonialism has taught us that to imagine is futile (a.m. brown, 2015).[15] Nevertheless, Black people are visionaries with deep imaginations for future

---

15 Two authors referenced in this chapter (adrienne maree brown & bell hooks) stylize their names in lowercase for ideological reasons. To be consistent with their

possibilities. There is power in "reclaiming the right to dream the future, strengthening the muscle to imagine together as black people" (a.m. brown, 2015, p. 6). As such, Black girls require imaginative spaces, or metaphysical configurations, within our radical imaginations that are also lived out loud. Imaginative spaces tap into our capacity to collectively dream of futures where Black people are loved, safe, and valued, where we make space to dream up our desires and envision what is possible (Kelley, 2002). As Dunn (2020) writes, "Black Imagination is a reclamation of our bodies, space, intelligence, care, and joy. Black imagination is a reclamation of our whole damn selves" (Dunn, 2020, p. 7). I learned that my Black Imagination was worthy of attention and inquiry in college and graduate school. Community building and storytelling exposed me to spaces unapologetically focused on my Black girlhood/womanhood.

If high school was a journey of losing myself, college and graduate school offered time committed to remembering myself. By reading Toni Morrison's work, I learned about the power of (re)memory and how Black women put themselves back together despite living in a world that attempts to flatten our humanity. Morrison taught me that to put myself back together, I had to engage in an intentional process of "reassembling the members of the body, the family, the population of the past" (Morrison, 2019, para. 4). Storytelling is one way that I remember myself and the worlds I inhabit. Like (hooks, 2009), I believe that stories hold "both the power and the art of possibility" (p. 53).

As I navigated each step of my formal education, reading texts by Black women and girls reminded me that we are worthy of intentional and unapologetic investment. I reveled in being exposed to ethnographies that urged me to reflect on my Black girlhood in graduate school. Texts like *Shapeshifters: Black Girls and the Choreography of Citizenship* (Cox, 2015) and *Hear Our Truths: The Creative Potential of Black Girlhood* (R.N. Brown, 2013) showed me that it was possible to engage in research with Black girls that was focused on their innovation and persistence across time and space. Cox's account of Black girls in Detroit reminded me of how I used performance and storytelling to shapeshift. Brown's reflection on her experiences as a Black woman navigating her commitment to Black girls alongside her position in academia pushed me to deeply consider the purpose and impact I wanted my research to have.

preferences, I defer to the authors and style their names lowercase both in the chapter and in the references.

Furthermore, Brown's commitment to honoring the narratives of both living and ancestral Black women and girls reminded me that being in academia gives us the privilege to act as if ideas are our own. Yet, we must also acknowledge that our work is informed by the personal, the political, and the women whose shoulders we stand on to elevate our people. Brown (2013) awoke in me a sense of urgency to foreground Black girls' lived experiences as I write. Her work reminded me that Black girls are saving ourselves, and we need each other.

Stories became how I made space for imaginative geographies to live within me. Both nonfictional and fictional accounts of Black girls urged me to continue piecing myself back together in the aftermath of the ways formal education attempted to dismember me. These stories reminded me that Black girls are worthy of places and spaces that honor the specificity of their lived experiences and adults committed to walking alongside them as they traverse oppressive systems.

Honoring Black Girls' Visions in the Black Girl Magic Crew

Black girls shift and create spaces in service of their safety, love, support, and development. Safe spaces center Black girls' epistemologies and honor their testimonies as valid and central to our understanding of the world. Sometimes, Black girls create spaces they wish they had when navigating the violent terrain of the education system. I was one of those Black girls who sought spaces that would love me in a world that told me I was unlovable. My wildest dreams came true in 2018 when I co-created the Black Girl Magic Crew (BGM), a safe space for Black high school girls at Magnolia High School (a pseudonym). The school is situated within an urban, majority-white (55.4%), middle-class (median income ≅ $60,000) community in the Southeastern United States. At the inception of BGM, the school had a student body of approximately 950 students, of which 10% were Asian, 42% Black/African American, 6% Hispanic/Latinx, and 40% White.

When I first sat in on a meeting between 20 Black high school girls and Dr. Monique Morris in February 2018, I attended with a curiosity to learn about the experiences of local Black girls. As the girls spoke, their needs were clearly articulated and consistent. These Black girls wanted to be heard, to feel comfortable being themselves in all spaces they occupied. They desired a school where responses to critical issues around race and gender were not "manufactured" but instead directly acknowledged and addressed their lived experiences. They wanted to feel like they had a sense of community and teachers they could trust. Perhaps most pronounced to me was their collective desire to have more Black women to serve as mentors and talk to them, not just about school, but life more broadly.

In the year leading up to that meeting, I had sought opportunities to get involved in communities that served and supported Black girls in my local community. At that moment, I realized I had found the space for which I had been yearning. I desired this space when I was a Black girl in high school. As I listened to the needs of the Black girls in the room, it became abundantly clear that as a Black woman pursuing my doctorate in community psychology whose research focuses on mental health and wellness, I was uniquely positioned to work with this group of Black girls who sought guidance in ways they had not yet experienced. Out of that conversation, the Black Girl Magic Crew was born.

The Black Girl Magic Crew (BGM) is an afterschool program that provides Black high school girls with a safe space to build community and discuss various topics (e.g., college prep, relationships, self-esteem, and mental wellness). BGM is a space where Black girls' needs are the sole reason the group exists. In this space, Black girls highlight their need for a space to have conversations about topics like self-love, stereotypes, and work-life balance. BGM offers an opportunity for Black girls to speak and be heard, challenge oppressive systems like schools and churches, and express themselves without judgment.

The work of BGM is done in community, with Black girls loving and working with Black women. The girls' interests and desires drive our work: they played an integral role in naming the group, constructing our community norms, and deciding the topics we discussed. Since its creation in Spring 2018, BGM has transformed from a gathering of four girls and me to a group of over fifty girls who have, over the years, collectively engaged in reflection, offered support, and uplifted one another during our meetings and programming both within and outside of the school.

During our time together, the girls in BGM have repeatedly discussed the need for space that supports their identity development as Black girls in a school for academically gifted students. Furthermore, our conversations often prioritize their mental health & wellness. We do this work through activities such as creating vision boards and collective affirmation boards; hosting panels of Black women to talk about their experiences in college; and reading a variety of books across genres written by Black cisgender and nonbinary folks who center Black girlhood experiences, imaginations, and possibilities.

The work of BGM is dedicated to helping Black girls envision what it can mean to be a Black girl today. BGM is a space that exists within and beyond physical space: Black girls create imaginative configurations for how they deserve to be loved, cared for, and tended to. Even amid a global pandemic, BGM continued to meet bi-weekly. We found ways to stay connected using virtual platforms, group messages, movies, podcasts, and books. BGM is evidence that Black girls create space where it is possible to love one another deeply.

BGM is an example of a space co-constructed with and for Black girls that centers their safety, love, and identity development. It is a space where their needs are heard and honored. There is a radical possibility in creating spaces where Black girls' desires are the point of reference. Black girls deserve more spaces like these, and as adults, we can serve as allies that hold space and redistribute resources so that these spaces can continue. As I reflect on my five years in community with BGM, I think of how deeply filling and satisfying this work has been. I think about how life-changing it would have been to be in a space like this one when I was an adolescent.

Doing Research with Black Girls

Engaging in research with Black girls reminds me that I am not alone in my struggle and perseverance. Being in community with Black girls allows me to envision a world where our imaginations and ways of knowing are prioritized. I prioritize Black girls' imaginations through participatory methodological approaches like photovoice. Photovoice centers participants' voices and perspectives by using photographs and critical group dialogue to identify, represent and enhance participants' lived experiences (Wang, 2006). I use photovoice as a tool for Black girls to share how they visualize mental health and wellness, community, and safety in the spaces they occupy and the memories they deem worthy of capturing on camera. My recent work (Inniss-Thompson, Butler-Barnes, Taaffe, & Elliott, 2022) demonstrates that the intentional use of participatory methodologies (such as photovoice, an approach that uses photos and critical dialogue as tools to identify, represent and enhance participants' lived experiences; Wang, 2006) can produce rich, grounded narratives that can contribute to a holistic understanding of Black girls' mental health and wellness. In this study, Black girls' narratives provided insight into how they defined and experienced mental health and wellness holistically, considering their internal experiences and external environment as central to their ability to be well. After exploring how Black girls defined mental health and wellness, we found that practices such as (1) spirituality, (2) resistance, and (3) community with Black girls and women were central to Black girls' sense of wellness. As I build the foundation of my career as a

Black girlhood scholar, I recognize that Black girls' priorities and needs must remain at the forefront of my work in academic and personal communities.

Conclusion

As Black queer scholar and activist adrienne maree brown writes, a vision is about "saying aloud what we long for" (a.m. brown, 2017). Visioning Black girls into the future requires an epistemic shift in conceptualizing community and anti-Blackness within society. We cannot continue to revolve around the suns that intentionally silence Black girls' epistemologies. Instead, we must orient ourselves around a new sun, a critical paradigmatic approach that centers Black girls' ways of knowing and understanding the world. Visioning is how we create new suns outside the system perpetuating violence against Black girls.

References

brown, a. m. (2015). *Afrofuturism and #blackspring.* http://adriennemareebrown.net/2015/05/02/afrofuturism-and-blackspring-new-school-afroturismtns/

brown, a. m. (2017). *Emergent strategy: Shaping change, changing worlds.* AK Press.

Brown, R. N. (2013). *Hear our truths: The creative potential of Black girlhood.* University of Illinois Press.

Cox, A. M. (2015). *Shapeshifters: Black girls and the choreography of citizenship.* Duke University Press.

Dunn, S. (2020). Introduction. In N. Marin (Ed.), *Black imagination: Black voices on Black futures* (pp. 1–7).

hooks, b. (2009). *Teaching critical thinking: Practical wisdom.* Routledge.

Hurston, Z. N. (1928). How it feels to be colored me. In A. Walker (Ed.), *I love myself when I am laughing: A Zora Neale Hurston reader* (pp. 152–155). The Feminist Press. https://doi.org/10.4135/9781483328539.n14

Inniss-Thompson, M. N., Butler-Barnes, S. T., Taaffe, C., & Elliott, T. (2022). "What serves you": Charting Black girl spaces for wellness through spirituality, resistance, and homeplace. *Journal of African American Women and Girls in Education, 2*(2), 37–64. https://doi.org/10.21423/jaawge-v2i2a113.

Kelley, R. D. G. (2002). *Freedom dreams: The Black radical imagination.* Beacon Press.

Morrison, T. (2019, August 8). "I wanted to carve out a world both culture specific and race-free": An essay by Toni Morrison. *The Guardian.* https://www.theguardian.com/books/2019/aug/08/toni-morrison-rememory-essay

Wang, C. C. (2006). Youth participation in photovoice as a strategy for community change. *Journal of Community Practice, 14,* 147–162. https://doi.org/10.1300/J125v14n01_09

10 Why I Do This Work: "I Was Built for This"

Tamika Gafford-Carter

Pinpointing the source of my inspiration to study Black girls has been a complicated journey. The process led me to reflect on the thirty-seven years I have spent growing, climbing, and sometimes clinging to this rotating rock. The call to write forced me to slow down and pay attention to the connections between numerous personal, academic, and professional experiences. As a scholar-practitioner, my purpose fulfilled through my work, sacrifice, and service, are deeply rooted in God's gifting and divine alignment. My primary career is counseling; I hold licenses and certifications in mental health, addictions, and school counseling. My research foci are self-image development and creating safe healing spaces for Black and marginalized girls. My studies encompass several areas: Educational Psychology of Black Girls, Gifted and Special Education; school refusal, intentional underachievement, and delinquency.

This chapter summarizes my personal and professional experiences with marginalization. Collectively it explains how my career and scholarship are influenced by my upbringing, work, motherhood and overall love for Black girls who operate in the spaces between social norms. The series of snapshots capturing my relationships with family, community, and work, tell the story of why I do this work.

Opening

Long before I earned a Master of Human Relations degree, a destiny to build people was imprinted in my psyche. At an early age I owned a keychain, likely purchased from a mall kiosk. Inside its plastic case was a flimsy, decorative, sky blue and purple card, displaying an interpretation of my name, Tamika, "the people's child". An Internet search sources my name to Japanese origin, meaning "beautiful child, people" and in Swahili, "sweet, flower of the rising". As a child, I thought the keychain was simply cute and crafty with a positive message. Decades later I would be directly and gently confronted by a spirit-filled woman who had quietly watched me advocate and counsel teens through desperate situations. When she told me that I was called to help youth, I awoke to a purpose that had been evident throughout my entire life.

The containers of my research and practice are counseling, education, and advocacy. In 2017, I founded Advantage Public Institute, a multi-state, non-profit organization using research to develop curriculum and programming. For nearly 10 years, I maintained international accreditation from The Joint Commission for Outpatient Behavioral Health Services. This allowed me to operate my small group practice with a community counseling model that provided behavioral health solutions for school climate and juvenile rehabilitation. My life paths have afforded me opportunities to serve girls of color from a young age. Still, this journey all began with the legacy with which my maternal ancestors blessed me from birth.

Family Roots

The lineage started with my Big Mama, Dr. Ellen Ruth Jones, the mother of my mother. Born in Louisiana, she maintained her Southern heritage, raising us on gumbo and boudin. I remember summers in her Los Angeles home eating cereal with goat milk. She refused my naïve puppy dog eyes requesting to run outside and buy from the ice cream man. Maturity and exposure brought understanding. Characteristic of many of her lessons, the wisdom that she shared digested best with time. I may not be able to say that I came from money, but certainly I was born into a legacy of learners. Education was everything with my beloved Big Mama. Only recently, I learned that at age 6 she was the youngest student in her schoolhouse. The Census documented that she was among a local group of peers who were three or more years her senior (U.S. Census Bureau, 1940).

My grandmother blazed trails across the South to the West Coast. She rests in the Midwest after she was called from Los Angeles, with her husband to pastor a church. The relocation was how I came to spend my adolescence and young adulthood in Oklahoma City. During that time, I witnessed her teaching and mentoring faith leaders. Sister Jones, as church members lovingly called my grandmother, was a nurse, culinary creative, and multi-talented entrepreneur. A single mother, she raised four productive, successful children in South Central Los Angeles. Her legacy, besides training ministers and first ladies across the Midwest, boasts five granddaughters who excel in academia and business. Big Mama's house was where we learned the elements of class. She equipped us with lessons in wearing and repairing pantyhose and slips, threading needles and quilting, transcribing sermons, organizing theology lessons, in addition to polishing everything.

As my grandmother lost pieces of her memory to illness, I was amazed that she retained her ability to recite scripture. Her mind was always so sharp, as were the words that she chose to lead people to conscientious living. Quite often her truths cut, especially while teaching humility, reflection, and self-awareness. It was after her passing, that I came to appreciate her way of communicating concern and offering guidance. By my mid 30's I realized that I too, was limited in my ability to "sugar coat" vital messages. Even later in life, I recall examining an old family photograph with a new perspective. I gazed deeply into her confident eyes; she with her four children had just migrated from Texas to California. Circa 1960, sans their father, she established herself in the West and purchased a home in Los Angeles. The woman who kept an extensive library, whose response for all of our questions was, "Look it up", planted seeds and taught me to water them myself.

Growing Up: Childhood and Adolescence

Representation matters immensely for marginalized girls. In 1991 there were few who looked like me in the media and far less in the areas that fascinated me: archaeology and astronomy. I remember when Janet Jackson's plastic surgery became visibly evident. I can never forget being wounded by a familiar adult's rant, "I use to like Janet, 'till she started chopping off pieces of her nose". The rant hurt me deeply. Ms. Jackson was one of the few celebrities with whom I identified. Undoubtedly gorgeous, her talent, verve, and grace were accents to her beautiful skin and Africanized features. I grew up singing and dancing to Rhythm Nation. Her rock and R&B vibes meshed perfectly with this Orange County girl who had been called an "Oreo". In her music and persona, I found a place where I could be comfortable in my eclectic existence. I saw myself in her; she made me, a little brown skinned, wide-nosed girl feel validated and valuable. So, when Ms. Jackson's "work" became evident, it impacted me personally. I felt like she was saying that my wide nose was unacceptable; that if I wanted to be recognized, loved, and appreciated, I needed to alter my appearance.

In childhood and even more in adolescence my identity was at war with social acceptance, reliant on perceptions of my peers. I was the Blackest girl in a white school in Orange County, and the whitest girl in the Black school in

Oklahoma City. Marginalized by the ways I'd experienced race, gender, and society moving from suburban liberal to rural conservative locale I wrestled with confidence. I engaged in shifting, noted by several authors to navigate unwelcoming social spaces (Gamst et al., 2020; Johnson, Gamst, Meyers, Arellano-Morales, Shorter-Gooden, 2016; Shorter-Gooden, 2004). I suffered from low self-esteem and resultant poor choices due to negative body image, hair struggles, colorism. Perfectionism impaired my self-perception, and I was paralyzed by stereotype threat (Anderson & Martin, 2018; Essien & Wood, 2021). As if being a nerdy, lanky, dark skinned suburban girl wasn't enough, our family moved from Southern California to Oklahoma City during a sensitive stage of my social development. Adjusting meant adopting a Midwest accent, diet, and urban vernacular. Several pieces of my identity were shaped, through the ways I processed my connection to the new environment and how I grieved my previous lifestyle. This phenomenon of gifted Black girls negotiating an agreement between their academic identity and social acceptance is documented by Dr. Ford (2011) a leading scholar of multicultural gifted education. Often accused of "acting white" by other Black students, girls struggle to balance the intersection of their individual attributes with sociocultural norms. I tried to "act Black", mimicking classmates, I practiced the "n"-word aggressively in the mirror. Representation matters immensely for marginalized girls establishing identity.

Combatting ignorance, through adolescence I engaged in difficult conversations with two mentors who shaped my cultural identity. My older brother inspired me to appreciate my Black girl features. While attending an HBCU he passed on essential knowledge. He challenged me to read critical race texts; Assata (1988) consumed my sophomore summer. Having a foundation in conscious perspectives helped me to avoid, or at least be aware of myself and others acting out stereotypical roles. These perspectives were further reinforced in my Black Karate School. At American Dragon we were raised on a creed and held accountable in the dojo for our choices at school and in community: reciting, "I will work hard to be the best I can be; I will not be a show off with my art". After achieving my green belt about age 15, my sensei appointed me to lead our dojo's girls, he named us the "Dragon Queens". My responsibilities were to circle them up during our stretch and check in mentally and emotionally before practice began. I racked up over 50 trophies over the 4 years I competed statewide. Martial Arts was pivotal in building my self-concept. Still eccentric and the odd one out in many spaces, I concluded that it didn't matter, because I was excelling at being the best version of myself, manifesting strength and grace.

I learned confidence develops with competence. Skill proficiency and opportunities for servant leadership are essential building blocks of Black girl self-image. At about 12 years old, I remember being positioned to effect change in youth. As a middle school cheerleader, I volunteered with my squad at local elementary schools. We taught motions, chants, and other basics to Black cheerleaders marginalized from their suburban counterparts by poverty. This sponsor arranged activity, built my leadership skills and love of service. In high school my squad strived to be twice as good as the suburban girls we met at camp, despite having half of their resources. This attitude contributed to me earning a scholarship and team captain in college.

College

I studied Psychology and Criminal Justice at The University of Oklahoma (OU). I had a knack for statistics and served as an undergraduate research assistant in Industrial and Organizational Psychology. My senior year, I was blessed with a well-paying, part-time work study assignment as a tutor. I worked at an elementary school founded by a professor of African American Studies. Marcus Garvey Leadership Charter School (MGLC) was revolutionary; the students wore red, black, and green uniform shirts, and spent time in specials learning Black History and African drumming. The students assigned to me needed several levels of support. Observing limited focus and self-regulation in my students, I shifted my tutoring approach. I incorporated behavior modification techniques to help them achieve academic and behavioral success. To support two boys in class, I assisted their new teacher, my OU classmate and friend. This evolved into partnering to provide a safe, productive learning environment for 3rd graders. Without teaching credentials, braving a group who had not had a dedicated teacher in six months, we co-taught by piecing together lesson plans and activities. Invoking my fourth year Psychology student skills, we agreed to be responsive, and to prioritize their socio-emotional needs when necessary.

On that assignment, I crashed into a little girl, we'll call her A'ja. From the unique spelling of her name to her eccentric behavior, A'ja existed in her own space; often in full disregard of the conventions of manners. By my arrival, second semester, she'd become the target of stares and jokes from classmates and the occasional teacher. Unlike many of her peers, A'ja was performing moderately well academically. It was the sitting in the corner talking and laughing with herself that marginalized her into being looked upon as a social pariah. I took her to my Karate school. Later that year, I would take a friend's orphaned 10-year-old cousin to the dojo as well. As I am writing this now, I realize that these were my first adult experiences reaching girls marginalized by their mental health. My efforts acknowledged both their eccentricities and reactions to the stigma of being othered by their Black classmates. Meeting the girls' connection needs through a culture rich community support became the basis for deterring attitudes, behavior, and labels that precede *Pushout*.

Adulting: Clinical Narratives

I cut my teeth in the counseling profession under the tutelage of three Black female entrepreneurs who taught invaluable lessons in staff and patient. As I transitioned through early stages of my career, I worked with low-income girls ages 6–18, who were afflicted by the Pair of ACEs; a combination of Adverse Childhood Experiences (abuse, addiction, abandonment) and Adverse Community Environments (poverty, divorce, crime) (Ellis & Dietz, 2020). For years, my workday was divided between school-based counseling, juvenile probation groups, and office-based individual work with women. From morning to afternoon, and evening, I went on a developmental journey from Black girlhood to womanhood. Throughout the course of each day, I heard recurring themes of anxiety and depression related to unrealistic expectation to perform strength. Regardless of socioeconomic status, the emotional dysfunction appeared to develop on a continuum of hardening, marked with microtraumas. Interrupting that process requires combating the normalization of trauma attached roles idealized by black teens and young women. The Black women I've counseled through addictive and mental disorders ignite my passion to apply a social justice framework to mental wellness prevention and intervention for Black girls.

Through practice I have encouraged and validated women at every developmental stage. Ending my day with women suffering from SBW, led me to strategize about how to interrupt the transmission of unhealthy behaviors from Black mother to daughter. Nelson, Cardemil, and Adeoye (2016) present a qualitative study of the strong Black woman (SBW) identity. They used thematic analysis to identify patterns within participant responses to explain: how Black women conceptualize strength within the Strong Black Woman schema. Five characteristics emerged in defining the Strong Black Woman: independent, caregiver, hardworking and high achieving, overcoming adversity, and emotionally contained. Underneath the Mask (Abrams, Hill, & Maxwell, 2019) established that characteristics of the Strong Black Women (SBW) Schema mediate depression. Researchers linked endorsement of the schema and perceived obligation to manifest strength to depressive symptomatology due to *self-silencing*, and externalized self-perceptions. Findings also point to significant familial, and social pressure for Black girls to perform as SBW. Importantly, the scholars offer evidence and clarification of the impact of the SBW Schema on Black women's mental health and identify specific points of intervention for practitioners. Prevention lies in examining self-image constructs and how caregivers and professionals can facilitate healthy development. Consistently across socioeconomic status and geography my adult clients' impaired self-image formed during girlhood. Over time, their emotional wellness dissolved in the pool of unhealthy traits used to characterize Black women's strength.

I've spent 20 years executing through career as a scholar-practitioner. Healing and supporting marginalized clients, I endeavor to better understand Black female self-image, identity, and emotional development. In addition to how we show up in the world, I am focused on enhancing the quality and inclusiveness of our healing and education. Young (2020) in addressing the racial achievement gap, points to a lack of empirical studies examining the challenges and strengths of Black girls. I help teen, adolescent, and girl children to become self-actualized through development of a positive self-image. Throughout my clinical practice, I've implemented age-appropriate evidence based therapeutic sister circles. Unlike many girl centered spaces, I invite girls with a wide range of experiences to gain understanding, empathize, ally, and contribute to the healing and socioemotional development of one another. Further I enlist tools that guide parents to model and facilitate socio-emotional wellness for their daughters. My goal is to measure, model, and practice using peer support to foster empowering interactions between Black girls. EMPOWER and CLASS are the psychoeducational programs I developed to meet their needs. I am proud that these programs are inclusive of girls from the hood to the 'burbs. In our circles they find common connection and learn techniques for affirming themselves and other girls.

E.M.P.O.W.E.R.: Education, Motivation, Personality, Overcoming, Wisdom, Effort, Responsibility

Reinvesting in my faith about age 20, I began to envision a youth center. In 2010 I opened Advantage Community Resources using a holistic community-based approach to redirecting teens in crisis. My primary referral base was the local public school system. Underserved by default, Black girls' mental health services were in a drought. Here, I developed the thirst to better understand the link between childhood trauma, personality, and Black women's identities. By 2012 I was running girls EMPOWER groups at 3 high schools.

My interest in overcoming with resilience was awakened while working with these teens and their families. The young ladies I served were experiencing poverty, kinship foster care, parental substance abuse, and domestic violence. One was bearing the weight of a juvenile sibling on trial in a high-profile racially and politically charged murder case. Repeatedly, the girls' wounds showed up in interpersonal relationships; they were either aggressors or victims of violence. In the face of complex traumas, their giftedness showed up as creative intelligence to survive and overcome. We met every Tuesday over pizza and constructed avenues to freedom.

Working with teen mothers in an alternative school I became acquainted with the image of intergenerational trauma, laced with racism (Bryant-Davis, 2007). Occasionally, I was frustrated with their stubbornness and perpetual engagement in self-destructive thinking and behavior. I told them, "If the decisions you make don't hurt, you are probably repeating a generational cycle'. This was to say that breaking unhealthy emotional and behavioral patterns would likely cause temporary mental or relational discomfort. After months of having criticized their own mothers' choices, several of the girls concluded that they were dealing with similar challenging role conflicts. My teen clients, unapologetically judgmental, expected their mothers to be all and provide all, while discounting their credibility at any sign of weakness. This was consistent with Nelson et al. (2016) findings that Black women feeling obligated to perform strength or characteristics of SBW, police Black womanhood in other Black women. I presented to mother-daughter dyads, "It ain't right, but its real, so how do we deal?". Applying family systems theory, I used clinical tools like the genogram (a visual generational family assessment) to highlight intergenerational patterns. Miraculously in session, defiant teens broke cycles by receiving the wisdom of their mothers.

Juvenile Probation Counseling
The same year I started an after school juvenile probation counseling program to bridge the gap in services between school truancy and city probation offices. My client centered insight came from the irony of my office overlooking the building where I'd completed community service as a juvenile. I soon learned that the city probation director was the same Black woman who I'd been assigned at 17. Our resulting partnership shaped seven years of specialized treatment for adolescent and teen girls labeled "at-risk". As a counselor and advocate, I approached the pessimistic families of teen addicts, thieves, and runaways feeling confident in my self-image reconstruction methods. The JPC program saw over three-quarters of the conduct disordered girls I gain empathy and self-efficacy through our targeted mediation sessions.

Reviewing district discipline reports I witnessed on a microlevel what Blake, Butler, Lewis, and Darensbourg (2011) notates, a dearth in data addressing the types and discipline of Black girl's behavioral infractions. I began to advocate against *Pushout* while showing young ladies paths out of generational cycles. I developed techniques for partnering with girl moms in ways that do not alienate or condemn them for their trauma or human mistakes. Armed with data, I combat inequities in education, healthcare, and policy for Black girls who are treated and feel as if they are invisible.

C.L.A.S.S.: *Confidence Leadership Academics and Social Skills*

My grandmother passed the same semester that I began a multi-year assignment at F.D Moon Academy as an embedded counseling agency. My counseling practice provided services for four years at an elementary school in 'the hood' of Eastside Oklahoma City. Inside were 200 girls gifted in all the ways schools and society tend to overlook. To understand and empower them from a humanistic approach, I utilized Dr. Donna Ford's F^{2}AME Model of Female Achievement (2013). Our discussions and activities emphasized selected factors within each sector: psychological, cultural, socioemotional, and academic.

In 2015, I named my closed format group of upper graders, CLASS, which stands for confidence, leadership, academics, and social skills. The tenets embodied my late grandmother's life lessons in love and ladyhood. Moreover, they represented containers for techniques from my theory of self-image development in Black Girls. CLASS began as an accessible alternative to the expensive, hyperfeminine, white-dominated girl offerings in the area. It evolved into a program based on eight years of direct therapeutic relationships with hundreds of girls of color in Oklahoma City. CLASS, a safe space for marginalized girls, became my test lab for assessment and techniques aimed at building self-image. Girls in my CLASS groups decreased depression, aggression, and suicidal ideation; they built relationships, attendance, and academic performance.

We hosted a conference to celebrate the girls. Before the event, I met with 100 girls individually or in small groups. I instructed them to write or draw on posters titled "Why I Rock". Even with probing, many girls could not name their positive qualities. Posttraumatic Slave Syndrome (DeGruy, 2005) intergenerational trauma, rape culture, and community silence had left all too familiar esteem scars. We continued to talk it out in CLASS on Tuesdays and sometimes Fridays dependent on school-girl-climate. Drawing on existential therapy, I crafted a lesson around Erykah Badu's "Bag Lady" (2001). Its objective was to highlight destructive intergenerational trauma response patterns. I was surprised that the girls' enjoyed this neo-soul classic. This group of 5th and 6th grade girls were able to identify examples of each woman in their lives: garbage bag lady, booty bag lady, etc. I paired the song explication with a worksheet, directing them to list their own bags. It was powerful. They saw within themselves the seeds of the *Sisterella* complex, a quiet depression experienced by Black women who work tirelessly to meet the expectations of their jobs, families, and society (Jones & Shorter-Gooden, 2009).

This activity was never an easy feat, facing their unquestioned adoption of their mothers' and aunts' hypervigilant attitudes and behaviors. Looking at these habits and beliefs with self-awareness was a delicate matter, especially as a school-contracted social justice-oriented clinician. Girls have a unique brand of loyalty tucked into respect for their mothers. Self-silencing leads Black girls to attach to beliefs that fuel imposter syndrome. In addition to battling pre-teen emotions, urges, and increased responsibility, establishing an identity while being marginalized is a struggle for many girls. My preteen culture shock of migration presented a unique vantage point on the experience of girls in the gaps of socialization. Working as a School Counselor, I became increasingly aware that the psychosocial conflict of moving was a common struggle with geographically transplanted youth. The trauma of loss and adjustment predisposed them to identity conflict, social isolation, and externalizing behaviors.

Reflecting on my relationships with A'ja and other early mentees, I sought to connect them to something that could help them center themselves enough to be comfortable in their own skin. Two degrees later I immersed myself in the study of Black girls marginalized by dual exceptionality (giftedness and disability), trauma, poverty, while maintaining the audacity to be magical.

First CLASS: Mothering the Marginalized Girl

My truest 'Aha moment' was the third girl. After already birthing two daughters, my hopes for a son were dashed by the sonographer's announcement. I fretted, because I was at a point in life, where I was recognizing my past gender-based trauma. I was still reconciling society's promise with its propensity to harm Black girls. I am grateful, now to have raised daughters; it was this experience that undoubtedly reigns as my influence in studying Black girls. My fears and hopes for Black girls are evident in my motherhood and research.

Motherhood carries concerns from the moment one chooses to conceive. We formulate questions around our child's appearance and make conjectures about their habits from their fetal responses to sound and light. At the same time, we worry about them: if they will be healthy, if we are eating the right foods, if they feel our emotions. As a pregnant college freshman, I joked with a friend that I might use my kids as experiments. During my second pregnancy I was enrolled in a college course, learning about birth defects. It was terrifying. The dangers associated with mothering a Black girl come from internal and external sources.

The marginalized, socially awkward Black girl is extremely sensitive to maternal emotions and communication style. Reducing the risk of breaking her spirit is paramount. Joy DeGruy (2005) offers an etiology for cultural roots of normalized verbal abuse. She begins conceptualizing Post Traumatic Slave Syndrome with stories and situations common to parenting. Describing verbal "denigration" of a daughter's appearance or character, she presents an all-too-common practice, as an historical protective defense from rape or sale (p. 9). In 2020, Mechell Guy linked highly anxious mother attachment to daughters' self-esteem. Guy illustrated the impact of traditional stereotypical Models of Black Femininity. Racially charged tropes like 'Mammy, Sapphire, Jezebel, and Strong Black Women' are destructive to adolescent girls' self-esteem and psychological functioning. Shaping girls from infancy to adulthood, through sensitive stages, critical periods, is difficult against the backdrop of racism and sexism.

I am thankful that my daughters each had a chance to know our Big Mama. Growing greys myself, I am still learning the twists and turns of her life. I am realizing its impact on my mother, her 4 granddaughters, and 5 great granddaughters. I, like my mother, am an only daughter; a family role which has undoubtedly shaped our development. I have witnessed how being an eldest or only daughter interacts with personality to shape temperament, and life choices. The conflict between non-familial roles of African American daughters in varied positions of birth order presented clinical notions during treatment with many of my youth and adult therapy clients. My hopes for my offspring are that they use the synergy of sisterhood to thrive. I want them to feel comfortable at the intersections of gender, sex, generation, and status. That the girls I refer to as "First CLASS" will flourish with the same teachings I share with my community daughters. Their tide-changing generation will be equipped to rebel from *Sisterella* complex, Strong Black Woman syndrome, and more aggressive stereotypes. Further I envision a society where my daughters and other Black girls will have a roadmap to success through intergenerational transmission of culture, family values, and strengths.

In *Imagining her future*, (Ramirez, Oshin, & Milan, 2017) Black, White, and Latina mothers' socialization goals for their daughters are compared.

Transmission of independence and strength to their daughters was valued more by Black participants than other ethnicities, who viewed the traits as externalizing behaviors. Black mothers wield a double edge sword in protecting and preparing our daughters for the world with meaningful, optimistic, honest guidance. Loving my daughters urged me to create a space that accepts their entire range of identities: autistic, sporty, musical, artsy, gifted Black girls who made me realize for whom I was sent. Their traits, needs, and experiences inform my work daily. My hope is that the world will behold them, but that they first embrace themselves. Ultimately, my ambition is for my work to give teachers, employers, and healthcare providers the inclusive data and training necessary to promote positive self-image and outcomes for young women of color.

Conclusion: I Was Built for This

I do this work for myself, my mother, grandmothers and daughters, and my legacy. My daughters who, remind me of myself, a Black girl in a white and Asian grade school, who choreographed, taught, and performed between my honors classes.

I do this work for myself and my teammates. The pre-teens who coached elementary school cheerleaders. I dreamed of helping Black girls access higher levels of excellence and wider ranges of opportunity. Playing on an uneven field, I inherently knew we were capable and deserved more.

I do this work to honor friends from oppressed communities who claimed state titles in backwoods midwestern towns, while the locals sneered. For us, the teen martial artists who instructed and mentored girls in our Black dojo. We stood out at tournaments, Black girls in Black guis (Karate uniforms) who were confident, disciplined while ethnic "af", and cleaned house. My homegirls were talented in everything from parliamentary procedure to free styling, track to triumphant resilience; we excelled before we were even seen. I proudly study Black girl excellence and the elevating, empowering, sustaining synergy that our sister circles produce.

In contrast to a culture bound colloquialism, "Ain't nobody studd'n you!", Black girls deserve to be studied, scientifically. Inspired by the A'ja's, the tenacious teens of EMPOWER, and sagacious lasses of CLASS, I study to do this work with excellence. My commitment to professional ethics propels me to search for roads through micro and macro level barriers to my clients' self-actualization. I know that establishing a healthy self-image prepares us to deal with personal, familial, and systemic traumas. The ways we challenge patriarchy, poverty, "Pushout', and "Strong Black Woman" syndrome continue to inspire my work. Collectively, our undeniable ability to navigate pressure and power activates a multitude of theoretical questions that inspires me to conceptualize, assess, cultivate, facilitate, and nourish Black Girl Magic.

References

Abrams, J. A., Hill, A., & Maxwell, M. (2019). Underneath the mask of the strong Black woman schema: Disentangling influences of strength and self-silencing on depressive symptoms among U.S. Black women. *Sex Roles, 80*, 1–10. https://doi.org/10.1007/s11199-018-0956-y.

Anderson, B. N., & Martin, J. A. (2018). What K-12 teachers need to know about teaching gifted Black girls battling perfectionism and stereotype threat. *Gifted Child Today, 41*(3), 117–124.

Badu, Erykah, & Erykah Badu|ARTIST. (2000). *Mama's gun*. Universal Motown Records, a division of UMG Recordings, Inc.

Blake, J. J., Butler, B. R., Lewis, C. W., & Darensbourg, A. (2011). Unmasking the inequitable discipline experiences of urban Black girls: Implications for urban educational stakeholders. *The Urban Review, 43*(1), 90–106.

Bryant-Davis, T. (2007). Healing requires recognition: The case for race-based traumatic stress. *The Counseling Psychologist, 35*(1), 135–143. https://doi.org/10.1177/0011000006295152

Charlies-names.com. https://charlies-names.com/en/tamika/

DeGruy Leary, J. (2005). *Post-traumatic slave syndrome: America's legacy of enduring injury* (p. 9). Joy Degruy Publications Inc.

Ellis, W., & Dietz, B. (2020). *Pair of ACEs tree*.

Ellis, W. R. (2020). Healing communities to heal schools. Educational Leadership, 78(2), 52–57.

Essien, I., & Wood, J. L. (2021). I love my hair: The weaponizing of Black girls hair by educators in early childhood education. *Early Childhood Education Journal, 49*(3), 401–412.

Ford, D. Y. (2011). *Reversing underachievement among gifted Black students* (2nd ed.). Prufrock Press.

Ford, D. Y. (2013). Ford female achievement model of excellence (FAME). Retrieved from http://www.drdonnayford.com/#!black-females/c1zop

Gamst, G., Arellano-Morales, L., Meyers, L. S., Serpas, D. G., Balla, J., Diaz, A., & Aldape, R. (2020). Shifting can be stressful for African American women: A structural mediation model. *Journal of Black Psychology, 46*(5), 364–387.

Guy, M. R. (2020). *The impact of the model of Black femininity and maternal anxious mother attachment to adolescent Black girls' self-esteem.* Liberty University

Johnson, J. C., Gamst, G., Meyers, L. S., Arellano-Morales, L., & Shorter-Gooden, K. (2016). Development and validation of the African American Women's Shifting Scale (AAWSS). *Cultural Diversity and Ethnic Minority Psychology, 22*(1), 11.

Jones, C., & Shorter-Gooden, K. (2009). The Sisterella Complex: Black women and depression. In Jones, C., & Shorter-Gooden, K. *Shifting: The double lives of Black women in America* (pp. 120–146). New York: Perennial.

Nelson, T., Cardemil, E. V., & Adeoye, C. T. (2016). Rethinking strength: Black women's perceptions of the "Strong Black Woman" role. *Psychology of Women Quarterly, 40*(4), 551–563.

Ramirez, J., Oshin, L., & Milan, S. (2017). Imagining her future: Diversity in mothers' socialization goals for their adolescent daughters. *Journal of Cross-Cultural Psychology, 48*(4), 593–610.

Shakur, A. (1988). *Assata: An autobiography.* Chicago Review Press.

Shorter-Gooden, K. (2004). Multiple resistance strategies: How African American women cope with racism and sexism. *Journal of Black Psychology, 30*(3), 406–425.

US Census Bureau. (1940). *Census of the United States: Population schedule* (16th ed.). Department of Commerce. Retrieved June 15, 2022, from https://ancestors.familysearch.org/en/L2DN-MWC/ellen-ruth-bell-1934-2015

Young, J. L. (2020). To heal our world, we must first heal our girls: Examining Black girl achievement. *Multicultural Learning and Teaching, 15*(2), 1–11.

11 Defining Ourselves, for Ourselves: The Embodiment of Critical Mentoring Pedagogy as Praxis in Black Girlhood Studies

TARYRN T. C. BROWN

> *I look at my environment*
> *And wonder where the fire went*
> *What happened to everything we used to be*
> *I hear so many cry for help*
> *Searching outside of themselves*
> *Now I know that his strength is within me*
>
> *And deep in my heart*
> *And deep in my heart, the answer it was in me*
> **And I made up my mind to define my own destiny**
>
> (The Miseducation of Lauryn Hill, 1998)

Noted in the Library of Congress (2015) as a culturally, historically, and aesthetically significant contribution to popular culture, the album *"The Miseducation of Lauryn Hill"* is a universal anthem in Black feminism that centers lessons, themes, and teachings in Black women and girls lived experiences (Sankofa et al., 2019). For mainstream audiences, the album brings into conversation experiences of *Blackgirls* [one word]; what Boylorn (2016) posits as the decompartmentalization of racialized and gendered lives of Black women and girls. It also engages with the ideologies of *memory work* (Ohito, 2021) and affirmations for Black women and girls that guides them into spaces of Black feminist futurity (Campt, 2017) and value that aims for Black and Brown bodies to feel accepted, welcomed, and comfortable to just *be*.

    A lyrical assembly of musical and visual disruption, *"The Miseducation of Lauryn Hill"* throws ideas of censorship and the politics of respectability out the window to demonstrate how Blackgirls have voices not only that should be heard, but that are also instrumental in supporting, healing, and affirming experiences in one another. This album was central to how I experienced my own evolution into the academy as faculty in the College of Education, and what I have come to posit in my own lived experience as a Blackgirl *musical mentoring framework* that blends the way we view boundaries in teaching and learning in spaces of Black girlhood. A blending of teaching and mentoring, that through my own experience creates space for intersectional pedagogies that account for cultures, histories, and possibilities of Blackgirl feminist futures.

Being and Experiencing Life as a Blackgirl in the Academy

"Tell me, who I have to be, to get some reciprocity..." (Lauryn Hill, 1998, Ex Factor)

Recognizing the situatedness of interpersonal and intercultural experiences of gender, race, and ethnicity within larger systems of power, oppression, and privilege, my experiences as a Blackgirl scholar have continued to be informed by and tethered together through networks of mentors and support. Aspects of my positionality that toggle between reflections of times past and present and that are heavily informed by dynamic Black women mentors across familial, academic and community spaces. With experiences across the humanities and social science disciplines, my approach to teaching and mentoring is situated in a solidarity and coalition building framework that centers the production of knowledge, cultures, resources, histories, and people. My teaching and mentoring, more directly, have always been rooted in cultivating critical consciousness for historically minoritized students in and outside of the classroom making way for pedagogical strategies for challenging students to consider Black feminism as an analytical tool to amplify intersectional identities beyond the minimum of survivability towards a generative frame of belonging, community, justice, and equity.

Lorde (1981) stated, "*I am not free while any woman is unfree, even when her shackles are different from my own.*" This persists as central in my positioning as Black feminism has, by necessity, emerged with political mobilizations and struggles that created the conditions of possibility for nurturing a politics of radical social transformation. The kind of radical transformative learning that can happen in a culturally informed classroom space that raises broader, foundational questions about the relationship(s) among theory, lived experiences, and the articulation of expansive visions of social change in the lives of Black girls. Through critically centering my own self-reflective story—the kind of stories we tell ourselves about ourselves that make ourselves—I aim to highlight through Blackgirl *critical auto/ethnography* (Boylorn, 2016) the harmony across my experiences in teaching and mentoring, centering my embodiment of critical mentoring pedagogy in my praxis in Black girlhood studies. As a methodology that makes space for an examination of behavior and ideas—critical auto/ethnography involves looking into the mirror and thinking critically about yourself across.

Inspired by the work of Black feminist geographers (Butler, 2018; McKittrick, 2006; McKittrick & Wynter, 2015) and my attention to critical considerations of teaching and mentoring pedagogies as praxis, this chapter aims to speak to what it means to teach and mentor in Black girlhood studies. As the field of Black girlhood continues to establish itself in tangentially from Black feminism, this kind of inquiry can further conversations of pedagogical strategy that can create safe and well spaces for those interested in studying Black girlhood. Through critical auto/ethnographic methodology, this chapter offers my internal reflections and highlights of Black girlhood praxis through embodied critical mentoring pedagogy (Johnson-Bailey, Lasker-Scott, & Sealey-Ruiz, 2015; Liou et al., 2016). Navigated both in and outside of the university classroom, these remembrances are framed both theoretically and analytically in both undergraduate and graduate courses of Black girlhood studies; the first offerings made available to students at my institution. Connecting aspects that are equal parts cultural, situational, political, and self-conscious (Boylorn, 2013; Matias & Liou, 2015), this chapter will use aspects of lived experience to explore how and why the tenets of critical mentoring pedagogy became central as a framework of consideration for praxis in Black girlhood studies. Building upon traditional definitions in both my teaching and mentoring, I use components of my critical mentoring pedagogy as a liberatory tool of praxis in Black girlhood where the deliberate goals of my teaching aim to further democratize education and the life opportunities that are central to the relationships developed in the Black girl-centered academic space. It is in the intersection of experience in my teaching and mentoring, that I lean towards critical mentoring pedagogy, as an assist in the development of Black girl pedagogical spaces of learning that center the rich and storied history of Black girlhoods.

Black Girls' Ways of Knowing and Humanness as Praxis

"It seems we lose the game before we even start to play-who made these rules? (Lauryn Hill, 1998)

Black girls are not a monolith. Black girls make up a heterogenous sub-group of youth culture whose symbolic representations appear in varied forms. Black girlhood, as a growing interdisciplinary field of study, stems from Black feminism and supports the particularity of Black girls' experiences. Black girlhood suggests that Black girls' knowledge and lived experience makes "*their personal political*" and distinct from while related to experiences of adult Black women. As Black girlhood as a field, continues to move towards more visibility in research and literature, my burgeoning work continues to create opportunities that expand my experiences of Black girlhood into the university teaching space through the design and development of courses in Black girlhood at both the undergraduate and graduate level. These course design and development experiences have challenged me as an educator to consider more explicit considerations for my praxis and what rises as foundational in my pedagogical vision for the Black girl-centered classroom. An acknowledgment of the exploratory space of Black girl critical auto/ethnography that centered my background informed in Black feminist pedagogies that often stylistically defined my approach in mentoring.

In the text, *On Being Human as Praxis* by Katherine McKittrick and Sylvia Wynter (2015), I was further encapsulated in an analysis that challenged my course development to reflect across three primary areas: (a) the power of the collective imaginary, (b) the "*call* and *response*" tradition, and (c) the embodied application humanity that centers who and how people move in and throughout spaces. This continued to be further informed by the scholarship of Tamara T. Butler (2018), in her work, "*Black Girl Cartography: Black girlhood and Place-making in Education research*," to center the importance of "transdisciplinary analyses of Black girls' sociocultural and geopolitical locations in education research" (p. 28). As educator, this relationship between humanity as praxis persisted as central in the collective imaginary and possibility for a academic learning space of Black girlhoods. In this reflective process I noticed the interactions I would have in the mentoring space outside of the classroom, which were simultaneously also negotiating critical discussions, engagement, and collaborations within Black girlhood. These exchanges ultimately started to frame the ways I was organizing my teaching and course development.

Defining Ourselves, for Ourselves   151

Table 12.1. *Components of a Conceptualized Black Girl Critical Mentoring Praxis*

Blackgirl Positionality (Boylorn, 2016; Hill, 2018)	Critical Auto/ Ethnography (Boylorn, 2013)	Critical Mentoring Pedagogy in Black Girlhood (Liou et al., 2016)
Blackgirl Literacies	Public/Private testimony for Black Women and girls	Anti-deficit framework designed to transform the mindset of the teacher.
Blackgirl Intersections of Lived Experience	Public/Private acknowledgment of Black Women and girls	Student's capital is centered and appreciated as community cultural wealth of all students.
Blackgirl Futurity	Public/Private empowerment of Black women and girls	Collective Praxis creates an environment focused on a strong collective purpose among students and teachers.

The Entanglement of Critical Mentoring Pedagogy and Black Girlhood

> *Everything is everything,*
> *what is meant to be, will be,*
> *After winter, must come spring,*
> *Change, it comes eventually"*
> (Hill, 1998)

The trajectory of Black Girlhood Studies, as an academic discipline, continues to grow and develop as its own interdisciplinary field of study that seeks to center the experiences and lives of Black girls (Halliday, 2019; Pratt-Clarke, Baldwin, & Brown, 2022). As not directly attended to in its predecessor field of Girlhood Studies, Black girlhood as a discipline seeks to counter the ways in which we understand experiences of Black girls within educational institutions. As a result, the interests in the pedagogies and practices of teaching and mentoring in Black Girlhood Studies continues to emerge as an important aspect of its growth as a field of study at the university level, in schooling spaces, and outside of formal academic settings. Previous scholarship most commonly has centered the dynamics of mentoring in community embedded initiatives in Black girlhoods which acknowledged the powerful dynamics present in the most successful mentoring relationships (Johnson-Bailey et al., 2015). These dynamics would strongly consider and keep central the benefits of the mentoring relationship as something that persist as mutually transformative. In considering praxis in Black girlhood, my attention as instructor truly sought to make consideration for a mutually beneficial learning environment, that would be connected to my previous experiences as a Black woman educator centering Black-girl centered work.

To teach in Black girlhood for me, aimed at building upon the scholarly contributions of Black girlhood scholars across disciplines that had created space for the non-monolithic realities that frame and shape Black girlhoods. Realities that are not a politically neutral or void of larger systemic and structural narratives to attempt to isolate and silence experiences of minoritized individuals. My teaching pedagogy sought to use the same intention to the goal of disrupting the dominant deficit discourses of Black girlhood to a space where one's social locations within systemic hierarchies of intelligence and dismantled to center more authentically the voices and epistemologies central to doing work in Black girlhood. In my teaching in Black girlhood, I came to better understand my desire to develop students' aspirational, navigational, and informational strategies as a central component in their own development of agency and consciousness-raising experience within the classroom. An experience in the classroom that called me as instructor to center the whole-student that rose as, in order to build upon my students' strengths, a strategy within the classroom space that resonated with the critical mentoring process I had used more directly in my role throughout mentoring relationships in other schooling and community spaces.

Knowledge is political and it is never produced in isolation. As Black feminists are communities of knowers of the Black women and girls' experiences, we continue to expand our funds of knowledge into wider communities of thought and praxis. The additional dimension that 'being' a Black feminist brings centralizes the role that our bodies and our politics are bound together under the symbol of Black feminism; and within the context of this manuscript, our Black girlhoods. As an educator at the university level for almost nine years, I have learned that central to my teaching philosophy is the centrality of collective and whole student development. My experiences have proven, no matter the subject areas, that in learning- especially in critical issues of education that account for lived experience at intersections of race, class-, and gender- my belief is the fact that together is better. Furthermore, in that togetherness, relationships matter and those true and authentic relationships in praxis, take work. I wholeheartedly believe in the power of developing and nurturing meaningful connections with my students. It's within this space that I am able to make room for this strategy within both my mentoring and teaching; noting explicitly the function of a teacher and mentor remain as increasingly significant in assisting historically minoritized populations to advance through the educational pipeline.

With an intentional centering of the collective, as mirrored in traditional orientations of Black feminist spaces of learning and engagement, critical mentoring places emphasis on relationships and ideas, rather than as a fixed and stable engagement structure that doesn't grapple with the complexities present in a whole-student centered approach. Critical mentoring pedagogy provides a broader theoretical framework to analyze the structural inequities that impact "achievement" and "opportunity" (Skrla, Scheurich, Garcia, & Nolly, 2004). From this pedagogical standpoint, I see critical mentorship as an important tool to bridge the intersection between learning opportunities and student achievement in the Black girl-centered learning space, as an informational framework situates the role of mentorship as an effective approach to addressing the needs of diverse students (Liou et al., 2016). Critical mentorship requires schools to function differently than in traditional compliance models, where the incentive structure for stakeholders is limited to test scores. That model promotes winners and losers and perpetuates a culture of deficit thinking where the racial ideology of academic achievement maintains low expectations (Skrla et al., 2004). Critical mentorship promotes an environment focused on a strong collective sense of purpose among students, teachers, and administrators and develops a culture of positive expectations for academic achievement. To cultivate a culture of high expectations for student success, the change process must engage all stakeholders in conversations about race, class, gender, sexuality, religions, and other markers that traditionally serve as predictors for academic outcomes.

As a pedagogy, critical mentoring rejects traditional orientations to the mechanical nature of mentor-mentee dynamic and rather centers an ethics of care and empathy towards the whole-student in engagement; within the Black feminist standpoint, I find this approach very similar to the womanist caring framework, coined by Beauboeuf-Lafontant (2005). An ethics of care that sees value in relationships within mentoring as not solely corrective or but rather purposeful in the accomplishment of discovery. This approach within critical mentoring translates seamlessly into praxis in consideration of a course design and development that isn't solely transactional in nature between teacher-student. In connecting the key ideas of critical mentoring to the practice of caring and school culture for Black girls, we lean into the future possibilities of the schooling and academic space that Morris (2016) suggests could be a "locus of learning" for Black girls which actualizes as a "mentor-rich" environment where teachers are available, informed, and committed to the well-being of Black girls. The task for a teacher-mentor being deliberately folded into mentoring practices within the university classroom and beyond. This freedom dream (Love, 2019) in designing academic spaces for Black girlhood studies creates opportunities for teachers to connect and draw from what we know about mentoring, towards the potential to provide students with what they need on a psychosocial level of being seen, heard, and able to thrive in our academic spaces. Moreover, in my own centering of the relationship between teaching and mentoring, I felt the necessary gateway that provided consideration that I could also share for those future Black girlhood scholars in my university classrooms to develop within themselves as they too aim to be more effective teacher-mentors in the classroom towards shifting the culture of the learning space to focus on the assets Black girls bring to the classroom.

Critical Mentoring Pedagogy and Black Girlhood

Black girlhood for interdisciplinary exploration, research and praxis continues to expand including Black girls' emerging identities and socialization across and within different spaces. Utilizing a Black feminist epistemological framework (Collins, 2000), coupled with tenets of critical mentoring pedagogy (Liou et al., 2016), this critical auto/ethnography centers experiences of developed pedagogies in teaching in Black girlhood. Critical auto/ethnography (CAE) is a form of qualitative research. Responding directly to the unique experiences of Black girls, as a Black woman educator, this chapter offers what Boylorn (2013) suggests as a, "a way for public/private testimony and acknowledgment" (p. 47), towards the way I developed and adopted critical mentoring pedagogy in my focus and centering of Black girls and Black girlhood in the course design and development process of space-making for the wholeness of complex Black girlhoods. Auto/ethnographers engage in cultural analysis through personal narrative that examines interpersonal and cultural experiences of identity from the inside out (Boylorn, 2013). The following sections will share more directly some of my auto/ethnographic reflective points that center the entangled relationship of my critical mentoring pedagogy and my praxis in university classroom. In my years of experience, as someone trained in college student development theory and also educational theory and practice, I have found over the years that the successful mentoring relationship consists of a space of empowering and equipping the mentee to reach their own professional goals, ambitions, and learning potential. This process is directly in alignment with the centrality of critical mentoring pedagogy. As two primary areas of attention in my course design, the following sections will discuss components of my praxis in the

Black girlhood studies classroom; (a) connectedness and (b) centering diverse perspectives within and about Black girlhood scholars.

Connectedness as a Part of Being Seen

As central in the embodied critical mentoring pedagogical approach, relationships and relationship building throughout the course design were important in Black girlhood studies. Attending intentionally to the development of both the collective identity and individual relational experience from student-student and instructor-student, spoke in retrospect to the disconnected sense of being that the students enrolled in the course and also mentored by me often communicated was their reality within their own academic homes across the institution. As Black girlhood courses being offered for the first time on a predominantly white university campus in a southern state rampant with political rhetoric set to attack the diverse histories of minoritized people, the role of relationship sought to not only establish the collective identity for the duration of our course time together, but to also create space for safety and wellness of those committed to the study of Black girl-centered ways of knowing.

Butler (2018) asserts, "Black girls and women's liberatory practices have been, and will continue to be, rooted in the spaces that we demand, seek, create, and cultivate" (p. 30). The centrality in relationship in the Black girlhood classroom created space for the needed emotional support of students, whom often reflected on their struggle with confidence in white-dominated learning spaces that not only lacked relational intentionality but often exacerbated its alternative in unwelcoming spaces shrouded in macro and micro racial aggressions that many students spoke to having to navigate. The power of the collective created space to speak words of possibility and hope the students, with reassurance that their interests and passions in Black girl-centered scholarship could align and compliment their academic ambitions. It also built a practical space of compassion, while also role modeling supportive engagements in the academic space that hopefully persist as useful in the increasingly complex world beyond the ivory tower.

Students in the course were able to build these relationships through engaging in critical questioning of critical perspectives from a myriad of topics central to Black girlhood and apply the tools of their disciplines, and experience first- hand within the complexity, uncertainty, and excitement of discovering possibility in Black girlhood as a field of study. For me, this experience continues to persist as transformative, especially accounting for my role as faculty teacher-mentor that has the privilege of guiding this experience, gathering collaboratively the resources and role modeling what could potentially be the catalysts for how these students come to create their own places in Black girlhood research. This aspect for me as teacher-mentor continues as truly fulfilling as I witness the future of Black girlhood in the perspectives of researchers, across the myriad of disciplines represented within the course through embodiment and enactment, moving beyond merely the consumption of the Black girl-centered knowledge and toward higher taxonomic modes of thinking—analysis, synthesis, application, evaluation, creation.

Price-Dennis, Muhammad, Womack, McArthur, and Haddix (2017) offer additional insights in the power of connectedness in the Black girl-centered learning space, "In our society, Black girl spaces are not strongly advocated for by those who intentionally or unintentionally promote anti-Blackness, but Black girls themselves deeply desire such collectivism" (p. 4). The role of relationship in implementation brought alive activities built within Black girlhood and Black feminist thought towards extended transnational global Black girlhoods through the perspective of Black girlhoods brought into the learning space by the students. The trajectory of this two-way relationship was made not only for the students within the course but also, unknowingly for me, as a Black girlhood scholar that continued to gain tremendously perspective and connectedness with students who had an interest and investment to learn about Black girl-centered interests, lived experiences, and issues.

Centering the Complexity of Black Girlhoods

In thinking about the types of critical reflective and prompting assignments that would frame the design of the course, I was led to another aspect of critical mentoring pedagogy that centered wholeness as central to our engagement, connection, and support learning. This aspect of critical mentoring pedagogy challenged me to ensure adequate representation of voice and lived experience in the vast complexity of Black girlhoods. Centering diverse perspective is found across a myriad of Black girlhood scholarship (Brown, 2009; Halliday, 2019; Muhammed & Haddix, 2016; Sealey-Ruiz, 2016; Sutherland, 2005), and challenges scholarship and praxis in Black girlhood to take up the mantel in disrupting monolithic narratives of Black girlhoods. Price-Dennis et al. (2017) assert, Black girl literacies are complex and are always situated in larger sociopolitical environments related to identity, power, and agency. These same ideas are realities in the university classroom, as teaching and learning in Black girlhood must also account for pedagogical approaches that write, speak, move, and affirm the multidimensionality of students of Black girlhood (Muhammad & Haddix, 2016; Pratt-Clarke et al.,

2022). An understanding of this approach in my teaching I believe moves us forward to spaces of possibility in an environmentally focused collective sense of purpose among students. With an intentional praxis in Black girlhood that acknowledges a myriad of perspectives layers the technicolored realities of the field of Black girlhood and creates an experience within the classroom that transcends teacher-student engagement into communal collective spaces for learning and support.

Blackgirl Pedagogical Futures in Black Girlhood

> *At long last love has arrived*
> *And I thank God I'm alive (I'm alive)*
> *You're just too good to be true*
> ***Can't take my eyes off you*** *(a one two, a one two)*
> (Hill, 1998)

My experiences within teaching and mentoring in Black girlhood continue to be guided by reflective processes in the classroom. As a teacher, one of my greatest joys comes from seeing my students use the skills they have gained to change the world around them for good, whether that be through landing that first job out of college, taking a position as a volunteer, or pursuing further education. As an approach to teaching and learning that is centered in the interest of the student, I believe critical mentoring pedagogy as praxis in Black girlhood is necessary in my overall engagement and persistence in the academy. Collectively, shared perspective, voice, and lived experience within teachings of Black girlhood, serves as a tool to assist students to work through both internal and external motivators and connections to Black girlhood studies and simultaneously equip them for advancing their research interests and aspirations for centering Black girls across many different disciplines. Thus, a critical mentoring pedagogical approach for praxis in Black girlhood can support the identification and building of students' strengths and needs and promote the advancement of a discipline grounded deeply in acknowledging and creating space for past, present, and futures of Black girls.

In this process of storying my praxis and mentoring I was reminded that teaching is not just about the transfer of knowledge. All students deserve to be recognized through a form of praxis that acknowledges the needs central to their ability to thrive. As an educator, it is extremely important to keep our eyes on the evolution of our praxis and recognize our role and capacity in the development and support of agency within teaching and learning. For it is within that support and agency that we can create possibilities for both the student and the teacher to build a reciprocal, respectful relationships with each other towards larger collective goals; goals that I believe will be instrumental in the continued growth and reach of Black girlhood.

References

Baldwin, J., & Lorde A. (1984). Revolutionary hope: A conversation between James Baldwin and Audre Lorde. *Essence Magazine*, December.

Barker, M. J. (2007). Cross-cultural mentoring in institutional contexts. *The Negro Educational Review, 58*, 85–103.

Bartolomé, L. I. (2004). Critical pedagogy and teacher education: Radicalizing prospective teachers. *Teacher Education Quarterly, 31*(1), 97–122. http://www.jstor.org/stable/23478420

Beauboeuf-Lafontant, T. (1999). A movement against and beyond boundaries: 1 "Politically Relevant Teaching" among African American Teachers. *Teachers College Record, 100*(4), 702–723. https://doi.org/10.1177/016146819910000401

Beauboeuf-Lafontant, T. (2005). Womanist lessons for reinventing teaching. *Journal of Teacher Education, 56*(5), 436–445. https://doi.org/10.1177/0022487105282576

Beauboeuf-Lafontant, T. (2009). *Behind the mask of the strong Black woman*. Temple University Press.

Boylorn, R. (2013). *Sweetwater: Black women and narratives of resilience*. Peter Lang Publishing.

Boylorn, R. M. (2016). On being at home with myself: Blackgirl autoethnography as research praxis. *International Review of Qualitative Research, 9*(1), 44–58. https://doi.org/10.1525/irqr.2016.9.1.44

Brown, R. N. (2009). *Black girlhood celebration: Toward a hip-hop feminist pedagogy*. Peter Lang.

Butler, T. T. (2018). Black girl cartography: Black girlhood and place-making in education Research. *Review of Research in Education, 42*(1), 28–45. https://doi.org/10.3102/0091732X18762114

Campt, T. M. (2017). *Listening to images*. Duke University Press. https://doi.org/10.2307/j.ctv1134dm3

Collins, P. H. (1996). What's in a name? Womanism, Black feminism, and beyond. *Black Scholar, 26*(1), 9–17. https:doi.org/10.1080/00064246.1996.11430765

Collins, P. (2000). *Black feminist thought knowledge consciousness and the politics of empowerment*. Routledge.

Crisp, G., & Cruz, I. (2009). Mentoring college students: A critical review of the literature between 1990 and 2007. *Research in Higher Education, 50*(6), 525–545. http://www.jstor.org/stable/29782942

DuBois, D. L., & Neville, H. A. (1998). Youth mentoring: Investigation of relationship characteristics and perceived benefits. *Journal of Community*

Psychology, 25, 227–234. https://doi.org/10.1002/(SICI)1520-6629(1997 05)25:3<227::AID-JCOP1>3.0.CO;2-T

DuBois, D. L., Portillo, N., Rhodes, J. E., Silverthorn, N., & Valentine, J. C. (2011). How effective are mentoring programs for youth? A systematic assessment of the evidence. *Psychological Science in the Public Interest*, 12(2), 57–91.

Evans-Winters, V. E., & Esposito, J. (2010). Other people's daughters: Critical race feminism and Black girls' education. *Educational Foundations*, 24, 11–24.

Fanon, F. (1986). *Black skins, white masks*. Pluto Press.

Halliday, A. (2019). *The black girlhood studies collection*. Canadian Scholars Press.

Hill, D. (2018). Black girl pedagogies: Layered lessons on reliability. *Curriculum Inquiry*, 48(3), 383–405. https://doi.org/10.1080/03626784.2018.1468213

Hill, L., Ruffhouse, & Columbia Records, Inc. (1998). *The miseducation of Lauryn Hill*.

Johnson-Bailey, J., Lasker-Scott, T., & Sealey-Ruiz, Y. (2015). *Mentoring while Black & female: The gendered literacy phenomenon of Black women mentors*. Adult Education Research Conference.

Lee, M., & Johnson-Bailey, J. (2004). Challenges to the classroom authority of women of color. *New Directions for Adult and Continuing Education*, 102, 55–64. https://doi.org/10.1002/ace.138

Liou, D., Nieves Martinez, A., & Rotheram-Fuller, E. (2016). "Don't give up on me": Critical mentoring pedagogy for the classroom building students' community cultural wealth. *International Journal of Qualitative Studies in Education*, 29(1), 104–129. https://doi.org/10.1080/09518398.2015.1017849

Love, B. L. (2019). *We want to do more than survive: Abolitionist teaching and the pursuit of educational freedom*. Beacon Press.

Matias, C. E., & Liou, D. D. (2015). Tending to the heart of communities of color: Towards critical race teacher activism. *Urban Education*, 50(5), 601–625. https://doi.org/10.1177/0042085913519338

McKittrick, K. (2006). *Demonic grounds: Black women and the cartographies of struggle*. University of Minnesota Press.

McKittrick, K. (Ed.), & Wynter, S. (2015). *On being human as praxis*. Duke University Press.

Morris, M. W. (2016). *Pushout: The criminalization of Black girls in schools*. The New Press.

Muhammad, G. E., & Haddix, M. (2016). Centering Black girls' literacies: A review of literature on the multiple ways of knowing of Black girls. *English Education*, 48(4), 299–336. http://www.jstor.org/stable/26492572

Ohito, E. (2021). What can we not leave behind? Storying family photographs, unlocking emotional memories, and welcoming complex conversations on being human. *Occasional Paper Series*, (45).

Pratt-Clarke, Menah, Andrea Baldwin, and Leticia Brown. (2020, October 27). Urban Teaching and Black Girls' Pedagogies. Oxford Research Encyclopedia of Education. Oxford: Oxford University Press. doi: https://doi.org/10.1093/acrefore/9780190264093.013.1349

Pratt-Clarke, M., Baldwin, A., & Brown, L. (2022). Urban teaching and Black girls' pedagogies. *Oxford Research Encyclopedia of Education*.

Price-Dennis, D., Muhammad, G. E., Womack, E., McArthur, S. A., & Haddix, M. (2017). The multiple identities and literacies of black girlhood: A conversation about creating spaces for Black girl voices. *Journal of Language and Literacy Education*, *13*(3), 1–18. https://doi.org/10.1177/1529100611414806

Sankofa, W. B., Evans-Winters, V. E., & Love, B. L. (2019). *Celebrating twenty years of Black girlhood: The Lauryn Hill reader*. Peter Lang Verlag.

Sealey-Ruiz, Y. (2016). Editorial: Why Black girls' literacies matter: New literacies for a new era. *English Education*, *48*(4), 290–298. http://www.jstor.org/stable/26492571

Skrla, L. E., Scheurich, J. J., Garcia, J., & Nolly, G. (2004). Equity audits: A practical leadership tool for developing equitable and excellent schools. *Educational Administration Quarterly*, *40*(1), 133–161. https://doi.org/10.1177/0013161X03259148

Sutherland, L. M. (2005). Black adolescent girls' use of literacy practices to negotiate boundaries of ascribed identity. *Journal of Literacy Research*, *37*(3), 365–406. https://doi.org/10.1207/s15548430jlr3703_4

Part IV Continuing the Work: The Future of Black Girlhood Studies

The contributors in this section forecast the future of Black girlhood studies and offer insight into the field and the research.

12 Continuing the Work of Black Girlhood Studies: Culturally Centered Program Development and Evaluation

Nisaa Kirtman and Kimberly Bryant

Introduction

> Sometimes I feel tired, not physically but mentally. I get tired of having to do more, say more…prove myself in ways that I know other girls in my classes don't. If I don't do well, then I have to deal with 'Oh well, we knew she wouldn't do well.' I have to correct people when they say things that aren't true about my history or my community. It's like I have more weight to carry and all I want to do is be a student. Sometimes I want to be invisible but I still want to be seen at the same time. Like I want to be me, but not me as the only one of my group.
>
> (Black Girls CODE Alumna, a computer science major at undergraduate at a predominantly White college, age 20)

The above interview excerpt captures our experience as Black women that spans educational or professional settings and contexts, age, grade levels, and areas of study—particularly STEM disciplines. As the comment suggests, we encounter learning and professional working environments, unlike others that require a kind of endurance to just do what we are there to do: learn and explore. We want our environments to be welcoming of us and our identity as Black women, but not stifle our ability to achieve. Instead of participating in environments without added layers that may chip away at our confidence self-esteem, and self-efficacy, we have to contend with societal stereotypes about us as Black girls and women: we are too loud, too assertive, too provocative, too mature, too disrespectful, too *alpha*, too lazy, too hard, and too defiant. Likewise, Black women are also within these same environments villainized if we present ourselves alternately as too self-confident, too self-assured, or *too cocky* while these same core attributes are seen as positives for our male peers.

Hence, how do you create learning environments, within educational programs, institutions, or corporate structures, that nurture Black women's full identities while allowing them to participate on the playing field as an equal to their peers? How do we ensure that both equity and fairness exist while maintaining high standards of achievement for all? Lastly, how are these environments created in a ways that we as Black females trust?

Recent models and frameworks for program development and evaluation for communities of color appear to be centered around culture, cultural relevance, and shared lived experiences of those responsible for designing such programs and research studies (Ingman & McConnell Moroye, 2019; Magee, Price, Ceran, Cervantes, & Willey, 2020; Chouinard & Cram, 2020). The current chapter represents a unique opportunity, from both the perspective of a Black female executive director of one of the first and largest coding programs for Black girls in the United States (Black Girls CODE) and the perspective of a Black female researcher and evaluator, to demonstrate how learning environments and research approaches can be designed to encourage *identity safety*, where the social identities of Black girls are assets rather than barriers to success.

Culturally responsive environments are free of triggering environmental cues that remind us of how society sees us in a negative light and, yet, encourage Black women to feel a sense of belonging and trust in STEM domains or any environment. Research indicates that a sense of belonging and trusted environments contributes to strong academic outcomes for Black youth (Butler-Barnes, Varner, Williams, & Sellers, 2017; Beasley, 2021; Challenger, Duquette, & Pascascio, 2020; Jolly, Cooper, & Chepyator-Thomson, 2020). We offer analysis, from a program-development standpoint and social psychological standpoint, of the challenges of retaining Black women in STEM fields, and also the challenge of diversity in STEM domains in general. We also propose some principles of remedy that are both by nature of program design and research design for historically marginalized groups (which causes underrepresentation) in any domain. We explore trust-building, identity safety, self-affirmation, intersectional identity, self-efficacy, and identity-safety threats that Black girls face in STEM-subject domains.

Black Women in STEM

Black women are among the most underrepresented groups in STEM disciplines. The systematic disparities in education have been prevalent in the U.S. educational system for centuries. Even today, studies point to the gender and racial disparities among female undergraduate and graduate students that pursue STEM disciplines, especially females in the Black community (Morton & Nkrumah, 2021; Park et al., 2022). While careers in STEM fields and related research fields are central to economic and national security, only 2% of practicing scientists and engineers identify as Black women (National Science Foundation, 2020). This acute disparity is correlated to issues that Black females face early on in their STEM-field career pathway, which may deter students from pursuing STEM subjects at all, including lack of mentorship from those with shared lived experiences, racism, sexism, stereotypes, and bias (McGee & Bentley, 2017). Until Black women are equally represented in all areas of STEM disciplines, our focus as program directors, researchers, and evaluators should be on the strategies that encourage Black female scholars to feel a sense of belonging, which is imperative for the effective recruitment, retention, and advancement of Black women as leaders in STEM domains. Being culturally centered and responsive for Black girls should include the (a) prioritization of the needs and cultural parameters of Black girls relative to program implementation and its outcomes, and (b) commitment to centering shared experiences and perspectives within the program and evaluation work.

Viable explanations exist that address the gender and racial disparities at the undergraduate and graduate levels. One way to frame this issue points to what Ladson-Billing (2006) termed the *education debt*, of which the historical, economic, sociopolitical, and moral decisions and policies have characterized our society. There seems to be an assumption that female scholars are not given the same STEM-subject exposure in K-12 education, and therefore, show less interest and lower achievement in STEM-subject classes. On the contrary, females and males show the same levels of interest in STEM disciplines and achievement in STEM-related classes (Xie, Fang, & Shauman, 2015). The *pipeline model* has been referred to as a viable explanation for understanding why women may move on from their STEM-domain pursuits. Xie, Fang, and Shauman (2015) point to the "leak" from the pipeline that women face during the end of undergraduate and graduate school and near the beginning of their professional careers, much later than expected.

The "leaky pipeline" in STEM Disciplines

The leaky pipeline for Black students happens earlier compared to their white counterparts, from the midpoint and the end of their undergraduate careers as they transition to graduate school (Riegle-Crumb, Morton, Nguyen, & Dasgupta, 2019). Based on a review of empirical studies of achievement in STEM disciplines, persistence, and attitudes among Black students at various educational levels, Collins (2018) argued that at the core of historically marginalized students' STEM-subject identities are defined by interactions centered around the cultural value of their skill sets related to STEM along with issues surrounding race and gender at different stages and in different learning contexts. As such, Black scholars' STEM identity development hinges, in part, on reciprocal interactions among various psychological factors and individual behaviors, contextual and environmental factors in STEM disciplines that embrace and promote the intersectionality of one's identity, and cultural factors (Collins, 2018). All of these factors impact decisions to pursue STEM fields academically, become innovators or entrepreneurs in STEM in disciplines, or move on to another subject area entirely. Due to the marginalization of Black scholars particularly, and their cultural values, Black students may need more than a developed *STEM identity* to exhibit academic success in STEM fields—an *environment* (or safe space) in which students belong and also embraces *whole-person learning* may also be needed to foster one's potential in STEM disciplines rather than success in STEM disciplines (Griffith et al., 2020).

Studies have attributed the leaky pipeline in college to the competitive, non-nurturing, and *chilly climate* where female students, and students of color, are treated as outsiders (Bystydzienski & Bird, 2006; Kerr & Robinson Kurpius, 2004; Lee & Mccabe, 2021). Black female students experience added layers of educational inequities compared to their White female counterparts, including lack of cultural or racial representation and role models in the field, lack of mentorship compared to their white counterparts, and high levels of stigma consciousness related to less anticipated belonging and trust, and overall structural, race-gender bias, and both resilience and trauma as a result (McGee & Bentley, 2017). In a recent study, Davis (2014) examined Black scholars' experiences in math courses in urban high schools using a critical race theoretical (CRT) framing of qualitative data; it found that characteristics that encouraged students' math interests included:

- Shared racial/cultural background with students,
- Passion for students and subject matter, and
- A caring and understanding approach to student engagement.

From the same study, characteristics that reportedly discouraged student engagement included:

- Lack of racial representation,
- Differential treatment of students based on race,

- Condescension and assumed incompetence, and
- Technology as a replacement for instruction.

This study points to the significance of social and emotional elements of teaching and learning *in addition to learning math*, such as caring and understanding with students, shared racial or cultural background between instructors and students, and engagement, which can contribute to Black student success in STEM.

Sense of Belonging, Navigating Stereotypes, and Identity Safety

Threats to our identity as Black women and girls, or stereotype threat, is an example of a social psychological contingency of identity. Being in a situation or doing something for which a negative stereotype about us and our identities is relevant. The stereotype about Black intellectual inferiority has been pervasive for centuries, and remains *in the air* even today as Claude Steele (1997) referenced. For instance, if a Black female student is worried that performing badly on a test will confirm people's negative beliefs about the intelligence of their race *and* gender, they are experiencing stereotype threat and may underperform as a result. We can be judged or treated in terms of it, and if what we're doing is important to us (e.g., our academic performance, our STEM major) or important to our future, then that pressure can be upsetting and distracting, might interfere with our functioning, and can deter us from that whole walk of life where we feel that pressure. As Black females, this is tied to us as a condition of life, especially in those situations where those stereotypes are relevant. Feeling threatened can lead to avoidance. It is widely known that Black girls and women may avoid classes and career pathways due to concerns related to *social identity threat*, particularly STEM classes and careers, out of fear that they may be stereotyped negatively and devalued due to their race and gender (Moss-Racusin et al., 2012; Remedios & Snyder, 2015). Hence, can in-school or even out-of-school programming that embraces both our racial and gender identities provide a buffer against such threats to our success, particularly in STEM domains?

Black Girls CODE

The Black Girls CODE (BGC) programming and learning environments address the many challenges faced by Black girls by offering learning experiences that bolster Black representation and imagery, led by instructors that encompass a shared passion for CS and STEM disciplines and implement culturally-centered engagement strategies often led by Black female mentors. BGC also offers Black girls the opportunity to network among peers in a technology-focused setting, while nurtured by a diverse staff of program facilitators and volunteers who are predominantly from historically marginalized communities much like the students. The overarching mission of BGC is to change the face of technology by introducing programming and technology to a new generation of coders who eventually may become builders of technological innovation and their own futures (BGC Mission Statement, 2011). Since its establishment in 2011, and in direct response to the lack of Black females in the tech industry, BGC sought to move beyond simply exposing girls of color to coding, but to increase their leadership and sense of self-efficacy for learning technology skills. Although the initial focus of the program focused on a broad demographic of students—girls of color; the program mission was adjusted to center Black girls in 2019.

BGC provided computer coding workshops and enrichment activities for girls from marginalized communities (ages 6–18), first in the San Francisco Bay area and eventually expanding to 15 cities across the US by the year 2017, and additionally extending the reach internationally to Johannesburg, South Africa. The programs offered included technical instruction in fields such as web design, game development, mobile application development, and even more novel technologies such as virtual reality and artificial intelligence. The curricula also explored holistic enrichment with workshops in storytelling, leadership, social justice, and other self-development topic areas. These coding and enrichment activities were designed to provide both exposure to STEM fields and to teach Black female scholars tangible skills to encourage the pursuit of CS as a potential career field and to provide a solid foundation for the social changemakers and leaders they will become. BGC endeavored to incorporate cultural queues throughout as many of its program practices as possible to ingrain the core values of self-efficacy and self-expression in ways of being in community with our students. Organizationally BGC understood that it was not enough just to teach it's girls to code; BGC understood that the organization must also teach how *to be and to thrive* as Black women in a society in which they were most often marginalized, criminalized, and dehumanized. One tangible example of cultural practices is the BGC pledge that students repeat during each coordinated session:

> **Who are we?**
> We are Black Girls CODE
>
> **What do we do?**
> We change the face of technology

> *Why are we here?*
> To innovate, to collaborate, to challenge ourselves
>
> *How do we do it?*
> Through community and self-love
>
> *What is our purpose?*
> To build our own futures
>
> *Who are we?(x3)*
> BGC! (x3)

This simple mantra is a rallying call. A way of knowing and connecting as a community. A self-affirmation that they are powerful and they are enough. Yes, how do we know that BGC's program model is effective? How do we at BGC know that what we are doing is truly having an impact? Who can best tell the story of BGC from an objective stance, yet share an understanding of what it means to be Black and female?

Program evaluations can be implemented in ways that are in service of Black culture, context, equity, and justice for Black girls. In order to tell our story accurately, there should be an acknowledgment of inequitable systems and the conditions that have led to the marginalization of Black women in STEM disciplines. Hence, the evaluator must be intentional in centering evaluations around Black girls, giving Black girls and our communities agency, and leveraging assets of our communities to improve the success and well-being of Black girls. It is time to challenge and interrogate traditional ideas of rigor and objectivity, and move towards creating a more authentic means of capturing data and evidence in order to define BGC's success.

Black-Centered/Equity-Centered Evaluation (Nisaa Kirtman)

As a Black female researcher and evaluator, what role does my shared identity with BGC students and alumna (and other programs designed for communities of color) play in using research and evaluation for greater social change, equity, and social justice? How do I use evaluation as a means of creating change and transformation through shared lived experiences accompanied by rigorous research? It is my belief that evaluations are stronger if the people or community being evaluated are not only included and engaged along the process, but tend to be more robust when Black evaluators play a key role in the evaluation and project and evaluations involving Black communities. Only we can tell our own stories. Lived experience provides a deep and profound understanding of a community in a way that other forms of learning cannot. To center equity in evaluation, we must have deep, inherent knowledge of the context, culture, the strengths, and the challenges that can help inform the research questions being asked, the assumptions being tested, and add nuance to findings in a way that doing a literature review cannot. Representation is critically important, both in the evaluation team and in the evaluation activities.

Brown (1949) described how Black Americans have *special and critical needs* that have grown out of differences in background and existing conditions in American society; hence, *special and critical* considerations need to be made when evaluating education and programming for Black Americans, and the Black experience overall, such as how history and culture may influence evaluation and programming design decisions. In the same vein, from 1940 and even today, my approach to research also considers how systemic racism and inequities have shaped education for Black Americans, including Black women and the vast number of intersectional identities in which we hold. As a Black woman, once majoring in physics, am I able to provide a more accurate analysis and evaluation of programming designed for Black girls in STEM? Who can best respond to the contextual, social, and mental imperatives of Black girls and women? As a Black female researcher with an intimate history in a STEM field, I have direct experiences with BGC students that may inform the evaluation of such a program, and, thus, tell a more accurate story of Black girls navigating STEM while also participating in the unique educational supports provided by BGC.

Additionally, what impact has BGC programming, educational, and social support had on students over short-term and long-term periods spanning ten years? How does BGC foster a sense of belonging and identity safety, in addition to mentoring and networking, that help sustain the connection of undergraduate alumna to the BGC program? These are the research questions that we at Rockman et al. Cooperative (REA), an independent and external research and evaluation cooperative, have helped answer over the past ten years in the form of eight formative and summative evaluations of BGC programming. Our synthesis of research findings using equity-centered approaches with Black girls, and ways that frameworks like CREE has enhanced and improved program outcomes, have been documented for over a decade, which includes (a) bringing the race and gender of Black girls to the forefront of research questions and program design; (b) co-creating research protocols and instruments with program stakeholders; and (c) viewing the culture, race, and gender of Black girls from an assets-based lens while recognizing the plethora of experiences these girls bring to STEM disciplines and their own STEM-subject identity development.

To properly assess program impact with a lens on equity, our evaluation approaches were designed in a manner that reflects equitable evaluation principles. The field of evaluation, which has been dedicated to righteous objectivity, can also become subjective and complicit. It has been argued that if a program or initiative were developed unjustly or unfairly from the beginning, that evaluation can also be used as a platform for those injustices (House, 2017). Hall (2018) argued that while evaluators of color have been contributing voices of the field since its inception, they have not been recognized. As a Black woman who has often limited my view of my own identity and role as a way to assimilate to a dominant perspective and not stand out amongst my colleagues and peers, what should evaluators of color like myself be looking towards beyond being compliance-driven and serving the pleasure of a funder? My inspiration to shift my view and recognize that my identities were assets to my evaluation work, not aspects of myself and my profession that needed to be hidden or downplayed, began in 2014 after two years working with BGC.

Dean-Coffey (2018) encourages funders, community-based organizations, researchers and evaluators, and communities as a whole to use evaluation as a tool and vessel to answer critical questions about unequal systems, populations, marginalization, contexts, and how issues of inequity influence the functioning of these. Finally, she calls for evaluative work to be multiculturally valid and focused on participant ownership and leadership. Coffey's work has helped me to personally define this unique approach and lens that I hold as an evaluator of color, and offer my analysis more critically and in ways that takes inequities, the low percentages of Black women pursuing STEM, my own experience, and uplifting the voices and stories of Black girls and women all into account.

The dominant evaluation paradigm includes definitions and expectations around validity, rigor, bias, and objectivity that honor particular types of knowledge, evidence, and truth. This looks for generalizable and scaled data and findings that may feel disconnected and not reflective of the values of many in the informal and formal education communities, especially those serving Black students. There is no one-size-fits-all framework to guide a culturally responsive or equitable participatory evaluation. BGC, and similarly designed programs, require a tailored evaluation framework that reflects the needs and interests of BGC stakeholders, program context, and the evaluation purpose. One of the pillars of CREE is participatory research is to involve key stakeholders (program staff, funders, communities served) at all points of a study design, implementation, analysis, and dissemination (Hood, 2015).

Participatory evaluations are equally process and outcome-driven, rather than focusing on outcomes alone. To guide the participatory evaluation processes, REA collaborated with the Kimberly (BGC founder) and BGC staff to inform and influence the evaluation designs, data collection processes, and implementation since 2012. This participatory approach helped increase the likelihood that REA's evaluation design and final products will best answer the highest-priority questions for all those with a vested interest in the program and outcomes, primarily students. Not only did we collaborate with Kimberly and BGC staff on instrument development and how to best present the evaluation activities to students, students were also given opportunities in the early stages of each evaluation to provide feedback on how items were worded and phrased, and if they wanted to review the final research reports and summaries of the data in which they contributed. Feedback and outcomes obtained through observations, surveys, focus groups, and interviews with students and parents have indicated positive short and long-term improvements in the areas of student confidence, self-efficacy for learning CS, interest in longer-term CS academic study and plans (e.g., declaring a major in the field), and CS and/or STEM-discipline career pursuits.

My decade-long participatory evaluations have demonstrated several key findings, and highlight the elements of BGC programming that contribute to students continued pursuits in STEM:

1. BGC Alumna have greater CS academic and career aspirations (e.g., majoring in CS or coding in college or wanting to pursue a career in coding) as a result of participating in the program for an average of at least 3 years and attribute these pursuits to having a Black female CS Founder and CEO of 14 years as a role model, and feeling *safe* to be who they are while coding;
2. BGC Alumna have benefitted from ongoing networking and longer-term mentorship experiences as a result of the program (e.g., self-reported improvements in confidence, feeling supported and guided, personally and when navigating professional events such as tech conferences);
3. BGC middle and high school students have demonstrated gains in confidence, coding ability, improvements in self-efficacy for learning CS, and attitude changes towards coding and STEM disciplines in general; and
4. Alumna have shown greater interest in pursuing a career in the tech industry because of BGC.

In light of such findings which have been demonstrated over long-term, more recently, we held a focus group with the same group of students that participated in one of the first focus groups in 2012.

In the fall of 2020, REA held three focus groups with eight BGC alumna between the ages of 17-22 who were all undergraduates at the time and participated in BGC consecutively for about eight years. The discussions centered around the significance of shared history and experiences, seeing role models that resemble themselves, and feeling judged at times within their own institutions, led to talks about stereotype threat. *Stereotype threat*, or the fear of being judged by a negative stereotype which may impact performance, and feel they are at risk of confirming a stereotype about their group. The participants talked about instances in which the particular stereotype of the "angry Black woman" is present, thus having to change behavior and be compliant in situations. One student described an incident that happened to her sister after being admitted into college, stating, "A white woman told her that she was only admitted into the school because of her race due to the fact that the school was required to admit people of color to keep the diversity." Further, participants in the focus group stated how such instances have or may stunt their individual growth as they have to limit themselves so that they would not be labeled or judged. Additionally, discussions of not belonging in certain spaces were present. Particularly, in their academic lives, they felt they sometimes did not belong or were placed in a box of limited expectations. For example, most of the participants admitted to having been accused of plagiarism because there was little to no expectation of them excelling in an academic space, especially in STEM domains, as well as being doubted or belittled based on their goals and achievements.

The participants of this focus group then praised how BGC has created safe spaces for them and other girls who wished to pursue STEM-subject careers. The technology field is filled with competition which coalesces many of these students into deep-seated feelings of not being good enough, especially for young Black girls who do not see themselves echoed within a traditional classroom. Within the BGC community, they have been able to feel safe, and comfortable—that they belong. The safe space that is created within the BGC community helps to dispel the feelings of incompetence by providing these girls a space not only to learn and grow, but a *safe space* to process failure. BGC reminds them that they are not alone in their struggles and that they can always rely on BGC as a home away from home when they are feeling lost or down, and simply want to talk to and be around other Black girls who have shared interests and a reciprocal bond. When asked why the group stays connected to BGC after several years, many since middle school, two participants commented:

> BGC is an organization that is very intersectional and is something I and I think the other girls are passionate about, and it is unique, a place where we can learn, connect and see representation.
>
> BGC events just have always felt very comfortable, and like home to me.

Alumna reported a greater sense of belonging at BGC versus other communities (including school environments) in which they were participants, and that their opinion matters. Fifty-one percent of students reported increased confidence in learning to code or computer science. About half (47%) of students reported already wanting to pursue coding or STEM disciplines prior to participating in BGC, but now want to pursue coding or STEM disciplines more than before; 29% of respondents had no interest in pursuing coding or STEM domains, but now do as a result of BGC. The alumna was asked to select one option between a set of positive and negative adjectives that best represents how they would rate BGC in comparison to their school environment based on their direct experiences. Overall, alumna reported the three most positive adjectives that represent BGC as friendly, non-racist, non-sexist, supportive, and non-homophobic. Alumna rated BGC higher on the following traits compared to their school experience, contributing to their overall sense of belonging at BGC: (a) unsupportive versus supportive (students rated BGC more supportive), (c) racist versus non-racist (students rated their schools as more racist than BGC), (d) elitist versus non-elitist (students rated their schools as more elitist), (e) sexist versus non-sexist (students rated their schools as more sexist than BGC). It is worth mentioning that all students rated BGC more positively than their schools on every trait of being a more welcoming and supportive climate in which they feel that they belong.

These findings speak to the unique elements that BGC provided for alumna that their school environment did not—a safe learning environment. The need for safety in learning environments that are not culturally-centered or responsive in school is what the author bell hooks may have hinted at, and if lacking in pedagogy, might contribute to either lack of engagement or a lack of voice.

> The experience of professors who educate for critical consciousness indicates that many students, especially students of color, may not feel at all "safe" in what appears to be a neutral setting. It is the absence of a feeling of safety that often promotes prolonged silence or lack of student engagement. (Hooks, 1994, p. 39)

This concept of creating a 'safe space' for Black girl genius to thrive is the secret sauce that makes the BGC experience unique as compared to some of its counterparts. On the surface, the organization's core mission is to change the face of the technology industry by encouraging Black girls to embrace the tech marketplace as builders and creators. However, we posit that the communal environment within BGC provides much more than technical instruction to the students who participate in its programs. The intentional and structured approach to embedding the program structure and evaluation methodology with cultural markers is beneficially important to codifying and measuring successful program outcomes for these Black female scholars.

These observations beg the question: how do programs and researchers alike develop practices and cultural norms that allow the community to develop *safety factors* which are restorative? The findings on the sense of belonging point to key elements of the BGC environments that contribute to Black girls' sense of belonging, a balance of soft-skill and hard-skill development, and also controllers of their own narrative and learning space: feeling heard and fully *seen* for the totality of their being within a societal structure in which they are most often marginalized, victimized, and even criminalized. The culturally-responsive and equitable approach to research and evaluation should be aligned with the ways in which programming is centered around equity and safety for Black girls. Hence, the successful collaboration between REA, myself, and BGC hinged on asking similar questions about how to create learning environments where Black girls can thrive, and how such environments involve the development of trust and confidence to be able to navigate pursuing STEM in the real world.

Modeling What We Teach (Kimberly Bryant)

As I reflect upon the past ten-plus years of nurturing this organization from an idea to a global movement, I am often confronted with questions about how our program structures, designs, core values, and practices have shaped the impact we've had on our scholars and many others. People seek tangible examples of how our teachings have provided a shield, enabling our students to engage and be received outside the safety of the Black Girls CODE community. These inquiries are pertinent and essential, necessitating a re-examination of what initially drove me to create this movement.

When I first conceived of Black Girls CODE in 2011, my dream was to create a community in which my young daughter could explore her passion for technology in a space with other young Black girls who shared a common bond and shared life experiences. As a Black woman who had spent over 25 years building her career in a predominantly male-dominated engineering field, I was keenly aware of the obstacles my daughter would inevitably face as a young Black woman venturing into the technology industry. Despite its rapid growth, this industry remains severely deficient in terms of strong female leadership and inclusion of individuals from historically marginalized communities (U.S. Department of Equal Employment Opportunity Commission, 2018). My own formative experiences as a Black woman beginning my career in Corporate America as an electrical engineer and technologist could best be described as *traumatizing*. My personal journey from a 'bench engineer' into the realm of engineering management was marred by bias, inequities, and constant marginalization. The work environments I encountered lacked social and psychological safety, which severely hampered my ability to flourish as a talented, driven, and ambitious young Black woman. I had an ardent desire to pave a safer, more compassionate, and potentially smoother pathway for my daughter and other brilliant young Black women who could potentially follow in my footsteps, venturing into the still predominantly male-dominated field of technology.

While most of the foundational aspects of the BGC program model since the organization's inception have been centered on teaching tangible computing skills to the more than 30,000 female scholars who have participated in our chapter-based and virtual programs, we recognized quite early that our girls needed to learn more than coding. One of the most significant aspects of their learning journeys was the cultivation of a profound sense of self within the protective embrace of this community—a space where, as scholar bell hooks eloquently puts it, they can be *safe to struggle*. The sense of psychological safety within the Black Girls CODE community is a key to the successful outcomes we have seen with students who may enter the programs as shy, self-conscious, or unsure learners and graduate as self-confident, self-assured leaders and innovators.

I was particularly moved by a conversation with one such student, Savanna, in early 2022 who requested her mother contact me directly to share her concerns regarding the future of Black Girls CODE. Savanna is a bright, inquisitive, 13-year-old who is not only a coder but a talented artist and poet who had been a long term participant in BGC NY chapter programs prior to our conversation. As I spoke briefly with Savanna, her words resonated so deeply that they brought me to tears. She passionately conveyed her righteous indignation at the mere thought of Black Girls CODE facing potential extinction or no longer serving as a sanctuary for little Black girls like herself. Savanna, like many of our girls, is impacted by the examples of inequality and unfairness that she witnesses in society particularly as they are directed to Black women. These experiences of injustice can be threats to their sense of self-efficacy and confidence during the formative years of their growth and maturity. To ensure that the impact of *safe space* extends beyond our classrooms, it is of paramount importance to embody the principles of fairness and justice within the program models, organizational practices, and core values espoused and practiced by organizational leadership. This call to "practice what we preach" is a broad call to action that requires us to model these values, from volunteers and program managers to the CEO and board directors.

As the creator of this movement, I find that the girls see themselves in me, just as I see myself and my own challenges mirrored in them. The influence of BGC mentors, facilitators, and fellow students plays a crucial role in shaping the young Black female scholars we aim to empower through our programs. It is not only what we teach them that leaves an impact but also the behaviors we exemplify and model for them. In fact, some of their most powerful lessons aren't actually *taught* explicitly; some of them are actually *caught* by observance. I believe this shared cultural connectedness is one of the greatest strengths of our program which perhaps has differentiated us from many others. We see each other. We share similar stories, and it is this deep connectedness at the foundation of the work as student and practitioner which creates the safe community in which learning is fluid, productive, and profound. When we juxtapose the Black Girls CODE program with traditional organizational models, a stark differentiation emerges. This contrast lies in the capacity to foster meaningful and sustainable growth in the abilities of Black girls to thrive and overcome systemic barriers within institutions that are riddled with obstacles rooted in white male patriarchal biases and prejudices. Scholar Kimberle Crenshaw has done extensive research in the area of intersectionality and belonging; focusing on the "double discrimination" which Black women encounter based on both race and gender. These biases and stereotypes present formidable barriers to the advancement of Black women, compelling them to endure an emotional tax. They face heightened pressure and the arduous task of navigating complex work environments while simultaneously managing the emotional toll of racial and gender biases. It is worth noting that these burdens may be imposed not only by individuals from the dominant class structure; but also by those from similar marginalized communities who exploit the tools of white patriarchal systems, further penalizing Black women throughout their careers. As a result, Black women and girls experience elevated levels of stress, burnout, and negative health outcomes. Additionally, these biases frequently manifest in perceptions of Black women as aggressive or lacking in leadership potential.

As I reflect upon the journey of Black Girls CODE, from its humble beginnings as an idea to its global impact as a movement, I am compelled to address the pressing need for reframing and transforming traditional systems. We must develop models that align with the needs of Black girls and hold existing systems accountable, even if they are the products of our own making. If our aim is to disrupt the barriers and biases deeply embedded within institutions that hinder the progress of Black women and girls, the values and core truths we stand for demand action and change. Through the lens of intersectionality, we must recognize the double discrimination faced by Black women—a confluence of both race and gender. These biases, stereotypes, and systemic obstacles create an emotional tax that Black women and girls unfortunately must shoulder as they navigate their educational pathways and careers. Leaders, practitioners, researchers, and community must remain steadfast in our mission to provide a safe space where Black girls can not only learn tangible skills but also cultivate a profound sense of self and resilience. By embodying fairness and justice within our program models, organizational practices, and core values, we extend the impact of these safe spaces beyond our classrooms and forge a path towards a future where the brilliance, potential, and leadership of Black girls are fully recognized and uplifted.

Concluding Thoughts from Kimberly and Nisaa

Black Girlhood studies can and should be centered around establishing trust and creating safe spaces for Black Girl Genius to thrive. Black girls can be treated with a symphony of real-time interventions to establish trust, a sense of belonging, and identity safety, without using our identity against us and our ability to succeed academically, specifically in STEM domains. Set high standards, directly convey the social capital needed to succeed, establish a very clear pathway forward to succeeding in STEM disciplines, and a lot of support in moving along that pathway. We thrive in environments that are trustworthy, where we can relax, learn, and succeed. Where we can be most fully our divine selves. While *Black Girl Magic* is something we celebrate, what we need is not magical. We simply want to be proud of who we are in learning contexts, without thinking about how we are stereotypically seen in such contexts. For instance, when STEM-subject mentors and evaluators have shared lived experiences, they can implement approaches and demonstrate outcomes that promote diversity, which can help meet the educational needs of Black girls in STEM domains and other fields. Black women possess a different perspective based on their lived experiences, adding richness to both the program and the evaluation, in design, technique, and reporting (Chouinard & Cram, 2020). Deep, inherent, and personal knowledge of the context, the strengths, and the challenges that Black girls experience can help inform the questions being asked, challenge the assumptions being tested, and add nuance to research findings—all of which underscores why representation is so important within the evaluation team, and among program partners and practitioners.

Solutions to support Black girls in STEM disciplines are more available to us than attempting to control everyone's bias. Building trust is simple enough that it invites all of us into this project of diversification and equity. We don't have to stand back, or be threatened by it because of all these forms of stereotype threat that we're subjected to in academic contexts, especially in STEM domains. There is a way forward that invites all of us to participate and lift up Black girls as a *solution* and not a *problem* whether we are creators of a program or researchers.

It begins with a spark of possibility, then interest, but ends with creating safe spaces where Black girls can be seen, nurtured, and celebrated.

References

Beasley, S. T. (2021). Student–faculty interactions and psychosociocultural influences as predictors of engagement among Black college students. *Journal of Diversity in Higher Education, 14*(2), 240–251. https://doi.org/10.1037/dhe0000169

Brown, I. C. (1949). *Race relations in a democracy* [BIE Vol. 5, Problems of race and culture in American schools]. New York, NY: Harper..

Butler-Barnes, S. T., Varner, F., Williams, A., & Sellers, R. (2017). Academic identity: A longitudinal investigation of African American adolescents' academic persistence. *Journal of Black Psychology, 43*(7), 714–739. https://doi.org/10.1177/0095798416683170

Bystydzienski, J. M., & Bird, S. R. (2006). *Removing barriers: Women in academic science, technology, engineering, and mathematics.* Indiana University Press.

Challenger, C. D., Duquette, K., & Pascascio, D. (2020). "Black boys: Invisible to visible": A psychoeducational group fostering self-efficacy, empowerment, and sense of belonging for African American boys. *Journal for Specialists in Group Work, 45*(3), 257–271. https://doi.org/10.1080/01933922.2020.1797444

Chouinard, J. A., & Cram, F. (2020). *Culturally responsive approaches to evaluation: Empirical implications for theory and practice.* SAGE Publications, Inc. https://doi.org/10.4135/9781506368559

Collins, K. H. (2018). Confronting color-blind STEM talent development: Toward a contextual model for Black student STEM identity. *Journal of Advanced Academics, 29*(2), 143–168. https://doi.org/10.1177/1932202X18757958

Davis, J. (2014). The mathematical experiences of Black males in a predominantly Black urban middle school and community. *International Journal of Education in Mathematics, Science and Technology, 2*(3), 206–222.

Dean-Coffey, J. (2018). What's race got to do with it? Equity and philanthropic evaluation practice. *American Journal of Evaluation, 39*(4), 527–542.

Griffin, E. K., & Armstead, C. (2020). Black's coping responses to racial stress. *Journal of Racial and Ethnic Health Disparities, 7*(4), 609. https://doi.org/10.1007/s40615-019-00690-w

Hall, M. E. (2018). Evaluation's race problem in the United States: A call to action for the profession and the *American Journal of Evaluation*. *American Journal of Evaluation, 39*(4), 569–583. https://doi.org/10.1177/1098214018792624

Hood, S. (2015). *Continuing the journey to reposition culture and cultural context in evaluation theory and practice.* Information Age Publishing.

Hooks, B. (1994). *Teaching to transgress.* Routledge.

House, E. R. (2017). Evaluation and the framing of race. *American Journal of Evaluation, 38*(2), 167–189. https://doi.org/10.1177/1098214017694963

Ingman, B. C., & McConnell Moroye, C. (2019). Experience-based objectives. *Educational Studies, 55*(3), 346–367. https://doi.org/10.1080/00131946.2018.1544900

Jolly, S., Cooper, J. N., & Chepyator-Thomson, J. R. (2020). An examination of culturally responsive programming for Black student-athletes' holistic development at division I historically White institutions (HWIs). *Journal of Issues in Intercollegiate Athletics,* 73–90.

Kerr, B., & Robinson Kurpius, S. E. (2004). Encouraging talented girls in math and science: Effects of a guidance intervention. *High Ability Studies, 15*(1), 85–102. https://doi.org/10.1080/1359813042000225357

Lee, J. J., & Mccabe, J. M. (2021). Who speaks and who listens: Revisiting the chilly climate in college classrooms. *Gender & Society, 35*(1), 32–60. https://doi.org/10.1177/0891243220977141

Magee, P. A., Price, J., Ceran, E., Cervantes, J. B., & Willey, C. (2020). The affordances and challenges of enacting culturally relevant STEM pedagogy. In Handbook of Research on STEM Education. Routledge.

McGee, E., & Bentley, L. (2017). The Equity ethic: Black and Latinx college students reengineering their STEM careers toward Justice. *American Journal of Education, 124*(1), 1–36. https://doi.org/10.1086/693954

Morton, T. R., & Nkrumah, T. (2021). A day of reckoning for the White academy: Reframing success for African American women in STEM. *Cultural Studies of Science Education, 16*(2), 485–494.

Moss-Racusin, C. A., & Good, J. J. (2013). "Measure of a man: Outcomes of gender stereotyping for men and masculinity": A special issue of *Social Psychology*. *Social Psychology, 44*(6), 414. https://doi.org/10.1027/1864-9335/a000166

National Science Foundation, N. S. B. (2020). *The state of U.S. science & engineering.* National Science Board Science & Engineering Indicators 2020. NSB-2020-1. In National Science Foundation..

Park, J. J., Zheng, J., Lue, K., Salazar, C., Liwanag, A. M., Parikh, R. M., & Anderson, J. L. (2022). Looking beyond college: STEM college seniors on entering the workforce and the impact of race and gender. *Journal of Diversity in Higher Education.* https://doi.org/10.1037/dhe0000433

Remedios, J. D., & Snyder, S. H. (2015). How women of color detect and respond to multiple forms of prejudice. *Sex Roles: A Journal of Research, 73*(9–10), 371. https://doi.org/10.1007/s11199-015-0453-5

Riegle-Crumb, C., Morton, K., Nguyen, U., & Dasgupta, N. (2019). Inquiry-based instruction in science and mathematics in middle school classrooms: Examining its association with students' attitudes by gender and race/ethnicity. *AERA Open, 5.* https://doi.org/10.1177/2332858419867653

Steele, C. M. (1997). A threat in the air: How stereotypes shape intellectual identity and performance. *American Psychologist, 52*(6), 613–629.U.S. Department of Equal Employment Opportunity Commission. (2018). *Diversity in High Tech: Special report.* https://www.oecd.org/digital/bridging-the-digital-gender-divide.pdf

Xie, Y., Fang, M., & Shauman, K. (2015). STEM education. *Annual Review of Sociology, 41*, 331–357. https://doi.org/10.1146/annurev-soc-071312-145659

13 Into the Future: Researcher's Role in Black Girlhood Methodology

JANELLE GRANT

Time for a Change

Researchers interested in Black girlhood studies cannot follow the status-quo of scientific research. Steeped in systemic racism, mainstream methods result in age-old discourses and policy suggestions germinating from reoccurring charges about Black deficits (Blatt, 2020; Ealey, 2021; McKittrick, 2021). For example, best-practice research about school discipline often coincides with the adultification of Black girls (Annamma, 2017; Ferguson, 2001). The adultification of Black girls refers to viewing Black girls as less deserving of protection and care—because researchers tell society that Black girls are "strong," "hyper-sexual," "loud," and "aggressive" (Toliver, 2018). These stereotypes not only result in real-life adultification of Black girls (e.g., a teacher punishing a Black girl harsher because of her supposed extra-human strength), but harmful notions of Black girlhood also affect how academics study Black girls. For example, the protocols and inventories measuring the "resiliency" that Black girls need to earn degrees and good jobs limit our expression of Black girls in our work by placing them on a binary of "good" or "ghetto" (Butler, 2018; Price-Dennis, Muhammad, Womack, McArthur, & Haddix, 2017; Theron, 2013).

According to the "research," I am one of the resilient Black kids. I know firsthand about performing whiteness as a means to fit in. As a young Black girl, I was not reading academic journals, but the results they produced about Black resilience affected the way I experienced schooling. For example, I did everything I could to hide my frizzy, curly hair and observed everything that the pretty white girls did to get positive attention from peers and people in charge. My respite from being resilient was coming home to my mom telling me that I was blessed and highly favored (Sheard, 2007), a favorite gospel motto from The Clark Sisters. I still felt inferior, but my observations told me to push through and not to ask questions. Prior to learning about the aforementioned research methods, dialectic relationships and other ideas about Black life were hard for me to explain because the research methods that I had been exposed to were not meant to approach Black life with complexity, nuance, and care (Price-Dennis et al., 2017). I am ready to notice genuine change from the past, present, and future research that Black women produce alongside Black girls that pushes against harmful stereotypical binaries. I am ready to put the kibosh on resilience research as a character trait of Blackness that centers whiteness—and any research that centers whiteness in Black girl identity.

Importantly, these "researched" claims are reckless and show no care for the treatment of Black girls. The aforementioned stereotypes (among others) play into controlling images of Black femininity and girlhood that pervade social norms of how teachers, law enforcement, doctors, and other social figures treat Black girls (Annamma, 2017). In other words, research produced about Black girls is not without consequence. Our work has the ability to perpetuate harm or demand a shift to caring for Black girls. Subini Annamma's (2017) book *Pedagogy of Pathologization: Dis/abled Girls of Color in the School-prison Nexus* taught me methodology that is dynamic, collaborative, and emotional as a way to honor marginalized truths. In addition, *Dear Science and Other Stories* by Katherine McKittrick (2021) contends with conducting considerate research. One of my aims as an early researcher is to challenge the status quo of research as a way to create spaces for Black girls that center their knowledge. In this reflection of method-making, I challenge academic traditions of the correct way to do research with conviction that research influences the real-life experiences of Black girls.

My conviction about method-making is personal, creative, and promising. I call for myself and others to produce work that aims to undo the harm that Black girls encounter in various spaces. My own understanding of power networks shows me how discipline (discipline in the form of standards/rules as well as confining academics to a particular field) affects the way I studied and viewed Black girlhood. For example, as a Black woman PhD candidate, I had been involved with many research projects about Black girlhood and feminism, in general, at various institutions. I recognized that researchers wanted to know how Black girls made it through life in light of many challenges. The researcher/university relationship is overarching, complex, and absolute in the development of our studies and decisions about what researchers do with the data (McMillian Cottom, 2018; Gould, 2021; McKittrick, 2021).

The academy finds it acceptable to report pain but not report about the greatness of Black girls. As examples, look at research from current studies. (To be clear, the following two studies cited are works that I find problematic in discourse and methodology.) Jernigan (2020) discusses obesity as a Black girl problem and worked to create programming about a healthy lifestyle. Jernigan reported considerations for the programming and suggested that facilitators "avoid Eurocentric or "White" food choices and recommendations;" instead, facilitators tell Black girls about the "use of alternative ingredients to make "soul food" (p. 890). Likewise, Opara et al. (2022) suggests that Black girls living in urban areas might feel unempowered due to lack of resources (…as if Black communities are not rich in resources). Opara et al. believe that finding ways to empower Black girls can save them from "risky behaviors and improve developmental outcomes such as educational, physical health, and mental health outcomes among Black girls" (p. 587). There are more studies like the two mentioned, and I cannot bring myself to give more space to them; however, the idea is that those studies are generally read as well-meaning.

Importantly, well-meaning work is not enough to actually celebrate Black girls as whole in their current state (Woodson, 2020). Centering whiteness as a credential of "goodness" in research does damage. The so-called objective methodologies often only describe pain, suffering, and deficit for Black girls (Nunn, 2018). In truth, methodologies are steeped in racialized discourses (McKittrick, 2021)—academics must be careful to recognize when their work repeats racist and damaging notions of Black girlhood. To make discursive and tangible changes in the way scholars approach Black girlhood, there is a need to honor the epistemic agency of Black girls and their cultures. Academics can do this through using various research methods and theories that honor marginalized epistemologies. Scholars cannot care for Black girls by suggesting that whiteness is needed for nourishment and confidence-building. Black culture is already good. Black girls are already empowered.

A New Vision: The Recommendations for the Future

Methods should be open to change and honor a wide variety of knowledge. The methodological approach described in this chapter does not have a name because it is not housed in one department or determined by the dominant discourse of "good" science. The recommendations are to be infused in the way you go about doing work on Black girlhood studies. According to McKittrick (2021), methods that center Black life use marginalized modes of inquiry (e.g., first-hand knowledge, cultural epistemology, family stories) as well as traditional methods (e.g., interviews, surveys, thematic analyses, regression analyses etc.). What is important is that findings and implications do not replicate racialized hierarchies.

When McKittrick (2021) calls out science/scientific methodology in *Dear Science and Other Stories*, she is not vilifying robust methods with rich description; however, the premise calls for researchers to think about what research produces in terms of real-life consequences. Accordingly, Black and Brown graduate students and faculty are adept at calling out those real-life marginalizing scenarios and consequences, but there is not much room for their firsthand experience that requires divergence from the scientific norms of method-making (Richardson, 2001). However, the consequences of racism are not the only aspects that shape Black girls' identities—Black girls have the epistemological authority to offer their lived experience expertise about the stratified ways societies function, and research methods need to prioritize that type of social power. As a researcher, I know it feels like there is a limited audience or influence, nevertheless, we cannot disregard stagnant and damaging images, discourses, stereotypes, and policy suggestions that are cultivated in the name of *publish or perish*.

Method-making is more than data collection and analyzation, as my approach guides personal convictions and actions that extend beyond research. For example, since I perform education research, I ask myself: do I advocate for Black girls in schools with what they have taught me and how am I taking care of Black girls? Through my work, I anticipate a better, more inclusive future where the subjective experience of Black girlhood is validated and protected. The following recommendations (in no way exhaustive) for method-making in Black girlhood studies are: (1) make it personal, (2) be creative, and (3) have hope.

Making Research Personal and Rethinking Subjectivity

I am unapologetically subjective. However, subjectivity does not align well with current approaches to the scientific method. The ways in which I experienced life and the observations gained watching my family navigate the world informs how I research Black girlhood. These experiences are valuable first-hand knowledge as it relates to how society works. Fundamentally, what it means to be a Black girl is set within the bounds of historically formed rules—Blackness, which affects Black girls, is a guiding concept informed by history that frames current Black life (Sharpe, 2016). Blackness is an identity that is not fixed (Browne, 2015). Therefore, Blackness, and in turn, Black girlhood are subjective experiences that tell stories of collective joy, pain, community, resistance, public and private life, and social orders that are experienced by individuals who embody Blackness (Browne, 2015; Sharpe, 2016).

Researching Black girlhood is personal. I cannot objectively view a collective life that I share the experience of living. Importantly, even if you never experienced Black girlhood, you learned about Black girls through your own cycle of socialization whether it be through news, songs, TV shows, schools, or churches. Thus, the way we all comprehend Black girlhood is not (cannot be) totally objective. Without holding ourselves accountable to changing the way we go about our methods, the misinformed and uncritical assumptions and biases against Black life portrayed as hard facts persist, rather than acknowledging that oppression is not a natural occurrence (Fayne, 2021; Porter & Haggerty, 1997).

Academia's standards concerning good research developed endogenously with organizational power that regulates methodologies. This means that the university and researchers within it train and have been trained to do scholarly work in a prescribed and racialized way. Ray (2019) asserts that social organizations in the United States are racialized, and universities are among those racialized spaces. Scholars and scholars-in-training are taught to understand Black girls from a non-Black epistemology. The racialized research training many scholars receive centers Black girlhood from a position of whiteness—whiteness being a credential of health, resiliency, success, and productivity. The rules for method-making are set by the academy, and scholars are taught that our job is to learn and pick from the list of set options—you are to be a quantitative researcher or qualitative researcher. Of course, the academy prefers that academics pick the quantitative route, as it is easier to point out the "objective science" behind methodology (Blatt, 2020). Accordingly, Blatt (2020) wrote

> Moreover, thanks to devices such as attitude scales and new survey methodologies (many developed in the course of wartime government research), individual behaviors and attitudes were measurable, could be aggregated into large data sets, and were susceptible to rigorous statistical treatment, promising both theoretical generalizability and a kind of apolitical, mechanical objectivity. (p. 210)

Nevertheless, my subjectivity (or standpoint epistemology, see Collins, 2002) has allowed me to see where methodologies have done Black girls a disservice by mostly placing us on a binary to achieve "generalizability." Black girlhood studies have no place for impersonal methods; rather, scholars in this space honor the marginalized knowledge of past and present Black girls, even if its personal. The personal, lived experience elucidates lives lived with rich with nuanced detail. Researchers must also tap into familial knowledge as part of their frameworks, which is useful for disrupting hegemonic statements.

Problematize the Way You Do Science

Making methods personal means holding yourself accountable for the social effects of your research. The important aspect of making methods personal is that researchers know they are personally accountable for the findings and themes they produce and disseminate. Findings and results from studies add to overall discourse and shape society. Many assumptions and biases researchers have about Black girls and their communities (e.g., resilient or not resilient) are related to research studies that claim an impenetrable scientific method that bolsters their results (Ealey, 2021). These methods are impersonal because, after all, it is hard to win an argument when it comes to science. Traditional scientific methods require academics to separate their lives and their participants' circumstances (or subjects) from the results to achieve objectivity (Blatt, 2020; Bower, 1998); therefore, researchers and the academy do not have to take full responsibility for the marginalizing traditions their work perpetuates. Again, researchers do not need to separate from method-making that is guided by tested theories and facts; however, it is imperative to know the history to make full sense of Blackness and Black life. Researchers must ask questions: what has this method been used to prove? Whose knowledge does this methodology honor? Am I "analyzing" others the way I want to be remembered?

If an academic chose to study Black life, they are encouraged to follow research examples that have worked to eradicate Blackness because of its threat to whiteness. Even though eugenics lost traction contemporarily, there are traces of that belief in mainstream methodologies—researchers are still treating Black girls as problems to solve, especially in education settings (Annamma, 2017). For example, Black girls are either "resilient" or "non-resilient" in schools, and the resilient students often do better in school and beyond (Clay, 2019; Finn & Rock, 1997; Theron, 2013; Gaztambide-Fernández & Angod, 2019; Winston, 2018). In reality, resilience means close proximity to whiteness and non-resilient means that they refuse to be something they are not (Annamma, 2017; Clay, 2019; McMillian Cottom, 2018; Matias, 2016). Using validated methods to figure out which Black girl is more resilient than another, in order to make them a posterchild for positive character traits is similar to eugenics statements, like "we shall identify those lines which supply our families of great men" (Davenport, 1910, p. 92). For example, Black girls who are labeled through research measures as resilient are not problems for society because of their proximity to whiteness (Keddie, Jacobs, & Nelson, 2020; Stovall, 2018; Matias, 2016). We must reject this whole disgusting line of thinking and studying!

Methods can either relate to the social order as it is currently, or researchers reject dominant discourse. Power structures (overarching disciplinary power of the academy) that limit critical and promising methodologies do so to maintain the status quo. For example, critical Black knowledge is stifled because Black girls—in our current social position—are vital to maintain the current social order (McMillian Cottom, 2018; Woodson, 2020). There is a saying that education is power. Yet when Black people speak up, society still does not systemically change. So, not everyone's knowledge is power or official (Baker-Bell, Paris, & Jackson, 2017). The academy, being amenable to larger societal desires of privileging whiteness, want Black girls and those that study Black girlhood to disassociate themselves from forms of racism because it then places the onus on Black people to change instead of holding the dominance of whiteness accountable (Blatt, 2020; Winston, 2018). Again, researchers do not need to separate from method-making that is guided by tested theories and facts; however, it is imperative to know the history to make full sense of Black girl identity. Researchers must ask questions: what has this method been used to prove? Whose knowledge does this methodology honor?

Be Creative

Creative methodologists ensure that their study participants are not subjects—or subjected to measures and analyzations that dehumanize them (Doharty, 2020). For example, Browne (2015) uses the narrative of an exslave to express how Black slaves acted in resistance—and had entertained himself in the midst. Browne re-tells the story of ex-slave Berry Smith fiddling and dancing with a group of Black people on a bridge to lure slave catchers to them, only to actually bring them to a trap that would trip the patrollers. The pranks and "such playful tricks were a means of self-defense" (p. 21). Browne then uses historical examples of self-defense to show how Black people deal with injustice yet still have full, complex, and enjoyable lives. Similarly, I envision that future work with Black girls explicates a complex picture of fullness, complexity, and enjoyment.

Importantly, the Blackness that Black girls embody is always under surveillance (Browne, 2015). Thus, researching Black girlhood is also under surveillance. Racial schemas of Black girls and their bodies are recycled stories that inform society that Black girlhood culture is a deficit and their knowledge is lacking. In efforts to produce non-recycled and damaging narratives, scholars identify cultural contradictions that help subvert simplistic ways of considering Black girlhood outside of the gaze of whiteness (White, 2021).

Discipline over research methods remain because societal norms and the power that enforces those norms go unnoticed (McKittrick, 2021). Research norms, and the workplace discipline to sustain them, goes unchallenged because the rules of trustworthy research are woven into society's organizations, like universities (Blatt, 2020; Bower, 1998). For example, early-career researchers observe punishments when their methods are not "scientific" or rewards when their methods follow Eurocentric ideas of scientific rationalizations. Significantly, researchers who study Black girlhood are under increased expectation to internalize and model methodologies in accordance with dominant U.S. cultural conceptions of how life is to be lived.

Uncritically using methods in the name of scientific trustworthiness unjustly perpetuates racialized scripts of deficiency onto Black girls. And, while I read creative and well-done articles displaying care for Black girls (see Ealey, 2021, Nunn, 2018, and White, 2021 to name only a few), it still shocks me how much work still follows a deficit framework. However, researchers have the opportunity to re-think the way we conduct science regarding Black girls—this sustained effort results in ideas about celebrating Black girlhood in its present form, directing systemic transformation, and changing the way scientists/scholars talk about Black girls for the better. Ladson-Billings (2021) sees the opportunity for a "hard re-set" (p. 68) of pedagogy to "reclaim and preserve our culture" (p. 68). Ladson-Billings is specifically applying the hard re-set to education systems, but the re-set cannot happen if there is not change on a macro-level of society. When people within social organizations like education shift, the way science and research is done changes, too.

Divergent or creative method-making recognizes the disciplinary network that officiates knowledge, and yet works to amplify marginalized knowledge as well as portray Black girls from a humanizing lens. Methodologies are relational because there is an unspoken contract between the researcher and the academy that allows for academics to keep their jobs and receive accolades, while the academy claims awareness of racial violence while doing nothing to upset the status quo (Blatt, 2020). For Black girlhood studies, our method-making recognizes the disciplinary network that officiates knowledge, and yet works to amplify marginalized knowledge, as well as portray Black girls from a humanizing lens. The embodied disciplinary effects (e.g., surveillance, punishments, and rewards) control what researchers do in the workplace, and especially if you are Black and/or if your research is relevant to Black life. Creativity in method-making is a sustained effort to learn new ways of informing each other about Black girls that centers their identity.

Have Hope

While I cannot define Black hope for everyone; however, I follow notions of Afropessimism that describe hope and freedom (Dumas & Ross, 2016; Woodson, 2020). Afropessimism is not looking for a solution to change current U.S. institutions because the racialized systems and organizations are doing exactly what they were created to do regarding reinforcing social status and racial hierarchy. Woodson rejects dominant discourse that claims that young Black children gain social mobility by going to schools meant to serve middle-class white families. Instead, Woodson explained that current methods purposefully ignore how "Black people's structural inferiority" (p. 16) is necessary to the public education system that upholds whiteness. Woodson suggested that instead of waiting for school systems to change based on data, researchers need to find ways that celebrate Black students in their current status. So, when I think about hopeful methods, I think about creating unique spaces where Black girls feel safe and celebrated. What these collaborative study spaces look like differs depending on who you are and who you are working with, and I believe that Black women have intuition of what is a good starting point in working with Black girls.

In my dissertation research, I called our space a "congregation meeting" because after getting to know them, I understood their conception of a church congregation—a lively place that is open to dialogue, emotion, thinking, caring, and confidential when it needs to be. I worked with Black girls and Black boys for my dissertation, and I while in the midst of everything, I found that the most important aspect of our congregation meetings was mutual gratitude. Going forward, when I create study spaces with Afropessimism in mind, I want gratitude to be a goal of our environment—gratitude of mutual storytelling, being present, and forming a special community. I have hope in the future of Black girlhood studies because humanizing and supportive work being done in Black girlhood studies foreshadows larger societal change. Reading works across various disciplines that center Blackness and Black girl identity reveal many possibilities toward getting the work done, and it is exciting to see so many academics taking the chance to change the way we study Black girlhood.

I am aware that having hope is a lot of emotional work on a researcher's part, and I want assert that research done by Black scholars can solely be for the efforts of healing ourselves and our community. I take this charge from Audre Lorde (2003).

> For the master's tools will never dismantle the master's house. They may allow us temporarily to beat him at his own game, but they will never enable us to bring about genuine change. And this fact is only threatening to those women who still define the master's house as their only source of support. (p. 26)

I know that Black girls do not benefit from traditional research methods, and I am hopeful that the collective efforts create new spaces for Black girls that are centered in Black girlhood from conception.

Into the Future…We Inspire Each Other

From the start of research careers, in particular for Black and Brown graduate students, scholars learn that there is no room for firsthand experience that requires divergence from the scientific norms of method-making (Blatt, 2020; Gould, 2021; Fayne, 2021). Scholars studying Black girlhood have to make space for studies that uplift Black girls and can tell a multi-faceted story of joy, pain, and self-exploration. I learned that "discipline is empire" (McKittrick, 2021, p. 39). Having such regimented and segmented fields of knowledge leaves little room for divergence or creativity. Segregating fields of knowledge by their methods is another way to keep Black girlhood studies obscured. So, when it comes to how I design my studies, I look to methodologists from many academic fields who honor and center Blackness. I imagine creating bridges between these scholars that move beyond simple collaboration and create a path toward compassion and justice for Black girls. Most importantly, how are we doing our part by taking care of Black girls through our work? The future of our methods, coalitions, and direct work with Black girls is a concerted effort to make known that our girls are "blessed and highly favored"—just as my mom did for me.

References

Annamma, S. A. (2017). *The pedagogy of pathologization dis/abled girls of color in the school-prison nexus*. Routledge.

Baker-Bell, A., Paris, D., & Jackson, D. (2017). Learning Black language matters: Humanizing research as culturally sustaining pedagogy. *International Review of Qualitative Research, 10*(4), 360–377.

Blatt, J. (2020). Institutional logics and the limits of social science knowledge. *History of Education Quarterly, 60*(2), 203–213.

Bower, B. (1998). Objective visions: Historians trace the rise and times of scientific objectivity. *Science News, 154*(23), 360–361.

Browne, S. (2015). *Dark matters*. Duke University Press.

Butler, T. T. (2018). Black girl cartography: Black girlhood and place-making in education research. *Review of Research in Education, 42*(1), 28–45.

Clay, K. L. (2019). "Despite the odds": Unpacking the politics of Black resilience neoliberalism. *American Educational Research Journal, 56*(1), 75–110.

Coles, J. A. (2021). Black desire: Black-centric youthtopias as critical race educational praxis. *International Journal of Qualitative Studies in Education, 34*(7), 1–22.

Collins, P. H. (2002). *Black feminist thought: Knowledge, consciousness, and the politics of empowerment*. Routledge.

Davenport, C. B. (1910). Report of committee on Eugenics. *Journal of Heredity, 1*(2), 126–129.

Davenport, C. B. (1931). The negro in American civilization. *The Eugenics Review, 23*(2), 160–161.

Doharty, N. (2020). The 'angry Black woman' as intellectual bondage: Being strategically emotional on the academic plantation. *Race Ethnicity and Education, 23*(4), 548–562.

Dumas, M. J., & Ross, K. M. (2016). "Be real black for me" imagining BlackCrit in education. *Urban Education, 51*(4), 415–442.

Ealey, J. (2021). Crushed little stars: A praxis-in-process of Black girlhood. *Girlhood Studies, 14*(2), 16–28.

Fayne, M. W. (2021). Advocacy journalism in the 21st century: Rethinking entertainment in digital Black press outlets. *Journalism, 24*(2), 1–18.

Ferguson, A. (2001). *Bad boys*. University of Michigan Press.

Finn, J. D., & Rock, D. A. (1997). Academic success among students at risk for school failure. *Journal of Applied Psychology, 82*(2), 221.

Foucault, M. (1979). *Discipline and punish*. Vintage.

Gaztambide-Fernández, R., & Angod, L. (2019). Approximating whiteness: Race, class, and empire in the making of modern elite/white subjects. *Educational Theory, 69*(6), 719–743.

Gould, E. (2021). Where does diversity go straight? Biopolitics, queer of color critique, and music education. In A. A. Kallio, H. Westerlund, S. Karlsen, K. Marsh, & E. Saether (Eds.), *The politics of diversity in music education* (pp. 151–162). Springer.

Holohan, K. J. (2017). Identification, language, and subjectivity: Reading Freire through/against Lacan. *Curriculum Inquiry, 47*(5), 446–464.

Howard, J. (2018). The White kid can do whatever he wants: The racial socialization of a gifted education program. *Educational Studies, 54*(5), 553–568.

Jernigan, M. M. (2020). Exploring Black girls' recommendations for healthy lifestyle interventions to address obesity. *Journal of Pediatric Psychology, 45*(8), 887–899.

Keddie, A., Jacobs, C., & Nelson, J. D. (2020). When you say diversity, do you mean Black students? Navigating challenges of racial inclusion in elite schools. *International Studies in Sociology of Education, 30*(4) 1–19.

Ladson-Billings, G. (2021). I'm here for the hard re-set: Post pandemic pedagogy to preserve our culture. *Equity & Excellence in Education, 54*(1), 68–78.

Masta, S. (2021). Classroom counterspaces: Centering Brown and Black students in doctoral education. *Teaching in Higher Education, 26*(3), 354–369.

Matias, C. E. (2016). "Why do you make me hate myself?": Re-teaching Whiteness, abuse, and love in urban teacher education. *Teaching Education, 27*(2), 194–211.

Mauldin, C., & Presberry, C. (2020). The world is ours: Mapping identity with Black Girl Cartography. *Journal of Educational Administration and History, 52*(3), 309–320.

McKittrick, K. (2021). *Dear science and other stories*. Duke University Press.

McMillian Cottom, T. (2018). *Thick: And other essays*. The New Press.

Nunn, N. M. (2018). Super-girl: Strength and sadness in Black girlhood. *Gender and Education, 30*(2), 239–258.

Ohito, E. O. (2021). Remembering my memories: Black feminist memory work as a visual research method of inquiry. *International Journal of Qualitative Studies in Education, 36*(9) 1–20.

Opara, I., Lardier Jr., D. T., Garcia-Reid, P., & Reid, R. J. (2020). Measuring intrapersonal psychological empowerment and ethnic identity: Highlighting strengths of urban Black girls. *Youth & Society, 54*(4), 573–592.

Porter, T. M., & Haggerty, K. D. (1997). Trust in numbers: The pursuit of objectivity in science & public life. *Canadian Journal of Sociology, 22*(2), 279.

Price-Dennis, D., Muhammad, G. E., Womack, E., McArthur, S. A., & Haddix, M. (2017). The multiple identities and literacies of Black girlhood: A conversation about creating spaces for Black girl voices. *Journal of Language and Literacy Education, 13*(2), 1–18.

Ray, V. (2019). A theory of racialized organizations. *American Sociological Review, 84*(1), 26–53.

Richardson, L. (2001). Getting personal: Writing stories. *International Journal of Qualitative Studies in Education, 14*(1), 33–38.

Sharpe, C. (2016). *In the wake: On blackness and being*. Duke University Press.

Sheard, K. (2007). Blessed & highly favored. [Song recorded by The Clark Sisters]. On *One Last Time*. EMI Gospel.

Smith, A. L. (2019). Theorizing Black girlhood. In A. S. Halliday (Ed.), *The Black girlhood studies collection* (pp. 21–44). CSP Books Incorporated.

Stovall, D. (2018). Are we ready for 'school' abolition?: Thoughts and practices of radical imaginary in education. *Taboo: The Journal of Culture and Education, 17*(1), 6–19.

Stryker, S. (1980). *Symbolic interactionism: A social structural version*. Benjamin-Cummings Publishing Company.

Theron, L. C. (2013). Black students' recollections of pathways to resilience: Lessons for school psychologists. *School Psychology International, 34*(5), 527–539.

Toliver, S. R. (2018). Alterity and innocence: The hunger games, Rue, and Black girl adultification. *Journal of Children's Literature, 44*(2), 4–15.

Warren, C. A. (2021). From morning to mourning: A meditation on possibility in Black education. *Equity & Excellence in Education, 54*(1), 92–102.

White, S. (2021). Black girls swim: Race, gender, and embodied aquatic histories. *Girlhood Studies, 14*(2), 63–79.

Winston, A. S. (2018). Neoliberalism and IQ: Naturalizing economic and racial inequality. *Theory & Psychology, 28*(5), 600–618.

Woodson, A. N. (2020). Afropessimism for us in education: In fugitivity, through fuckery and with funk. In C. A. Grant, A. N. Woodson, & M. J. Dumas (Eds.), *The future is Black: Afropessimism, fugitivity, and radical hope in education* (pp. 16–21). Routledge.

Notes on Contributors

Editors

Toni Denese Sturdivant, Ph.D. is a scholar-activist whose work focuses on positive racial identity development in young Black girls, anti-colonial child development practices, and how societal messages related to social identities are internalized by young children.

Altheria Caldera, Ph.D. is a teacher educator and scholar-activist who advances educational equity in the areas of linguistic justice, Black girls and school discipline, and anti-racist pedagogies.

Contributors

Charlene (Charli) M. Brown, Ph.D. is a transformative transpersonal strategist focusing on the well-being of the whole person. She specializes in integrating psycho-socio-emotional tools into the everyday and teaching others how to utilize this for their highest impact and engagement. In her research, Dr. Brown concentrates on the complexities of identity for Black women and girls in the numerous spaces they occupy. She has been working with and interested in Black girls for over 10 years. Dr. Brown currently serves as an adjunct professor at Widener University.

Taryrn T. C. Brown (she/her/hers) is an Assistant Professor and Program Coordinator at the University of Florida. Her program of research has three major foci: the intersection of gender, race, and class in the lives of Black women and girls in and out of school settings; the amplification of Black women and girls' voices in prevention science; and the role parents, schools, and communities play in Black girls' socialization, literacies, and identity construction.

Kimberly Bryant is the Founder of Black Girls CODE, a non-profit organization dedicated to "changing the face of technology" by introducing girls of color (ages 7–17) to the field of technology and computer science, concentrating in entrepreneurial concepts. She is an electrical engineer who worked in the biotechnology field at Genentech, Novartis Vaccines, Diagnostics, and Merck. In 2011, Bryant founded Black Girls CODE, a nonprofit organization that focuses on providing technology and computer programming education to Black/African-American girls. After founding Black Girls CODE, Bryant was listed as one of the "25 Most Influential African-Americans In Technology" by Business Insider. More recently, Kimberly founded Ascend Ventures Tech and the Black Innovation Lab. ASCEND Ventures and its flagship Black Innovation Lab ("The Lab") builds upon Kimberly Bryant's trailblazing work of helping marginalized founders and entrepreneurs build pathways to financial freedom and ownership.

Dr. Loren S. Cahill is a cultural worker, artist, and Assistant Professor at Smith College's School of Social Work. Her current research interests include Black Girlhood Studies, Black Feminist Geographies, and Womanist Futurities. She is also quite interested in Freedom Dreams, Radical Love, Sacred Spaces, Intergenerational Healing, Community Archives, and various forms of Artistry. She works in close collaboration with The Colored Girls Museum and Our Mothers Kitchens. She has her bachelor's degree in Africana Studies from Wellesley College, MSW from the University of Michigan Ann Arbor, and her Ph.D. in Critical Social Personality Environmental Psychology from CUNY's Graduate Center.

Tamika Gafford-Carter, a licensed alcohol, drug, and mental health counselor, has 20 years of work with youth and adults in a variety of settings. She serves as an advocate for many issues that affect women and girls and runs API a multi-state non-profit supporting practical solutions to pressing issues. Carter's body of work draws on a compilation of studies from treating African American women across the lifespan.

Dr. Rashida Govan is an educator, activist and writer who has worked for more than 20 years in education and youth development. She completed a postdoctoral position as project director of the International Study on Youth Community Organizing. Her other research interests include African American girls' adolescent development and college readiness, access and success. Rashida is deeply engaged in the New Orleans community and is credited with facilitating a number of community education programs including parent leadership trainings with the Fatherhood Consortium and the PRIDE Parent Leadership Academy, the Trayvon Martin Teach-In and the Assata Shakur Teach-In. Govan is the founder and executive director of Project Butterfly New Orleans, an evidence-based, African-centered girls rites of passage program.

Janelle Grant, Ph.D. recently graduated from Purdue University with her doctorate in Curriculum Studies. Her research lies within the intersections of critical theory, race, and education. She has experience teaching multicultural education, research methods, and educational foundations courses.

Misha N. Inniss-Thompson, Ph.D. is a Black girlhood scholar whose work honors the glory of Black girls' ways of knowing and being in the world. Her research uses participatory and critical approaches to consider how Black girls curate physical and imaginative spaces that center their ability to feel well, safe, and free. At this book's release, Inniss-Thompson is an Assistant Professor in the Department of Psychology at Cornell University.

Janine Jones is an Associate Professor of philosophy at UNC-Greensboro. She is co-editor of Pursuing Trayvon Martin: Historical Contexts and Contemporary Manifestations of Racial Dynamics and the special editor of the *Simone de Beauvoir Studies Journal (SdBS) Sites of Coercion: Plantation, Colony, Metropole.* Jones is interested in the study of Blackgirls and, more generally, problems that lie at the intersection of imagination, language, perception, epistemology, and socio-ontology, especially as applied in the racist, classist, race-gendered, eugenicist realms in which we live.

Noor Jones-Bey is a transdisciplinary educator, researcher, and artist. She is pursuing a Ph.D. in Urban Education at the Steinhardt School and serves as a program director of EXCEL at NYU, a critical literacy, and college access program. Noor received an M.A. in Sociology of Education from New York University and a B.A. in American Studies from the University of California, Berkeley. Her dissertation work examines intergenerational knowledge of Black women and girls navigating in and out of schools. In her spare time, she loves to cook, dance, run marathons, travel, and stir up good vibes.

Nisaa Kirtman, Ph.D., is a researcher and evaluator with over twenty years of experience designing and conducting research in educational settings, and the public health sector. She is a Research Principal at Rockman et al. Cooperative, a San Francisco-based research and evaluation cooperative. She uses an equity centered approach to both research and evaluation, and believes that communities and partners have a fundamental role in redefining what a study or evaluation should be informed by Nisaa strives to help programs and organizations use evaluative thinking, and understand larger contexts and culture for their program processes and outcomes.

Dr. Lateasha Meyers is an Assistant Professor in Multicultural and Gender Studies with a focus on African American Studies at California State University Chico. Her research centers education and Black girlhood. She specifically focuses on how Black girls construct their educational worlds and how the intersections of class, race, gender, and age affect their constructions.

Imani S. R. Minor is a budding intellectual activist who views creativity as the foundation of intellectuality. She is currently a Master of Divinity student at Howard University. Passionate about laughing, loving, and liberating, Imani Shakirah Raanee embodies the fullness of her name.

Dr. Stephanie Power-Carter is the daughter of Walter and Bobbie Power. Faculty in The Ohio State the Department of Teaching and Learning and director for the Center for Discourse Analysis and Video Ethnography

darlene anita scott is a writer and visual artist who explores corporeal presentations of trauma and the violence of silence, especially in Black girls. She is co-editor of the creative-critical volume Revisiting the Elegy in the Black Lives Matter Era (Routledge 2019), and her debut poetry collection, Marrow (University Press of Kentucky 2022) reimagines people lost in a mass murder-suicide at the Guyanese settlement of the Peoples Temple founded by James "Jim" Jones and popularly known as Jonestown.

Dr. Danielle Wright is a licensed clinical social worker, therapist and public health practitioner with 13 years of experience in the areas of trauma, toxic stress, infant mental health, social and emotional learning and disaster mental health. She is the Founding Director of Navigate Nola, the child well-being division of the Deep South Center for Environmental Justice. In addition to her role at Navigate NOLA, Dr. Wright is also a therapist, in private practice, at Atlas Psychiatry, and a Tulane University School of Social Work adjunct instructor.

A published author, Dr. Wright's work is featured in the book, Therapeutic Cultural Routines to Build Family Relationships Talk, Touch & Listen While Combing Hair.

Index

A

ACEs 71, 138
Adultification 16, 41, 91, 100–101, 110–111, 117, 121, 183
Afropessimism 191
Agency 17, 74, 78, 152
Anzaldua 2
Autohistoria 2
autobiography, Black women's 2
Autoethnography 28–29
    Black feminist 2
    Critical 149, 154

B

Black Feminist Theory, *see* Black Womanist Theory
Black girl, special 21
Black Womanist Theory 5, 28–29
Black women's logic of inquiry 60

C

Colorism 38–40, 84
Counterstories 7, 8, 101, 116–118, 127–128
Criminalization 6–7, 16, 18, 19, 41, 81–82, 92, 98

Critical Race Feminism 5

D

Debt, education 165
Disembody: 23, 30, 44–45, 128
Dismember *see* disembody

F

Femininity 19, 46, 74, 90, 184
Framework,
    musical mentoring 148
    womanist caring 153

G

Geographies, imaginative 125, 128
Girlhood, Black 16, 47–48
Grooves 83

H

hooks, bell 54–55, 73, 176

I

Images, controlling *see* stereotypes

Indivisibility of Black girlhood and womanhood 29–30, 38, 40–41, 43, 91
Intersectionality 46–47, 69, 76, 148, 152, 166

J

Jezebel, *see* stereotypes

K

Knowledge, visual oppositional 103

L

Literacies, multiple 27

M

Mammy, *see* stereotypes
Memories 2, 53, 55, 59, 61, 96, 123, 127
Misogynoir 26
Model, pipeline 165, 166
Morrison, Toni 124, 127
Multiplicity 29–30, 46, 51

O

Oversexualization 5–6, 7, 19–20

P

Patriarchy 7, 37, 41, 44
Pedagogy, critical mentoring 149, 153–154
Perspective, cultural asset 7
Phenomenological Variant of Ecology Systems Theory (PVEST) 4
Photovoice 99, 130
Plurality, *see* multiplicy

Policing, over *see* criminalization
Politics, respectability 67, 74–75, 90, 91, 100, 103
Positionality 5, 11
Power 41, 74, 91, 187, 189
prose, womanist 2

Q

Qualitative inquiry 3, 29

R

Reflection, self 4
Reflexivity, critical 3–4
Research,
    Participatory action 26, 82–83
    women of color intimate 5
Responsiveness, cultural 164, 165

S

Sapphire, *see* stereotypes
Sexualization, over 19, 68, 77, 111
Silences 54, 58, 87, 97, 103, 131, 139
Sisteralla *see* stereotypes
Spaces, imaginative 127
Stereotypes 15, 16, 18, 21, 44, 45–46, 99, 100, 102, 111, 116, 120, 138–139, 142, 143, 165, 167, 183–184
Stories,
    Origin 109
    thinking 52–53, 57
Subjectivity 8, 58, 186
Syndrome
    Imposter 41
    Post Traumatic Slave 141, 143

T

Testimonio 2
Trope, *see* stereotypes

W

Whiteness 39, 52, 54, 55, 61, 98, 102, 185, 187–190

Womanhood, Black 16, 42

www.ingramcontent.com/pod-product-compliance
Lightning Source LLC
Chambersburg PA
CBHW061714300426

44115CB00014B/2683